TALES OF GREAT LAKES
LIGHTHOUSES

GUIDING LIGHTS
TRAGIC SHADOWS

Copyright © 2005 by Lynx Images Inc.
Copyright © 2005 text Edward Butts
P.O. Box 5961, Station A
Toronto, Canada M5W 1P4
Web Site: http://www.lynximages.com
First Edition: July 2005

Exclusively distributed in the United States by

Holt, Michigan

Editor: Barbara Chisholm
Cover and page layout: Andrea Gutsche

Front Cover: Composite by Andrea Gutsche;
                      photograph by Donna Sigmeth
Back Cover: Oswego Lighthouse, courtesy of Erwin Mole
Ship in fall, courtesy of Metropolitan Toronto Reference Library

Printed and bound in Canada by Transcontinental Printing Inc.

Library and Archives Canada Cataloguing in Publication

Butts, Edward, 1951-
    Guiding lights, tragic shadows : tales of Great Lakes lighthouses / Edward Butts.

Includes bibliographical references.
ISBN-13: 978-1-894073-57-6
ISBN-10: 1-894073-57-6

    1. Lighthouses--Great Lakes--Pictorial works.
2. Lighthouses--Great Lakes--History. I. Title.

VK1023.3.B88 2005   387.1'55'0977022   C2005-903183-2

TALES OF GREAT LAKES LIGHTHOUSES

GUIDING LIGHTS
TRAGIC SHADOWS

by Edward Butts

Thunder Bay Press

For my uncle, Tom Butts, who has sailed the Arctic,
the Atlantic, and the Great Lakes

The Lighthouse Keeper

by Smoke in the Eyes

Over the lake the sky hangs low,
A seagull screams in the faraway;
Like wraiths in the dusk the boats ply slow
Through the mists that curtain the bay;

Then over my heart there's a shadow falls,
Blacker, denser than shadows of night,
For the siren voice of the city calls
And I must guard the light.

What is it to me that a white moon gleams?
So near, yet far, and the streets shine bright,
For the keeper there's only darkness and dreams;
Someone must watch the light.

Toronto *Globe*, July 8, 1916

Two wrecks, the schooner Chattanooga *and the steamer* Bielman, *lie just beneath the water off Great Duck Island in northern Lake Huron. The Great Duck Lighthouse, built in 1877, was replaced by an 89-foot tower (26.7-m) during the First World War, making it the tallest in the region.*

TABLE OF CONTENTS

TABLE OF CONTENTS

TABLE OF CONTENTS

The Detroit Reef Lighthouse under construction in 1931. The lighthouse sits on a massive pier.

The William H. Truesdale *on Lake Erie. Saltwater sailors were often contemptuous of freshwater sailors— until they sailed the Great Lakes. (Page right) Among the lightkeeper's chores was the constant cleaning and polishing of lenses. Here, keeper Alex Herron tends to the lamp in the Hope Island Lighthouse, Georgian Bay.*

The Mataafa *aground off Duluth. Due to the storm, the crew had to spend a nerve-wracking night aboard the ship before rescue came in the morning.*

Much has been written of the "wilderness" of North America. The word brings to mind images of Daniel Boone's wild Kentucky, or the Northern Ontario bush. But there has been another wilderness in the story of North America, a wilderness of water. The Great Lakes, while being a highway to the heart of the continent, have at the same time proved to be as difficult to tame as any wild land.

The earliest Great Lakes mariners learned at considerable cost in ships and lives that sailing the Lakes was every bit as hazardous as sailing the saltwater sea. Ships' captains had to be wary not only of the suddenness with which storms could build up, but also of the deadly reefs and shoals that lurked along shorelines and even in seemingly open water.

Lighthouses, of course, were the surest means of warning ships away from danger points, or guiding them into safe harbour. In the era before automation, the lighthouses had to be maintained by keepers. Lightkeeping required more than just lighting the lamp every night and keeping it refuelled. There were endless tasks to be done, like polishing the lenses and brass fittings. It was often a lonely job, especially in the more remote regions of the Upper Lakes. Unless a lightkeeper had his (or her) family at the site, or was fortunate enough to have an assistant, he might see very few other human souls for the entire navigation season, from spring thaw to winter freeze-up.

A lightkeeper's job called for vigilance, for if a ship were in trouble, the keeper was often the first person to alert rescuers. The keeper might even be the only person on hand to render assistance. On both the Canadian and American sides of the lakes, the men and women who tended the lights took part in daring rescues and witnessed the tragedy of shipwrecks. They themselves experienced perilous journeys just travelling to and from isolated posts.

The lighthouses that line the freshwater shores of Canada and the United States, from the Thousand Islands to the western end of Lake Superior, have been the scenes of many dramatic events: war, great feats of engineering, even murder. Most important, the lighthouses were welcome sights for sailors and the passengers on their ships. Every person who sailed safely past a lighthouse was grateful for the beacon. They knew that somewhere in the waters beneath them quite likely lay the bones of ships and people who had met unfortunate ends because, at one time, that reassuring light did not exist. Sailing the Great Lakes was still a risky business, but with those guiding lights in place, the mariners at least had a better chance of making it safely across the water to the next port of call.

A QUESTION OF FIRSTS

In any given community, of any given region, in any given country in the world, there are people who look for things in their history of which to be proud: a famous son or daughter; a remarkable invention or discovery; a world-shaking event; or something they can point to as a "first". Sometimes, however, the claims can conflict. For example, three countries—Scotland, Canada, and the United States—have claims to the great inventor Alexander Graham Bell. Santo Domingo in the Dominican Republic proudly calls itself "The First City in the Americas", but similar claims are made by St. Augustine in Florida and St. John's, Newfoundland. Santo Domingo also says it has the bones of Christopher Columbus. So do Cuba and Spain.

Facts become confused or lost. Civic or national pride dismisses documented evidence. Legend is accepted as fact. Then the legend is carved in stone, or inscribed on a bronze plaque. Just as it has elsewhere, so it has gone with the history of the Great Lakes.

One could compose a very long list of "firsts" about the five huge lakes and their connecting waterways that make up North America's Inland Seas. But the question posed here is: where was the first Great Lakes lighthouse? Several communities have claimed the honour in articles, books, even on websites. In the long-run, it probably does not matter, because all of the lighthouses in question were important in their time, and made their contributions to commerce, navigation and history. It would be worthwhile, however, to settle the question, if only for the sake of accuracy.

For simple reasons of geography, the first of the Great Lakes to be navigated regularly by vessels large enough to be called ships were Lakes Ontario and Erie. Claims for the "first light" on the lakes have been made for Galloo Island, Toronto, and Fort Niagara on Lake Ontario; and Buffalo and Erie on Lake Erie.

The first light—that is, something other than a lantern hung from a pole or a tree branch—to shine on the Lakes was at Fort Niagara, at present day Youngstown, New York. But it was not a lighthouse, nor was it American. In 1781 the British, who still held the fort, put a light in a small structure

The British, and later the Americans, placed lights on rooftops at Fort Niagara. A fifty-foot (15.2-m) stone tower was built in 1872. In 1900, 11 feet (3.3m) were added to its height.

on the roof of a building called the French Castle (from the days when it had been a French fort) so British ships would not sail too far west of the fort at night. The Americans used this light from the time they took over the fort in 1796 until 1803, when it was apparently discontinued. In 1823, a light was built on the roof of the Fort Niagara mess hall. Like the earlier British beacon, it was certainly useful, but it was still not a lighthouse.

In 1804, the British built the first actual lighthouse on the Lakes when the 49th Regiment of Foot erected an octagonal stone tower on Point Mississauga, about half a mile (.8km) from Fort George at the mouth of the Niagara River (Niagara-on-the-Lake). They also built a house for the keeper, a retired soldier named Dominique Henry. He had the distinction of being the very first lighthouse keeper anywhere on the Lakes. He was also the only keeper of the Point Mississauga Light, because that light was permanently extinguished by the War of 1812.

On May 27, 1813, American troops captured and occupied what is now called Niagara-on-the-Lake, and held it until December 10. Before their retreat, they burned most of the town. The lighthouse was one of the few buildings they did not destroy; in fact, they had given it a wide berth throughout the occupation because they feared it had been mined with explosives. (During the April 27, 1813 American attack on York (Toronto), the British had detonated their powder magazine. The explosion killed or wounded scores of American soldiers, including the noted explorer General Zebulon Pike. The Americans did not want a repeat of that calamity.)

In 1814 the British pulled down the lighthouse and used the stones in the construction of Fort Mississauga. The first lighthouse on the Great

(Top) American General Zebulon Pike was killed when the British blew up their powder magazine at York in April 1813. (Middle) The Point Mississauga Light at what is now Niagara-on-the-Lake, Ontario. Built by the British in 1804, this was the first lighthouse on the Great Lakes. It was demolished in 1814. (Bottom) Toronto's Gibraltar Point Lighthouse, built in 1808, was the first permanent lighthouse on the Great Lakes.

Lakes is now an integral part of Fort Mississauga, a Canadian National Historic Site. Unfortunately, the Point Mississauga Light (sometimes mistakenly called the Newark Light) has been overlooked by many Great Lakes chroniclers.

The first *permanent* lighthouse to be built anywhere on the Great Lakes was the Gibraltar Point Lighthouse on what is now Toronto Island, off the settlement of York (Toronto), on Lake Ontario. The stone tower was built in 1808, and though it is no longer operational, it is still standing. It has been marked as a historic site.

A lighthouse was built on Galloo Island, just off Sackets Harbor, New York, at the eastern end of Lake Ontario in 1820. It was a wooden structure that was replaced with a stone tower in 1867. The Galloo Island claim to be site of the first lighthouse on Lake Ontario quite likely caused the confusion that led to the claims from Buffalo, New York; and Erie, Pennsylvania, to lighthouse "firsts" on the Great Lakes. Buffalo and Erie both had lighthouses in 1818, two years before Galloo Island, but a decade after Gibraltar Point. No one is certain which port had a lighthouse first, so Erie and Buffalo will have to share the honours of first lighthouse on Lake Erie. Galloo Island can still be called the site of the first American lighthouse on Lake Ontario. All have something of which to be proud.

The second Buffalo Lighthouse, as printed in a local newspaper. Completed in 1833, this second tower replaced the earlier one built in 1818. (Inset) To install a more powerful Fresnel lens, workmen had to remove the lantern room and build an addition of stone encasement windows, 1856.

Oswego harbour and lighthouse, 1850. The Lower Lakes were relatively well lit by the mid-nineteenth century. (Inset) Close-up of the tower.

(Above) Christian Island Lighthouse in Lake Huron's Georgian Bay is one of six Imperial Towers built by the Canadian Government. (Right) The crowded harbour at Detroit in 1869 indicates the growing need for navigational aids.

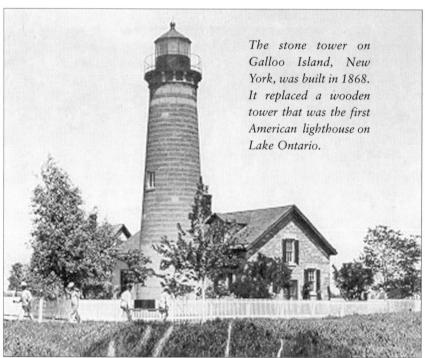

The stone tower on Galloo Island, New York, was built in 1868. It replaced a wooden tower that was the first American lighthouse on Lake Ontario.

The Imperial Towers: John Brown's Legacy

Scottish-born John Brown (1808–1876) was a man born to build. He apprenticed as a stonemason in Glasgow, then emigrated to North America, where men of his skills were in great demand. He went first to New York, but in 1838 moved on to Thorold, Upper Canada (later Canada West, and then Ontario). There he became involved in the operation of the Queenston Quarry, source of some of the finest building stone in colonial Canada.

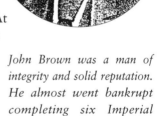

Over the next two decades, Brown earned a reputation as a master builder, and became relatively wealthy. He was involved in the construction of railroads, canals and harbours. He built cement and plaster mills, lime kilns and a sawmill. He owned shipyards in which he built tugboats, dredges and scows. At World Fairs held in Paris in 1855 and in London in 1862, his plaster and cement products won medals. Perhaps Brown's work did not have the kind of glamour that accompanied the building of an opulent mansion or a magnificent bridge, but it proved him to be a solid, dependable man who, when he took on a job, did it right. In 1855, the Public Works

John Brown was a man of integrity and solid reputation. He almost went bankrupt completing six Imperial Towers.

Commission for Canada West offered Brown the opportunity to construct buildings that would be both utilitarian and beautiful: a series of 11 lighthouses on Lake Huron and Georgian Bay.

The Upper Great Lakes country was opening up to settlement and development. Pioneers were moving up the Lakes to start new lives. Timber and ore were moving down the lakes to more populated centres. Soon shiploads of grain would follow. And trade with the United States was growing steadily. But so far, the only Canadian lighthouse above Lake Erie was the one at Goderich, built in 1847. The Americans had embarked on an extensive lighthouse-building program along their Great Lakes shores. The Canadians had to try to keep pace, to help make the Lakes safer for the shipping of both nations. The Public Works Commissioners decided to do it in style.

John Brown had already built the lighthouse on Mohawk Island in Lake Erie, near Port Maitland, so he was experienced with that unique type of structure. He eagerly accepted the project, which was authorized by the Canadian government, and had at least partial financial support from Britain. The lighthouses would be called Imperial Towers. It was the sort of grand project for which a man would be remembered.

Sites for the towers were chosen according to the presence of dangerous shoals or reefs, or because they were guiding points to deep channels or safe harbours. Though 11 sites were selected, Imperial Towers would rise at only six of them: Point Clark, 20 miles (32km) north of Goderich; Chantry Island, near Southampton; Cove Island, where Lake Huron meets Georgian Bay; Nottawasaga Island, near Collingwood; Griffith Island, at the entrance to Owen Sound; and Christian Island, in southeast Georgian Bay. Brown also built a lighthouse at Burlington Bay on Lake Ontario, but it has never been listed as an Imperial Tower, even though Brown allegedly considered it his finest work. Imperial Towers planned for White Fish Island, Mississagi Strait, Isle St. Joseph, Clapperton Island and Badgeley Island were never built, though most of those locations did eventually get smaller, wooden lighthouses.

Brown selected the finest white limestone from Canadian quarries, and employed the best stonecutters, masons and other craftsmen. But procuring materials and hiring men was one thing; transporting them to the work sites was quite another. The lighthouse locations were remote, and Lake Huron seemed determined to keep them that way. Supply boats were delayed by storms and a few were even sunk. Gales and blizzards delayed construction. Men who were being paid top wages to work in such isolated locations had long periods in which they had nothing to do, because of overdue ships. Delivery of special equipment from France was held up because the French were obliged to fill American orders first. Then, when equipment was available, French specialists had to travel to Canada to assemble and install it. All of which was incredibly expensive.

Even though John Brown had greatly underestimated the cost of the project, he was a man of unshakeable integrity and was determined to complete the six lighthouses he had started, even if it bankrupted him. The towers would be monuments not only to his skill, but also to his sense of principle.

Each tower rose from a base seven feet (2.1m) thick. The walls tapered to a thickness of two feet (.6m) at the top. The interior diameter was ten and a half feet (3.1m) from top to bottom. The towers were all 80 feet (24.3m) high, except the one on Christian Island, which was 55 feet (16.7m). At the very top of the walls, granite was used instead of limestone, to support the great weight of the lantern room, which was made of iron, copper and glass. A bronze gutter-spout in the shape of a lion's head was installed to drain off water that resulted from condensation on the lantern room windows. The exterior stonework on all of the buildings was of exceptional quality, and each lighthouse was given a slightly different window placement in the sides of the tower to suit the specific location. Each had its own distinctive light characteristics so that it would be easily recognizable by sailors.

The first completed Imperial Tower, at Cove Island, went into operation on October 30, 1858. The last to be completed, at Christian Island, first shone its beacon on May 1, 1859. The cost of erecting these six towers was a shocking $223,000! That was more than the colony of Canada West could afford, even with financial help from Britain. Brown did, in fact, almost go bankrupt finishing the project. He must have been able to recoup at least some of his losses, because he remained in business until the day he died.

The six Imperial Towers, all of which are still standing, are unique among Great Lakes lighthouses. There are no lighthouses quite like them in the United States. However, the cost of these elegant structures was such that there would be no more like them in Ontario, either. Realizing that it would take many towers to light the long Canadian shore all the way to the Superior Lakehead, the Canadian government chose to build wooden lighthouses that were

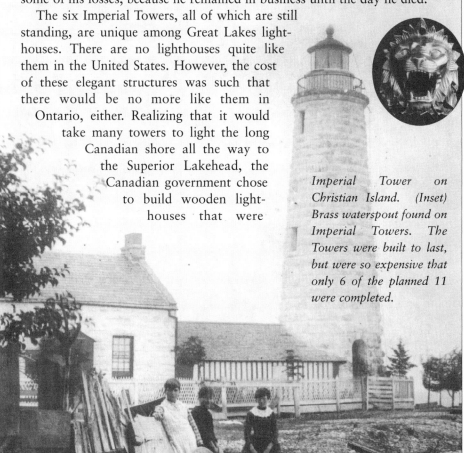

Imperial Tower on Christian Island. (Inset) Brass waterspout found on Imperial Towers. The Towers were built to last, but were so expensive that only 6 of the planned 11 were completed.

(Above) Fixing a Fresnel lens at the Buffalo Harbour depot. (Left) Fresnels came in a variety of sizes or "orders". These lenses range from the 4th to 6th orders.

cheaper, but adequate for the job. They would not stand the test of time and the elements, however, in the stately manner of the Imperial Towers, all of which are still in (automated) operation.

THE LIGHTS AND THEIR KEEPERS: LAMPS, LENSES AND OILS

ILLUMINATION

By the time American and British (later Canadian) lighthouses began to appear on the shores of the Great Lakes, considerable advances had been made in the technology of marine illumination. The very first European lighthouses were towers that were open to the sky. Attendants burned wood, charcoal or tar. Of course, these lights were useless in bad weather, when they were needed most. By the 1600s, lightkeepers were using oil lamps or huge candelabras that held dozens of tallow candles. These lighting systems required constant maintenance, produced only a feeble light, and were fire hazards. Moreover, there was no effective way to make the light flash, in order for mariners to distinguish one light from another.

In 1765 a French chemist, Antoine Lavoisier, developed the parabolic beacon reflector, a disc lined with polished tin that greatly enhanced the amount of light cast by a lamp. Less than twenty years later, a Swiss physicist, Aimé Argand, designed an oil lamp that had a hollow wick, allowing a smokeless flame that burned ten times brighter than previous lamps. Further modifications to the Argand lamp gave it several wicks and enabled a clock-work-driven pump to feed oil to the burners. Another clockwork-driven system, developed in 1784, turned reflectors back and forth in a timed sequence, thus giving a "light characteristic" to a lighthouse. This meant that if a constant beam was not suitable for a particular lighthouse, the light could be made to "blink" with a predetermined span of seconds between the flashes. Sailors now had a means by which to identify a lighthouse at night. The lightkeeper had another chore, however, as the weights for the clockwork mechanism had to be rewound during the night.

In 1812, Winslow Lewis of Boston, a former ship's captain, took out a patent on what he said was a new invention, the Lewis lamp. This device was simply an Argand lamp with a few of its components rearranged, and was in fact inferior to the original. It tended to soot up easily and required

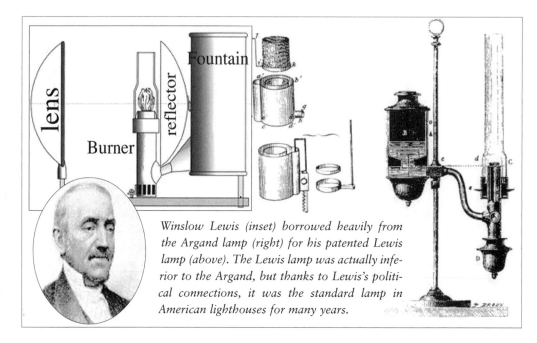

lens

Burner

reflector

Fountain

Winslow Lewis (inset) borrowed heavily from the Argand lamp (right) for his patented Lewis lamp (above). The Lewis lamp was actually inferior to the Argand, but thanks to Lewis's political connections, it was the standard lamp in American lighthouses for many years.

constant cleaning and adjustment. Compared to the high quality of the European-made Argand lamp, the American-made Lewis lamp was shoddy. But Lewis had friends in high places. He was a personal friend of Stephen Pleasonton, the Fifth Auditor of the Treasury, the government department that was at that time in charge of American lighthouses. At Pleasonton's insistence, Lewis lamps went into American lighthouses on the Great Lakes and elsewhere, and stayed there for a long time.

The big breakthrough in lighthouse illumination came in 1822 when another French scientist, Augustin Fresnel, invented a revolutionary new device called the Fresnel lens. Fresnel's invention looked like a huge glass beehive. At the focal plane (centre) of the lens was a single large lamp. Surrounding the lamp were concentric rings of glass prisms and mirrors that bent the light to a narrow beam. The lens at the centre was shaped like a magnifying glass, so that the light was even more concentrated as it was cast seaward. The old reflector lamps lost 83 percent of their light; the Fresnel lens lost only 17 percent. Fresnel developed several orders (sizes) of his lens, to suit the power of light required at a given location. The largest of them could cast a beam 20 miles (32km) or more. A Fresnel lens was big—some of them 12 feet (3.6m) high—and heavy. It had to be taken to the lighthouse in pieces and assembled by a team of experts. Needless to say, this state-of-the-art lens was very expensive.

The Fresnel lens from the Nottawasaga Light. Fresnel lenses were very expensive, and had to be assembled by a team of experts from France. (Inset) Augustin Fresnel, inventor of the Fresnel lens— state-of-the-art lighting technology before the coming of electricity.

Money was little object, however, when governments considered the ships, cargoes and lives to be saved. France, Great Britain and other maritime nations began replacing their old lighting systems with Fresnel lenses. But not the United States. Stephen Pleasonton was strongly against bringing the French invention to the U.S. He dismissed it as an expensive fad. As far as Pleasonton was concerned, the American-made Lewis lamp did the job nicely. Sailors disagreed. They complained that American lighthouses were far inferior to those of other nations. But Pleasonton, who had never been a mariner and knew little about the sea, was stubborn. It would take many years and a congressional investigation before the United States finally began to convert to Fresnel lenses in 1841.

While American lightkeepers on the Great Lakes were burdened with the sub-standard Lewis lamps, the British acceptance of the Fresnel lens did not necessarily mean that all Canadian lightkeepers were equipped with Fresnels. Some had Argand lamps, or variations of it. Some locations did not require a light as powerful as a Fresnel. When the Imperial Towers on Lake Huron were built, they were equipped with Fresnel lenses. But because of the high cost, and a backlog of orders the French manufacturer had once the Americans began to convert to Fresnel, other Canadian lighthouses sometimes had to wait.

Before scientists learned how to harness electricity, the only way to create artificial light was by burning some kind of fuel. For many years, Canadian and American lightkeepers relied on whale oil, of which sperm whale oil was considered the best. It burned brightly, and made little or no smoke. It was expensive, however, and the price just kept going up as the whale population dwindled. Some American lightkeepers used lard, which had to be heated first.

(Above) Nineteenth-century oil lamps. For many years, whale oil was used for illumination. Kerosene (coal oil), invented by Abraham Gesner featured on the 46-cent stamp (right), burned more brightly than whale oil,

Then, in 1846, Abraham Gesner, an English doctor who had emigrated to Halifax, Nova Scotia, invented kerosene (coal oil, as Canadians came to call it). Kerosene burned brighter than whale oil, and was cheap to produce. Many lightkeepers objected to the use of kerosene because they felt it was taking away the livelihood of whalers. Nonetheless, coal oil was soon being used in Canadian lighthouses. American lightkeepers, too, eventually adapted to kerosene, though some did so reluctantly, claiming to prefer lard.

LIGHTKEEPERS: ROUTINE AND REGULATIONS

Whatever fuel a lightkeeper burned, he had to carry heavy barrels of it up the long stairway to the lantern room at the top. Regardless of the type of lamp or lens in use, the keeper spent endless hours cleaning and polishing glass and metal. He had to trim wicks, oil the clockwork mechanism and paint the lighthouse and other buildings. If there was a foghorn at the site, that was his responsibility, too.

Not only was the lightkeeper's day one of routine, it was also one of strict observation of regulations. Lots of regulations! Some regulations, such as those regarding the storage and handling of fuel, were necessary for safety purposes. Others seemed to be little more than the product of bureaucratic tyranny, such as the rule stipulating the kind of brush strokes to be used in painting the lighthouse. To ensure that lightkeepers obeyed the rules, inspectors made unscheduled visits. If a lightkeeper knew that an inspector was making the rounds, he would often try to spread the word to his colleagues.

On the Canadian side of the Lakes, lighthouses were the responsibility of the Department of Public Works, and later the Department of Marine and Fisheries. In the United States, lighthouses first came under the authority of the Treasury Department, then the United States Lighthouse Service. Great Lakes lighthouses today are maintained by the Coast Guard services of their respective countries.

American lightkeepers were generally better paid than their Canadian counterparts. They were also more likely to have assistants who were paid by the government. Canadian lightkeepers frequently had to pay assistants out of their own pockets. In both countries the keepers' wives and children often filled in as assistants, usually unpaid.

To the assistant often fell the more menial jobs—the never-ending cleaning and polishing. This sometimes led to conflict in the tower, with assistants writing letters of complaint about overbearing head lightkeepers. But if an assistant did the job well, and faithfully kept the light burning when the keeper was absent or ill, he (or she) could expect to be rewarded with his (or her) own lighthouse. It was not uncommon for the keeping of a lighthouse to become a family vocation, passed on from generation to generation.

(Left) Many Canadian lightkeepers worked in inexpensive, wooden lighthouses and relied upon family as unpaid assistants, as was the case at the Janet Head Light on Manitoulin Island. (Right) The American government built more stone and brick lighthouses, and provided keepers with paid, uniformed assistants.

The position of lightkeeper was much sought-after, and at this time the applicant stood a better chance of securing the job if he were a captain, a war veteran, or had political connections. Captain George Collins, Canadian lightkeeper at Cove Island and then Nottawasaga Island in Lake Huron, was also a Mason; quite likely an additional advantage.

Sailors passing a lighthouse in the night "read" the light just the way modern drivers read a highway sign. Therefore, the "light characteristic" had to be accurately kept. A slight variation in the timing of the flashes could cause a skipper to mistake one lighthouse for another, resulting in disaster. An excerpt from a regular column called "Schooner Days", carried by the Toronto *Evening Telegram* from 1931 to 1956, reveals how a captain could "read" a light. The lighthouse the narrator describes was at Port Darlington, east of Toronto.

> The lighthouse is 54 feet high [16.4m] and shows from the south a red light, and approaching from the east and west a bright light. The arrangement of the harbour light made it most useful for [a] seaman to enter the harbour at night, straight ahead with the red light which showed you were south of the harbour and the piers were in line, a flash of white showing when you were off course to the east or the west.

Great Lakes lightkeepers came from a variety of backgrounds. Some were retired sailors. For others, the job came as a political reward (which meant that the position could be lost should there be a change of administration after the next election). After the First World War, the Canadian government handed out lightkeeping positions to disabled veterans, with mixed results. Some of the heroes of the trenches performed admirably, others, less so.

Whether a lightkeeper was an extrovert who welcomed one and all to his tower, or a recluse who preferred solitude; whether he had a city like Toronto or Buffalo at his back, or was stationed at a remote island or shoal in Lake Superior, the lightkeeper was of a special breed. With the technology that was available—sometimes the best, sometimes not—he (or she) had to keep safe the shipping lanes of the freshwater seas shared by Canada and the United States.

Children of the Light! Beth and Lois, daughters of lightkeeper Arnold Wing and his wife Lillian, pose with assistant Jerry Emery by the boat cable at Georgian Bay's Western Islands Light.

(Top left) Buller, the lighthouse dog of Presqu'ile, Georgian Bay. Every morning at five a.m., Buller would go into lightkeeper John Mackenzie's bedroom with the lighthouse key (left) in his mouth and awaken his master with a touch of his paw. (Top right) The McKenzie family of Strawberry Island Lighthouse in the North Channel, c. 1887–88. Little Donald, held by his father, William, was born at the lighthouse in 1883.

(Above) Julia and John Malone with the 11 children they raised on Menagerie Island in Lake Superior between 1881–1910. The eight boys were all named after lighthouse inspectors. John Malone, Jr. was the last lightkeeper at the Menagerie Island Lighthouse (right).

Anna and Robert Carlson of the Michigan Island Lighthouse in Lake Superior endured four days of fear in the winter of 1891 when Robert's fishing party was trapped on an ice floe. Robert was lucky to survive the ordeal; Anna thought her husband was dead.

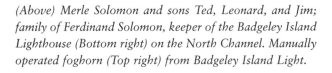

(Above) Merle Solomon and sons Ted, Leonard, and Jim; family of Ferdinand Solomon, keeper of the Badgeley Island Lighthouse (Bottom right) on the North Channel. Manually operated foghorn (Top right) from Badgeley Island Light.

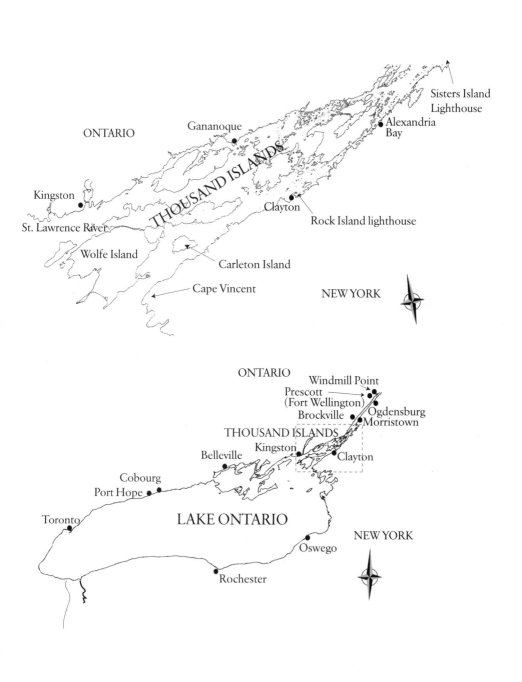

ONTARIO

Gananoque

THOUSAND ISLANDS

Alexandria
Bay

Sisters Island
Lighthouse

Kingston

St. Lawrence River

Clayton

Rock Island lighthouse

Wolfe Island

Carleton Island

Cape Vincent

NEW YORK

ONTARIO

Windmill Point

Prescott
(Fort Wellington)

Ogdensburg

Brockville

Morristown

THOUSAND ISLANDS

Belleville

Kingston

Clayton

Cobourg

Port Hope

Toronto

LAKE ONTARIO

NEW YORK

Oswego

Rochester

PART ONE
THE THOUSAND ISLANDS

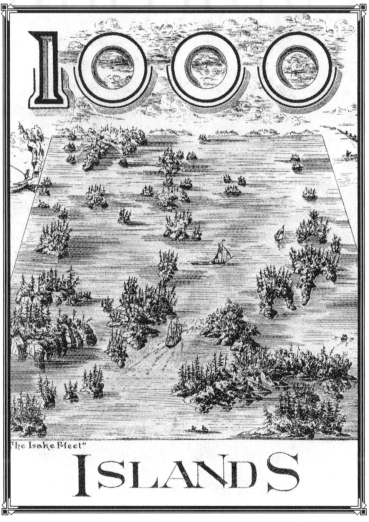

The Thousand Islands, a beautiful waterway made deadly by hidden reefs and shoals, and the islands themselves.

The windmill at Windmill Point, scene of a bloody battle in 1838. It would eventually be converted into a lighthouse.

WINDMILL POINT LIGHTHOUSE: THE HUNTERS' INVASION

Just to the east of Prescott, Ontario, stands the old Windmill Point Lighthouse. Originally constructed as a windmill in 1822, in 1838 the stone tower almost became, in the American imagination, a northern version of the Alamo.

Tyranny! It was a word oft spoken by Americans in the mid-1830s. While black slaves laboured in the shadow of the Stars and Stripes, and Native people, uprooted from their homes east of the Mississippi, were driven along the Trail of Tears to the dry lands of the West, Americans spoke contemptuously of the military dictatorship in Mexico to the south. In 1836 there had been a revolution in the Mexican state of Texas. American settlers who had gone there at the invitation of the Mexican government rebelled when the dictator Santa Ana seized power and began to impose his harsh rule. A small band of rebels led by such larger-than-life figures as James Bowie and David Crockett made a gallant but futile stand against Santa Ana's army at the Alamo in San Antonio. The Alamo defenders were massacred, but their sacrifice inspired their comrades to fight on to victory. A Texan army led by Sam Houston defeated Santa Ana. Now Texas was an independent republic, awaiting an opportunity to become a state in the American Union.

At the same time, Americans spoke with even greater contempt of British tyranny to the north, in Canada. The very existence of the British flag in their hemisphere seemed a threat to what Americans called Manifest Destiny, a God-given right to occupy the entire continent of North America. In the War of 1812, the United States had invaded Canada, mistakenly believing that its conquest would be "a mere matter of marching". The Canadians, they thought, would leap at the chance to be free of "British tyranny". But the Canadians, many of them from Loyalist families that had fled persecution in the States after the Revolutionary War, fought alongside the Redcoats to drive the Yankee invaders back. Americans had to look to their huge victory over a British army at New Orleans in 1815 to convince themselves that they had "won" that war.

Then, in 1837 and 1838, came rumblings of trouble in Canada. There was widespread discontent among the general population with the autocratic, corrupt, self-serving colonial administrations. But discontent did not necessarily mean a desire to sever ties with the British Crown. Armed insurrections sparked by William Lyon Mackenzie in Upper Canada (Ontario), and Louis-Joseph Papineau in Lower Canada (Quebec) did not gain popular

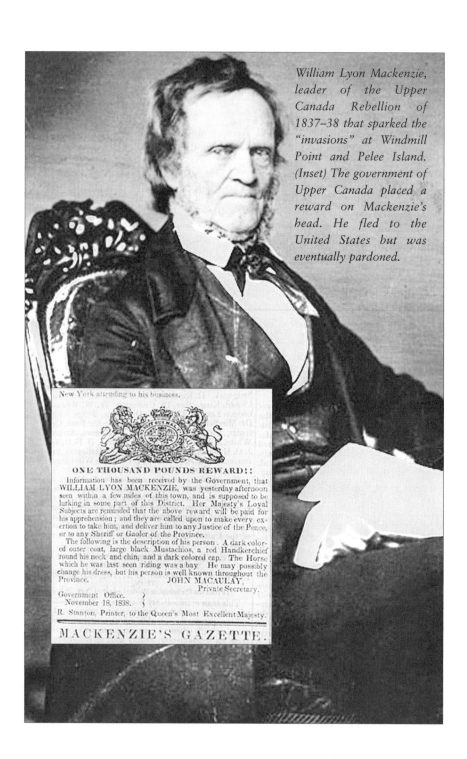

William Lyon Mackenzie, leader of the Upper Canada Rebellion of 1837–38 that sparked the "invasions" at Windmill Point and Pelee Island. (Inset) The government of Upper Canada placed a reward on Mackenzie's head. He fled to the United States but was eventually pardoned.

New York attending to his business.

ONE THOUSAND POUNDS REWARD!!

Information has been received by the Government, that WILLIAM LYON MACKENZIE, was yesterday afternoon seen within a few miles of this town, and is supposed to be lurking in some part of this District. Her Majesty's Loyal Subjects are reminded that the above reward will be paid for his apprehension; and they are called upon to make every exertion to take him, and deliver him to any Justice of the Peace, or to any Sheriff or Gaoler of the Province.

The following is the description of his person. A dark colored outer coat, large black Mustachios, a red Handkerchief round his neck and chin, and a dark colored cap. The Horse which he was last seen riding was a bay. He may possibly change his dress, but his person is well known throughout the Province.   JOHN MACAULAY,

Private Secretary.

Government Office.
November 18, 1838.

R. Stanton, Printer, to the Queen's Most Excellent Majesty.

MACKENZIE'S GAZETTE.

support and were quickly suppressed. Still, there were those in the United States who believed that the inevitable was about to happen. The long-suffering Canadians wanted to throw off the yoke of British tyranny, they thought. All that those unfortunate victims of British injustice needed was a little help from liberty-loving Americans.

Mackenzie and Papineau had, in fact, received support from American sympathizers. Officially, the American government discouraged any interference in British North American affairs by United States citizens. But beneath the surface there was that tantalizing prospect that plump prizes like Upper and Lower Canada, and then the Atlantic colonies, could be annexed by the Union—as Texas would surely be.

An organization known as the Hunters' Lodge, allegedly named for one of Mackenzie's followers, began to recruit members in American communities along the Canadian border and in port cities on the Great Lakes. The Hunters were said to have over a thousand individual lodges, with up to 80,000 members and a war chest of $300,000. The figures are probably an exaggeration, but the Hunters were nonetheless growing into a force to be reckoned with.

Like the Freemasons and other "secret" societies, the Hunters had oaths, ceremonies, special signals, and a hierarchy within their ranks. They were dedicated to the "liberation" of Canada and the banishment of the British tyrants from North America. There was a scattering of disaffected Canadians among the Hunters, but the majority of them were Americans, most of whom knew as much about Canada as they did about Mongolia. The membership included a few idealists, and a large number of adventurers and characters who could best be described as riff-raff. When they took the Hunters' oath they were promised rewards of money and free land in Canada, once the British tyrant had been overthrown. They truly believed that when they crossed the border, their ranks would be swelled by grateful Canadians. At a convention held in Cleveland in September 1838, they elected a president, vice-president and cabinet for the new Republic of Canada—all of them Americans. They also elected military commanders, one of whom was among Canadian history's most colourful rogues. The Commodore in the East of the Hunter Navy was Bill Johnston. Johnston was a Canadian expatriate with a deep-seated hatred for the British going back to the War of 1812, when he had been charged with desertion and treason. Years of activity as a bandit and smuggler had earned him the name Pirate of the Thousand Islands. Just a few months before the convention, Johnston had looted and burned the Canadian steamer *Sir Robert Peel* on the St. Lawrence River.

Among those drawn to the Hunters' cause was a 31-year-old mercenary named Nils Gustaf Von Schoultz. His comrades believed him to be a Polish-

The rebel navy captured and burned the Sir Robert Peel *as revenge for the burning of the ship* Caroline.

born revolutionary. More than a century later his great-grand-daughter, Ella Pipping, would reveal that he was, in fact, a Swedish national, born in Finland. Von Schoultz had indeed fought in a Polish revolt against Russia, and had escaped imprisonment by the Russians. He had served with the French Foreign Legion, and had lived in Italy and England before sailing for America. He settled in Salina in Onondaga County, New York, where he joined the local Hunters' Lodge. He believed wholeheartedly their arguments that the Canadians, like the Poles, were an oppressed people crying out for a liberator. He was made a colonel in the Hunter army, and was probably the only "officer" in that bizarre force with any military skill, or any sense of honour, as would become evident when the fighting started.

Early in November 1838, Hunters began to drift into Sackets Harbor, Oswego, Salina, Syracuse, Ogdensburg, Cape Vincent, Clayton and other New York communities. They kept a low profile, so as not to attract the attention of American authorities. On the Canadian side of the water, people had long been expecting a Hunter attack. The commanders of British garrisons throughout the colonies had established pickets at key locations and the Canadian militia had been called up. Just where the attack would be launched, though, no one could be sure.

BATTLE ON THE RIVER

On the morning of Sunday, November 11, the American steamer United States, downward bound for Ogdensburg from Oswego, put in at Sackets Harbor on her regular passenger run. Captain James Van Cleve did not know that among the passengers already aboard were about 100 Hunters. At Sackets Harbor, 70 or 80 more came aboard, including Nils Von Schoultz. At each stop the United States made as she steamed from Lake Ontario into the St. Lawrence River, more Hunters went aboard. Among them were Bill Johnston and "General" John Ward Birge, the commander of the invading army. Birge had predicted that once Americans knew that the invasion to liberate Canada was underway, thirty to forty thousand volunteers would swarm to the Hunters' banner. He had a plan that would have had the British foe rolling with laughter had they known of it. He was going to seize lightly garrisoned Fort Wellington at Prescott and, in his reasoning, effectively blockade the St. Lawrence River, thereby preventing British forces in Montreal and Quebec City from supplying and reinforcing the garrisons in Upper Canada. Birge evidently did not know that after the War of 1812, the British had constructed the Rideau Canal in case of just such an emergency. It was part of a waterway that linked Lower Canada to Kingston and Ottawa via the Cataraqui, Rideau and Ottawa Rivers. There was much about the Hunter invasion that would have been laughable, were it not for the fact that it cost so many men their lives.

As the *United States* passed Cape Vincent, two schooners approached: the *Charlotte of Oswego*, and the *Charlotte of Toronto*. A passenger asked Captain Van Cleve to take them in tow, a common practice at the time. Van Cleve was behind schedule and didn't want to lose time, but the passenger offered him one hundred dollars. The captain had lines tossed to the sailing vessels, and they were soon hauled alongside the big steamer.

Then the hatches of the schooners were thrown open and scores of men who had been hiding below decks swarmed out and climbed aboard the *United States*. They were heavily armed and quickly took possession of the steamer. Out of a cabin came the Hunter officers, resplendent in their new, homemade uniforms. No two looked alike, but all were dazzling with their brass buttons, epaulets, swords and red sashes. Bill Johnston preferred a bowie knife to a sword and had five pistols stuffed into his waistband.

Birge told the astonished Captain Van Cleve that they were commandeering his vessel for the invasion of Canada. There were now about four hundred Hunters on the *United States* and the two schooners, so Van Cleve knew that resistance would be unwise. Instead, he told Birge that if the *United States* failed to make its next scheduled stop, suspicion would be aroused. The Hunters agreed, and piled into the two schooners. It was the last time the leaders of the disorganized "army" would agree on anything. The two *Charlottes* sailed for Prescott on the Canadian shore, while Captain Van Cleve steamed into Morristown, New York, where he immediately informed American authorities of the Hunters' intentions. They, in turn (and to their credit), sent a warning across the river.

Accounts vary as to exactly what happened next, but clearly things went badly for the Hunters right from the start. Bill Johnston, who was much better at handling a small, speedy sloop than larger craft, ran the *Charlotte of Oswego* onto a sandbar at the mouth of the Oswegatchie River just west of Ogdensburg. Birge came alongside in a rowboat and the "general" and

The Hunters planned to capture Fort Wellington at Prescott and shut Upper Canada off from Lower Canada. Perhaps they didn't know that the British had built the Rideau Canal in the event of just such an emergency.

the "commodore" argued over what to do. Then Birge headed back to the American shore, saying that he was going to send more men across the river. Once there he complained of feeling ill, and took no further part in the invasion. Johnston and other Hunter leaders would attribute his "belly ache" to cowardice.

With the departure of Birge, Nils Von Schoultz assumed command of the *Charlotte of Toronto*. Rather than wait for the *Charlotte of Oswego* to get unstuck, he headed straight for Prescott. He intended to go ashore and take Fort Wellington by surprise, unaware that the British Commander there, Colonel Plomer Young, had already been alerted that the Hunters were coming. Von Schoultz landed his men above Prescott at a place called Honeywell's Bay, where they captured two sentries and destroyed a bridge. Then they returned to the schooner and continued on to Prescott.

It was now past midnight and into the small hours of November 12. Von Schoultz tied the *Charlotte of Toronto* to the Prescott dock, but the rope broke and the schooner began to drift downstream. Some nearby Canadian militia opened fire with a cannon, but the vessel was out of range. However, the shot was heard at Fort Wellington and in Brockville, and alerted the officers there as to where the action would be.

The *Charlotte of Toronto* ran aground on a sandbar a mile and a half (2.4km) downstream, just off Windmill Point. With her heavy load of men, arms and ammunition, the vessel could not be dislodged. There was no choice but to use the ship's boat to ferry men and armaments ashore.

Von Schoultz reconnoitered the area, and decided that it was the perfect beachhead for the invasion. The eight-storey-high windmill, with stone walls three-and-a-half feet (1m) thick could be converted into a fortress. Its high, small windows would be excellent firing platforms for snipers. There were a number of stone buildings near the tower—actually, the hamlet of New Jerusalem—that offered shelter for defenders. Von Schoultz believed that if he held this position, he could provide cover for the reinforcements he expected from across the river. He had just under two hundred men (22 of them Canadians); almost the same number that had held the Alamo for 13 days just two years earlier. Von Schoultz undoubtedly knew about the Alamo. All of America was talking about the courageous stand of William Barrett Travis, David Crockett and James Bowie. Those men, too, had expected help; help that never came. But Von Schoultz, firm in his belief that his cause was righteous and that America would mobilize now that the gauntlet had been thrown down, knew that help was just across the river. And when the Canadians saw his flag snapping in the light of dawn, they would hail him as their liberator.

Von Schoultz put his men to work building stone walls and gun emplacements. From the top of the windmill he flew the Hunters' own flag, a blue silk banner with an eagle and two stars and the words "Liberated by the Onondaga Hunters". It had been made for him by the ladies of Salina. This was his way of announcing to the local population that deliverance was at hand. Then he sent men out to forage for food and bring in some of the newly liberated citizens for questioning. The Hunters did round up a few bewildered Canadians. The civilians were polite to their captors, but evidently did not even realize how oppressed they had been.

As the *Charlotte of Toronto*'s cargo piled up on the shore, the schooner lifted off the sandbar. Bill Johnston arrived in a scow with more arms and news that five hundred Hunters in Ogdensburg were waiting to cross the water. Then a small British patrol boat appeared. Johnston and the crew of the schooner—men who had been pressed into service by the Hunters—hoisted sail and retreated upriver in the *Charlotte of Toronto*.

By daybreak Colonel Young in Fort Wellington knew of the Hunters' occupation of the windmill. Across the river the *Charlotte of Oswego* was still stranded on a sandbar, but the Hunters had commandeered the *United*

Nils Von Schoultz, European mercenary and Hunter leader. His misplaced idealism would cost him his life.

The Battle of the Windmill as seen from the American side of the St. Lawrence River. Some American chroniclers tried to turn the sad affair into a northern version of the Battle of the Alamo, fought in Texas just two years earlier. (Inset) Lieutenant Colonel Ogle Cowan brought the 9th Provisional Battalion from Brockville to fight the invaders.

States to try to pull her free. Young did not have enough troops at his disposal to attack the windmill, and at the same time guard the shore in case of another landing. He sent a few Canadian militiamen to watch the windmill from the cover of the woods, while he kept the main part of his small force in readiness for an assault elsewhere.

The Hunters who had pirated the *United States* were having difficulties. They were not experienced sailors, and were having no luck at all in getting the *Charlotte of Oswego* off the sandbar. Another vessel of the Hunter "navy", the little steamer *Paul Pry*, came to lend assistance. After considerable effort, the *Charlotte of Oswego* was pulled free.

Then trouble showed up in the form of the British steamer *Experiment*, commanded by Lieutenant William Fowell of the Royal Navy. Armed with an 18-pounder cannon and a 3-pounder swivel gun, the *Experiment* opened fire on the Hunter fleet. The *United States* retreated to Ogdensburg Harbour, but the *Paul Pry* and the *Charlotte of Oswego* made for Windmill Point, the *Charlotte* answering the *Experiment*'s fire with her own cannon. The duelling ships must have swung close to the Canadian shore, because it was reported that some of the cannonballs actually landed in Prescott.

The more disciplined fire of the British gunners must have disheartened the Hunters, because they turned and made a dash for Ogdensburg.

No sooner had Fowell chased the schooner and the little steamer into American waters than he found his vessel in the path of the much larger *United States*, which had returned to the fray. The big steamer was bearing down on him at full speed, obviously with the intention of ramming the *Experiment*. Fowell ordered a hard turn, and as the British steamer swung about, her 18-pounder belched fire and iron. The big cannonball smashed into the wheelhouse of the *United States*, beheading her pilot. Young Solomon Foster was the first casualty of the Hunter invasion. The *United States* once again fled for the safety of Ogdensburg harbour.

Fowell could not fire into American territory, so he withdrew to a position off Prescott and maintained a patrol there to protect the town from any further Hunter action. This left the crossing at Windmill Point temporarily unguarded, and Bill Johnston took quick advantage. He used a small boat to deliver three small cannons to Von Schoultz.

By this time, U.S. federal troops had arrived in Ogdensburg. They seized the vessels the Hunters had been using, as well as their stocks of arms and ammunition, and placed them under armed guard. Von Schoultz and the men on Windmill Point would get no more help.

The situation was just the opposite for Colonel Young. Lieutenant Colonel Ogle Gowan arrived from Brockville with his 9th Provisional Battalion. Two gunboats, the *Victoria* and the *Cobourg*, came down from Kingston. On board were officers and men of the 89th Regiment and the Royal Marines. Young now felt he had enough men to take the position on Windmill Point.

Von Schoultz, who still expected reinforcements, thought otherwise. The veteran of European battlefields had dug in well and positioned his men skillfully. When the battle commenced on the morning of November 13, he proved to be a tough adversary.

The *Cobourg* and the *Victoria* began lobbing shells at the windmill, but the six-pounders only bounced off the thick, stone walls. The *Experiment*, with her powerful 18-pounder, had been forced to withdraw because of engine trouble. Three hundred British troops and Canadian militiamen under Young and Gowan charged the Hunter position. Riflemen behind stone walls and high up in the tower poured volley after volley of lead into them, and Von Schoultz's field pieces hurled iron at point blank range. Some of the attackers were victims of "friendly fire" as cannonballs from the two gunboats missed the windmill and fell among the British and Canadians. Von Schoultz had set up a "dummy" cannon to fool the British, and Lieutenant William Johnson was killed in an attempt to capture it. After twenty minutes of thunder, smoke and blood, Young called off the attack. His force had suffered 21 dead and 64 wounded. It was obvious that it would take heavier artillery than his six-pounder pop guns to dislodge the fortified Hunters. He kept his troops in a semi-circle around the windmill—out of the range of the sharpshooters in the tower—and sent to Kingston for bigger guns.

In the Hunter camp, Von Schoultz had 13 dead and 29 wounded (3 of whom would die from their injuries). He had no medical supplies. The Hunters had been certain that once they landed, the adoring Canadians would happily provide them with everything they needed. Von Schoultz sent a few men out to try to slip through the British cordon and bring back medical supplies, but they were quickly captured.

On the American shore, hundreds of people had gathered to watch the battle, about 1.2 miles (2km) away, on the other side of the river. They cheered heartily when the Hunter fire drove back the British advance, but no one attempted to cross the river to help the beleaguered liberators. When darkness fell, Von Schoultz had his men gather the dead and wounded of both sides that littered the ground around the windmill, and had them placed in a barn. The British and Canadian prisoners would later speak highly of the kind treatment they received from the gallant European. But some of the Hunters, apparently without their commander's knowledge, vented their anger on the corpse of Lieutenant Johnson.

The night was cold and it snowed, but an American named Meredith paddled across the river on a plank and sneaked past the British to speak to Von Schoultz and then report back to the U.S. side. He told the "ailing" General Birge that Von Schoultz had wounded and no medical supplies, and had exhausted the ammunition for his field pieces. He was keeping his men busy scavenging the windmill for nails and bits of iron they could use as grapeshot. Birge suggested that Bill Johnston create a diversion by attacking the town of Gananoque, but the dreaded river pirate had disappeared from the scene.

Colonel Young kept the windmill under siege with only occasional firing, but would not commit his troops to another assault until his big guns arrived. He arranged a truce with Von Schoultz so he could retrieve his dead and wounded. Von Schoultz would not even consider surrender. On November 15, Young met an American colonel aboard the steamer *Telegraph*. The American tried to convince Young to let the Hunters leave the windmill and return to the U.S. He promised that American courts would deal with Von Schoultz and his men, and that the U.S. Army would prevent any further invasion attempts. Young refused. The Hunters had killed British troops and must therefore face British justice. Moreover, Young could not make such a deal without the permission of the Lieutenant-Governor of Upper Canada.

The windmill, sometime after the battle. The Hunters surrendered when the British pounded their position with heavy artillery. "...The roof crumbled to pieces over our heads", Von Schoultz wrote.

That night the *Paul Pry* managed to slip across the river to Windmill Point. On board were the Ogdensburg Postmaster, Preston King, and other officials of the town. King tried to convince Von Schoultz to abandon the windmill while he had the chance. But someone else in the Ogsdenburg party told Von Schoultz that help was coming. All would be well if he and his men could hold out just a little longer. Amazingly, Von Schoultz and his men believed this lie. King and his party left with just a few of the Hunter wounded. The invaders were now truly alone, and their fortress was about to become a trap.

The next day, November 16, Colonel Young's artillery arrived: two 18-pounders and a howitzer. His command had been beefed up with the arrival of the 93rd Regiment of grenadiers from Montreal. Looking out from the windmill at the red-coated columns, Von Schoultz finally realized that his position was hopeless. He sought to surrender under terms, but Young would accept only unconditional surrender. Then, to demonstrate that he was holding all the cards, he ordered his big guns to open fire.

The windmill and the stone buildings the Hunters had incorporated into their defensive works had withstood the fire of six-pounder cannons, but it was soon evident that they could not stand up to the battering of the big eighteen-pounders. Von Schoultz later wrote, "I kept my position, though the roof crumbled to pieces over our heads".

As round after round slammed into the windmill, setting it afire, British troops formed a perimeter, keeping just out of rifle range. The Hunters waved a white flag, but still the bombardment continued. One Hunter tried

British penal colony in Van Diemen's Land (Tasmania), where sixty of the captured Hunters were imprisoned.

to haul down their flag and was immediately shot. Then the cannonade stopped, and the British troops began to close in. The shell-shocked and terrified Hunters poured out of the windmill and surrendered. Von Schoultz was not among them. He and a few others had slipped out and tried to escape, but they were soon caught and taken to Prescott.

The prisoners were roughly handled by Canadian militiamen and civilians before British regulars could intervene. The people were furious that their country had been subjected to an unprovoked attack. Moreover, word had got out that the body of the slain Lieutenant Johnson had been stripped and mutilated by the Hunters. When the prisoners were shipped off to Kingston for trial, a regimental band further humiliated them by playing "Yankee Doodle".

Fifty of the prisoners were found to be under 21 years of age, and they were eventually paroled to their homes. The rest were held for a military trial. Twelve, including Von Schoultz, were sentenced to death. Von Schoultz was defended by none other than future Prime Minister John A. Macdonald. The young lawyer advised Von Schoultz to plead not guilty, but the soldier insisted on entering a guilty plea. His only argument in his own defence was that he had been deceived by others. From his cell, Von Schoultz wrote to a friend in Salina, "Let no further blood be shed; and believe me, from what I have seen, that all the stories that were told about the sufferings of the Canadian people were untrue". In his will the doomed man left four hundred pounds to the dependents of the Canadian militiamen who had been killed. He was hanged on December 8. Eleven others met the same fate over the next few weeks. Sixty Hunters were transported to the

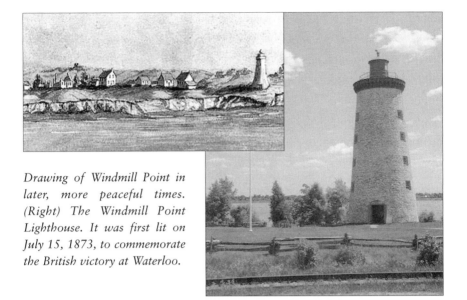

Drawing of Windmill Point in later, more peaceful times. (Right) The Windmill Point Lighthouse. It was first lit on July 15, 1873, to commemorate the British victory at Waterloo.

penal colony at Van Diemen's Land (Tasmania) and 22 were discharged from jail and sent back to the United States.

Had the defenders of the windmill all died fighting, they might have found themselves a place in American legend similar to that of the heroes of the Alamo. As it was, American chroniclers did try to squeeze some glory out of the sorry affair. One writer greatly exaggerated the size of the British force arrayed against the "lion-hearted Patriots", and inflated the number of British dead to 450. In his narrative, Von Schoultz fights heroically to the very end, finally being overwhelmed by a horde of British soldiers who "pounced upon him like a pack of bloodhounds". Seventy-five years after the event, another American author wrote that the Hunters failed because they did not have a Washington or a Sam Houston to lead them and, "with the aid of American sympathizers, wrest a province from the hands of an oppressive ruler".

For years the windmill stood as a battered reminder of those bloody November days in 1838. Then, in 1873, the Canadian government decided that a lighthouse was needed to warn mariners of Windmill Point and of those same shallows that the *Charlotte of Toronto* had run onto. Since the windmill tower was already there, it was simply repaired and converted to a lighthouse. Its lamp was first lit on June 15 to commemorate another battle, the British victory over Napoleon at Waterloo in 1815. It remained in service for 105 years, a beacon of light in a place where men had died for a cause that never was.

ROCK ISLAND LIGHT: A PIRATE AND A WRECK

A PIRATE KEPT THE LIGHT

Rock Island, near Clayton, New York, is just a speck in the great maze of the Thousand Islands, but a major shipping channel ran past it in the nineteenth century and there was a deadly shoal nearby. A lighthouse was built on the island in 1848. Bill Johnston, the notorious pirate of the Thousand Islands, was not, as is sometimes claimed, the first lightkeeper there. Two other men kept the light before he took over in 1853. But Johnston was certainly the most colourful of the keepers to occupy the small house with the beacon on the roof.

Canadian-born Johnston had been a pirate and a smuggler all his life, and had been declared a traitor in Canada for going over to the American side in the War of 1812. After his involvement in the Patriot fiasco at Windmill Point (see p.35), he had a $5,000 reward on his head in Canada, and a $500 reward in the United States. Johnston surrendered to American authorities and was sentenced to a year in prison, of which he served only six months. He was pardoned by President William Henry Harrison.

Johnston was 71 years old when he became the Rock Island lightkeeper, and in all likelihood was still involved in smuggling. An island in the St. Lawrence was a perfect spot from which to conduct such operations—while being paid $350 a year to keep the lighthouse. The old pirate lived alone on the island, but liked to entertain visitors with tales of his exploits. Many years earlier, in 1838, Johnston's gang had pirated the Canadian steamer *Sir Robert Peel*, and Johnston took the ship's silverware as part of his share of the loot. It was said that in later years, on festive occasions, Johnston would set his table with the stolen silverware. Quite possibly, visitors at the Rock Island Lighthouse ate their meals with the *Sir Robert Peel*'s silver.

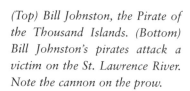

(Top) Bill Johnston, the Pirate of the Thousand Islands. (Bottom) Bill Johnston's pirates attack a victim on the St. Lawrence River. Note the cannon on the prow.

The Rock Island lighthouse when Johnston was keeper.

People who met Johnston during his lightkeeping years commented on how agile and robust he was for a man of such advanced years. They said he could still jump from rock to rock like a schoolboy. Since his island home was mostly bare rock, Johnston hauled boatloads of soil over from the mainland so he could plant vegetable and flower gardens.

In 1861 Johnston, now past 80, was relieved of his lightkeeping duties. Then the Civil War broke out. Johnston went to U.S. Army headquarters in Washington D.C. and offered his services, but was turned down. He retired to Clayton, and died there in 1870 at the age of 88.

THE CAPTAIN PULLED A GUN

In 1882, a new lighthouse was built on Rock Island, this one a sixty-foot (18.2-m) white stone tower. A boathouse, workshop, carpenter's shop, smokehouse and generator house were also crowded onto the little island. Michael Diepolder, a son of German immigrants, was the lightkeeper there when the wreck of the three-masted schooner *Vickery* took place on August 15, 1889. The accident almost resulted in murder.

The *Vickery* was en route from Chicago to Prescott with a cargo of grain. On board were Captain John Massey, six crewmembers and two female passengers. It was night when the *Vickery* entered the St. Lawrence, and Captain Massey was worried that the lights from the many cottages in the Thousand Islands might confuse him. He decided that he needed a pilot, so he stopped at Clayton to pick one up.

Once the home of a pirate, Rock Island is now the site of a museum.

The Vickery *on the bottom of the St. Lawrence River. After the ship ran onto a shoal, Captain Massey tried to shoot the river pilot.*

The pilot Captain Massey found was Henry Webber, allegedly an experienced riverman. However, veteran that he may have been, that night Webber had bad luck. Within 15 minutes of boarding the *Vickery*, he piloted the ship right onto the shoal by Rock Island. And Webber's luck almost got worse! An enraged Captain Massey swore at the pilot, pulled a revolver, and was about to shoot him. The first mate, Massey's brother, grabbed the captain's arm just as he pulled the trigger. The bullet buried itself in the deck, and the gun fell onto a hatch cover. The first mate grabbed it and threw it over the side.

The ship was filling with water, so all on board took to the lifeboats and rowed to Rock Island. (We can probably assume that Webber was not in Captain Massey's boat.) Lightkeeper Diepolder took the castaways in. There is no record of what went on in the lighthouse that night, but the atmosphere must have been tense, with Captain Massey fuming and Webber probably trying to keep out of his sight.

In the morning, Diepolder's guests went to Clayton. In reporting the loss of the *Vickery*, Captain Massey said that he most certainly would have shot Webber if his brother hadn't interfered. However, now that he'd had time to calm down, he said, he was glad that he hadn't shot the pilot.

It is possible that the accident was not the pilot's fault. Diepolder had always said that the light was too low, and that from certain angles the house blocked it from view. He felt that it should be raised to make it more visible from the water. It took years of petitioning, but finally, in 1895, the government had a new stone base made for the tower, raising it by five feet.

Diepolder remained at the Rock Island Light until July 1901, when he died suddenly of a heart attack after a swim. His widow, Emma, tended the light until the following September, when a new lightkeeper took over. The Rock Island Light was in service until 1958, when it was deactivated. It is now a museum operated by the Rock Island Lighthouse Historical and Memorial Association, and a museum now occupies the site that was once home to a pirate.

Lightkeeper Michael Diepolder complained for years that the Rock Island Light was too low. The American government finally had it raised, six years after the wreck of the Vickery.

SISTERS ISLAND: LIGHT ON THE BORDER

The Sisters Island lighthouse is about 12 miles (19km) from the small town of Alexandria Bay, New York. The name of the island likely derives from the fact that it was originally three tiny islands that were eventually connected by concrete walkways. A stone wall was built around the perimeter of the entire island.

Before the lighthouse was built, Sisters Island was situated right on the international boundary. On the Canadian side of the island there was an important shipping channel that hid a dangerous shoal. The Americans wanted to build a lighthouse to warn ships of the hazard, but it required nine years of negotiations before the border could be slightly altered. Once the Americans had title to the land, they built one of the most picturesque lighthouses in the Thousand Islands. Constructed of native limestone in 1870, it is a two-storey house with a tower rising from the roof. The cast-iron lantern room is sixty feet (18.2m) above the surface of the river.

A Civil War veteran named William Dodge was appointed lightkeeper, and for the next half century the Dodge family tended the Sisters Island Light. For twenty years, the presence of the lighthouse helped prevent any major accidents. Then one night in 1890 the Dodge family was awakened by a loud crash just outside their home. The passenger steamer *Ocean* had collided with the barge *Kent*. With water pouring into his vessel, the captain of the *Ocean* ran the ship at full speed onto Sisters Island to avoid sinking. There does not appear to have been any loss of life. Over forty years later, however, the waters off Sisters Island were the scene of a calamity.

The Thousand Islands. Even before construction began on the St. Lawrence Seaway, the Canadian and American governments worked to widen and deepen the shipping channels by blasting the riverbed with dynamite.

With traffic on the St. Lawrence steadily increasing, and the freighters themselves being built larger, collisions like the one between the *Ocean* and the *Kent* became a growing danger. For many years before construction began on the St. Lawrence Seaway in 1954, the Canadian and American governments had been deepening and widening channels on their respective sides of the St. Lawrence. Since the river bottom was bedrock, this required much blasting. A specially designed vessel called a drill-boat would be positioned above the area to be blasted, and a drilling platform was extended from the deck. Using heavy equipment on the platform, workmen would drill a series of holes into the riverbed. Then a machine called a loader was used to pack the holes with dynamite, much the way a ramrod was used to push a bullet down the barrel of a musket. The charges were attached by a cable to a detonator on the ship. When the explosives were in place, the ship would move off about a thousand yards (over 900m), and the charges set off. Then the rubble on the river bottom could be dredged out.

Working with explosives, of course, is always hazardous. In 1930 there was a tragic, freak accident on the Canadian side of the river, near Brockville, when the drill-boat *John B. King* was struck by lightning and exploded, killing 31 men. On July 19, 1932, a similar disaster occurred on the American side.

THE DAY THE *AMERICA* EXPLODED

The 150-foot (45.7m) drill-boat *America* had been ramming dynamite charges into the riverbed in the vicinity of Sisters Island. By late afternoon there was a ton and a half of explosives packed into the rock beneath the

The Sisters Island Lighthouse is one of the prettiest in the Thousand Islands, but it was near here that disaster struck the drill-boat America *in 1932.*

ship. Suddenly there was a blast that shook the St. Lawrence Valley for miles around. Men, ship and machinery were blown sky-high. Newspaper accounts said that the *America* simply disappeared. When the smoke cleared, all that remained of the drill-boat was some bits of floating debris to which a few injured survivors were clinging. Seven men were dead, and nine more were left with broken legs and crushed ankles.

The crew of a passing freighter, upbound for Lake Ontario, tossed life jackets to the men in the water, but the ship did not stop. It wasn't necessary, as dozens of boats from nearby islands were rushing to the scene to pick up the injured and the dead.

Water would have absorbed much of the shock, so there was no damage done on land. However, many people said they had felt the concussion. The sound of the explosion brought people from miles around on both sides of the river.

The disaster was particularly tragic for the community of Alexandria Bay. Five of the dead men were from that town. One of them, 27-year-old James Priestly, had just started the job that very day, filling in for his brother.

No one was sure exactly what caused the explosion, but one survivor said that the loader might have accidentally struck the cap on one of the charges in the river bottom. Because the charges were all connected, that would have set off all of the dynamite directly beneath the ship.

It is quite possible that on the river bottom, not far from the shore of Sisters Island, there are still some rusted fragments of the *America*. But there is no other evidence of that terrible July day in 1932. The lighthouse still stands, a private residence now and no longer an operational beacon. The building of the Seaway eliminated the need for a lighthouse on Sisters Island.

ONTARIO

Prescott

Thousand Islands

Brockville

Ogdensburg
Morristown

Prince Edward Peninsula

Kingston

Clayton

Bay of Quinte

Belleville

East Charity Shoals Light
Cape Vincent

Brighton

Presqu'ile Lighthouse

Tibbetts Point

Cobourg

Grenadier Island

Port Hope

False Duck Island

Stoney
Point

SacketsHarbor

Main Duck Island

Toronto

Frenchman's Bay

Galloo Island

NEW YORK

Toronto
Island

LAKE ONTARIO

Burlington
Hamilton

Oswego

Point Mississauga Light

Syracuse

Port Dalhousie

Rochester

Youngstown

Fort George

Niagara River

Welland Canal
(to Lake Erie)

PART TWO
LAKE ONTARIO

The image of a lighthouse was often used in nineteenth- and early twentieth-century advertising. Here a lightkeeper says that going four days without his favourite pipe tobacco is "too much for any man".

Gibraltar Point Lighthouse, the first permanent lighthouse on the Great Lakes, and the scene of a legendary murder.

Toronto Island was actually a peninsula until a storm in 1858 washed out the spit of land connecting it to the mainland. In the mid-nineteenth century, it was still a wild and lonely place.

York, Upper Canada. The lighthouse that guarded the harbour bore witness to events that would shape the history of Ontario.

GIBRALTAR POINT LIGHTHOUSE: THE PARADE OF HISTORY

The era of the lightkeeper on the Great Lakes began in 1808, when a light-house was built at Toronto's Gibraltar Point, on the peninsula (now an island) that shelters Toronto Harbour from the storms of Lake Ontario. That era lasted for over 180 years, until electronic automation, solar power and other technological advances made the lightkeeper's job obsolete. As one of the longest operating lighthouses on the Lakes, the Gibraltar Point Light has borne witness to a dynamic procession of events that helped shape the history of Ontario. It saw little "Muddy York", a miserable collection of log huts and tents, grow into a great metropolis. Its glowing light warned generations of captains and sailors away from the deadly shoals that lay off Toronto Island; guiding graceful schooners under sail, smoke belching steamers, and eventually ocean-going freighters.

Perched on an island on the doorstep of a growing colonial town, the Gibraltar Point Lighthouse was not as lonely as some of the more remote lights, but it was lonely enough. In the early days, when Toronto itself was but a speck of "civilization" in the midst of a wild frontier, the peninsula was heavily forested, and off-limits to settlement because it was Crown land. The lightkeeper and his family were pretty much on their own, with the wide lagoon of Toronto Harbour between them and the mainland. Even that harbour could be a dangerous challenge to a few souls in a little sloop or rowboat.

There were times when the lighthouse rose above the smoke and fury of war. In the eventful summer of 1812, it saw General Isaac Brock sail off in the *General Simcoe* for his appointment with destiny. (He captured Detroit, and then was mortally wounded repelling an American attack at Queenston.) In 1813 American raiders drove outnum-bered and poorly led British Redcoats out of York, and then sacked the town. The lighthouse was the only important building left undamaged by the looters

John Graves Simcoe, governor of Upper Canada and founder of York (Toronto).

and arsonists. This could have been because the lighthouse was out on the peninsula, some distance away from the actual town, and the American troops simply overlooked it. Or they might have thought that the British had mined it with explosives. Then, at the close of the war, the lighthouse was the scene of violence of a different nature—at least, according to legend. The tale has become one of Toronto's best-known ghost stories. (The full story of John Paul Radelmüller, first keeper of the Gibraltar Point Light, is told by this author in *Tortured Souls: the True Stories Behind Twenty Ontario Hauntings* [Lynx Images, 2005]. Only a brief scenario is given here.)

JOHN PAUL RADELMÜLLER: MURDER, BONES AND A GHOST

John Paul Radelmüller (whose name is often spelled incorrectly as Rademuller) was a German-born servant in the houses of British Royalty. After many years of service to the Royals and in the home of the Governor of Nova Scotia, he arrived in York, Upper Canada, in January 1804, looking for land. Radelmüller could not acquire the land he wanted, but he did secure the plum position of lightkeeper in 1808. Though Dominique Henry at the short-lived Point Mississauga Light was the very first lightkeeper on the Great Lakes, Radelmüller was the first to tend a permanently established lighthouse. And the likeable German, who was now in his mid-fifties (an old man by the standards of the time), did the job very well.

Then, one January night in 1815, some drunken soldiers from the York garrison beat him to death in a dispute over beer, or so legend has it. All that is known for certain is that John Paul Radelmüller vanished from the face of the earth. The story has it that the guilty soldiers, suddenly sobered by the enormity of their crime, dismembered the body and buried the parts all over the island. It has been said that Radelmüller's ghost still haunts the lighthouse and the island, mindful of his duties as the lightkeeper, while searching for his lost bones.

The peninsula was still a wild and lonely place in 1832 when James Durnan accepted the post of lightkeeper. His mother, upon hearing the news, exclaimed, "Oh, James! Will you be safe? Do the people who live there wear clothes? Are there Indians on the island?" Indians did, in fact, visit the Durnan family in the lightkeeper's cottage one Sunday morning. They joined the family in prayers, and then asked for a quart of milk.

The Durnans became something of a local institution. When James retired from the post in 1853, his son George took it over and held it until 1905. The parade of history past the lighthouse continued during George

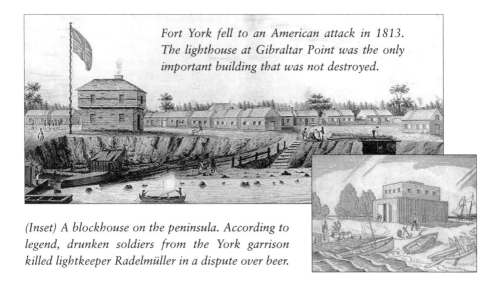

Fort York fell to an American attack in 1813. The lighthouse at Gibraltar Point was the only important building that was not destroyed.

(Inset) A blockhouse on the peninsula. According to legend, drunken soldiers from the York garrison killed lightkeeper Radelmüller in a dispute over beer.

Durnan's tenure. In 1866 the Queen's Own Rifles sailed past it on their way to fight Fenian invaders. In 1883 the steamer *Luella* landed 58 orphans on the island, the first wards of the new Lakeside Home for Little Children, an auxiliary of the now world-renowned Hospital for Sick Children.

In spite of George Durnan's unfailing dedication to his duties, there were times when Lake Ontario would not be denied, and ships were wrecked in the waters off Toronto Island: the *Monarch* and the *J.C. Beard* in 1856; the *Pacific* in 1861; the *Jane Ann Marsh* in 1868; the *Anne Bell Chambers* in 1873; and the *Fearless* and the *Olive Branch* in 1875. Durnan participated in many a rescue, not only of sailors in distress, but also of swimmers and pleasure boaters who went out to the island for recreation.

When George Durnan retired from his post at Gibraltar Point in 1905, he was honoured with the Imperial Service Order medal, presented to him by the Governor General on behalf of King Edward VII. It was a decoration created by that monarch to reward civilians for long and meritorious service to the Empire. But even though George Durnan kept the Gibraltar Point Light shining longer than any other keeper, his is not the name most readily associated with the lighthouse. Rather, it is that of the first keeper, John Paul Radelmüller, who vanished under such mysterious circumstances. Ironically, it was Durnan himself who inadvertently helped to make Radelmüller's name a Gibraltar Point legend.

In 1893 Durnan discovered an old grave with a few human bones in it. The remains could have been those of some long forgotten soul, but Torontonians immediately assumed that they were the bones of John Paul

Lightkeeper George Durnan (right) found some human bones—supposedly Radelmüller's—that gave rise to the stories of a haunted lighthouse.

Radelmüller. The discovery enhanced the rumour that the lighthouse was haunted, that the ghost of Radelmüller was wandering about Toronto Island at night. Tales of murder and the supernatural proved to be of much greater interest to the public than George Durnan's gold medal and long years of service. Radelmüller's ghost would, in fact, be the subject of an unusual debate in the middle of the supposedly non-superstitious twentieth century.

In the winter of 1957, the Gibraltar Point Lighthouse was decommissioned when a fully automated light on a simple iron tower was erected. The Department of Transport, seemingly lacking a sense of history, intended to demolish the tower. Canadians were going to destroy that which even the Americans had spared in 1813. Radelmüller's ghost, if indeed it haunted the building, was going to be left homeless. Rescue came in the form of the Metro Parks and Recreation Committee, which saved the lighthouse from the wrecker's ball and had it declared a historic site. A plaque would give a brief outline of the tower's history, including a few words about the alleged haunting. The wording for the plaque was suggested by the Archaeological and Historic Sites Advisory Board of the Ontario Department of Travel and Publicity. But the Metro Parks and Recreation Committee, after saving the structure itself, wanted no part of its most enduring legend. "Ghosts and haunted buildings have no historical significance", they declared. One committee member said he didn't believe the lighthouse was haunted at all. A reeve of Metropolitan Toronto asked if historians had established whether the discovery of a

For five months, a war of words raged in Toronto over whether or not the historic plaque on the Gibraltar Point Lighthouse should mention the alleged haunting.

skeleton on the island was a fact or a myth. Radelmüller, if he were listening, must have felt slighted.

From December 1957 until April 1958 the argument rocked the offices of the Committee and the Board. Did the vagaries of legend and superstition deserve to be stamped on a plaque along with the hard facts of history? Was an alleged ghost entitled to that kind of official recognition? The Committee demanded that the wording be changed, eliminating all mention of ghosts and haunting. But the members of the Board stuck to their guns and refused to make the change.

On April 12, 1958, *The Globe and Mail* announced, "Lighthouse Retains Right To Its Ghost". The Metro Committee, the short article concluded, "surrendered". The ghost of John Paul Radelmüller had a home, and recognition. The Gibraltar Point Lighthouse remains the only official official historic site in Canada marked as a haunted place.

A stiff wind blows boaters past the Queen's Wharf Light, one of a pair of light-houses at Toronto Harbour's Western Gap.

The well-protected harbour was one of the principal reasons the site was chosen for settlement. Lighthouses guided ships to the Western Gap, off Queen's Wharf (seen far left). Eventually lights were built to mark the Eastern Gap as well.

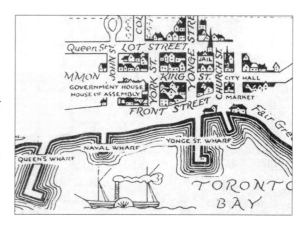

The Queen's Wharf Lighthouse, just visible above a warehouse.

TORONTO'S EASTERN GAP AND QUEEN'S WHARF LIGHTS:

STANDING WITNESS

Ships entering or leaving Toronto Harbour must pass through one of the gaps at the eastern and western ends of the Toronto Islands. In 1861, the Western Gap was marked by two 20-foot (6-m) wooden lighthouses, one on either side of the water. These lights were in service until 1916. One was torn down, but the other, known as the Queen's Wharf Light, was moved inland to be the centrepiece in a park at the

Toronto Harbour appears idyllic in this picture, but stormy weather could make the crossing between island and mainland perilous.

foot of Bathurst Street. Like the Gibraltar Point Light, these sentinels sometimes witnessed unfortunate accidents.

In 1924, an anonymous Toronto writer recalled that, in his childhood, he and other boys from Toronto's poor neighbourhoods would go skinny-dipping in the Western Gap by the Queen's Wharf Lighthouse. Evidently, rules about swimming in the harbour were lax at that time, and nobody objected to a bunch of naked boys cavorting in the water. The writer said that when other boys, "dudes" from more affluent parts of town had the nerve to show up wearing bathing suits, the poor boys, wearing only "nature's garb" would chase them away. But sometimes there would be trouble of a more solemn nature, and a small body would be found floating in the Gap.

The Eastern Gap, too, has been the scene of tragedy. Two lighthouses guided ships into this entrance to the harbour: a 22-foot (6.7-m), white, square wooden tower on the inner end of the East Pier; and a 40-foot (12-m) steel tower at the outer edge of the pier. In January 1959, one of these lighthouses might have been the last chance for survival for Gordon Miles, a Toronto Island resident who worked on the mainland. Miles crossed the Gap everyday in his skiff, regardless of the weather. Just two weeks before his disappearance, Miles was blown two miles (3.2km) out on Lake Ontario during a storm, and was able to row back only with great difficulty. In yet an earlier brush with disaster, he had crossed the water by leaping from ice

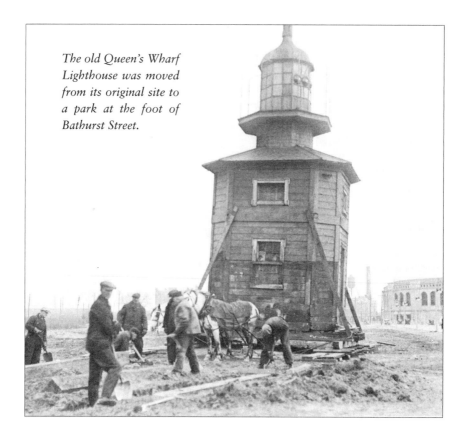

The old Queen's Wharf Lighthouse was moved from its original site to a park at the foot of Bathurst Street.

floe to ice floe, dragging his boat behind him. Miles' luck ran out when he tempted fate one time too many.

A storm was blowing, with winds gusting up to forty miles (64km) an hour. Lake Ontario was in a foul mood. Sometime after eleven p.m., Miles set out from the Toronto shoreline in his eight-foot (2.4-m) boat. He was never seen again. When he failed to arrive home, two tugboats were sent out to search for him. Even they were driven back by the violence of the gale. Later, searchers found Miles' duffle bag and lunch pail on a seawall near one of the Eastern Gap Lights. (Accounts do not specify which lighthouse.) They believed he might have been trying to climb onto the seawall, or to get the attention of the lightkeeper. But visibility was nil that night, and ten-foot (3-m) waves were hurling themselves against the Toronto shore. The only traces found of Gordon Miles' final encounter with Lake Ontario were an oar and some wreckage from his boat.

THE OLD RED LIGHTHOUSE, QUEEN'S WHARF, TORONTO

by J.B. Rittenhouse

There stood a beacon on Ontario's shore
That guided sturdy mariners by night.
When storms assailed and waters fiercely rolled,
It warned them with its never-failing light.

It stood in state for over fifty years,
Through heat and rain and winter's icy blast;
It bravely did its work and never failed,
And looked with pride on thousands
passing masts.

If this old lighthouse could only speak,
Many thrilling tales of shipwreck it
could tell.
Of dangers passed—of loss of human
life—Of anxiousness when light on
raging waters fell.

But now its day is passed, its
usefulness s o'er,
The march of progress has usurped
its place.
When moved, it muttered not a
murmur of complaint,
For Ontario's waters it will always face.

Most carefully 'twas placed (which tells
of passing worth),
And worthily the honour it assumes
It stands today a monumental work,
As honoured as any hero's sacred tomb.

So let it stand, that all who pass may see.
And let it speak in its own silent way.
To thousands that it guided it gave
its very best,
And earned repose in its declining day.

Toronto *Globe*, December 19, 1929

*Newspapers in the nine-
teenth and early twentieth
centuries often published
amateur poetry. In this
example, a would-be bard
pays homage to the Queen's
Wharf Lighthouse.*

THE FRENCHMAN'S BAY LIGHT: MIXED SIGNALS

For many years there has been a story in circulation about a young naval officer on the bridge of a destroyer one night, who sees a light some distance ahead of his ship. He believes he is on a collision course with another vessel, so he has a message flashed, telling the other ship to change course. A reply is flashed back, telling the officer that he must change *his* course. The communication goes back and forth for several minutes, with the distance between the two narrowing. The now-angry young officer finally sends the message: "CHANGE YOUR COURSE IMMEDIATELY. I AM A DESTROYER".

He gets the response: "CHANGE YOUR COURSE IMMEDIATELY. I AM A LIGHTHOUSE".

This story, in several versions, has been set in American, Canadian and British warships, and is no doubt fictional. But it does serve to illustrate the fact that sometimes a ship's master can be confused by a light. Captain Johnston of the *Mary Ward* allegedly mistook the light from a tavern or boarding house for the lighthouse on Nottawasaga Island in Lake Huron, and ran his ship onto a shoal (see p.157). If he did, indeed, make such an error, he was not the only skipper to do so. Another captain apparently thought that he was seeing the gleam from a lighthouse, when in all probability he was looking at a light on a train.

Frenchman's Bay, to the east of Toronto in what is now the suburb of Scarborough, was a busy port in the 1880s. But it was not

The schooner Marysburgh *ran aground when a skipper mistook a green railway light for the Frenchman's Bay Light.*

Frenchman's Bay, five miles (8km) west of where the Marysburgh was wrecked. This was reputed to be a smugglers' lair.

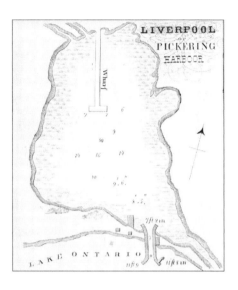

a registered port. Private funds built the dock, and maintained a lighthouse as far back as 1857. In 1880, a brand new wooden lighthouse replaced an older structure. The coal oil that fuelled the lamp was paid for out of tolls collected in the harbour. At that time, the Frenchman's Bay Lighthouse had a distinctive green light.

Five miles (8km) to the east of Frenchman's Bay was a makeshift harbour called Port Union. This was roughly at the line where the suburbs of Scarborough and Pickering now meet. Port Union no longer exists, but in the 1880s it had a dock, a farmer's market and a railway station with a water tower. The water tower was particularly important, because westward bound locomotives stopped there to take on water before climbing the steep grade up to Scarborough. That stretch of shore between Frenchman's Bay and Port Union was also reputed to be a smuggler's coast. Ontario farmers didn't just sell their potatoes and onions there; they also bought duty-free American goods.

The night of October 31, 1881, would have been a miserable Halloween for the children of Toronto. It was, in fact, a dark and stormy night. Out on Lake Ontario, to the east of Toronto, the schooner *Marysburgh*, 99 feet (30m) long and two-masted, was looking for the Frenchman's Bay Light, the only green light on the lake. It is not known what was in her hold, and the name of the skipper has been lost. But the schooner was not in a normal navigation channel, which could indicate that her cargo was not entirely legitimate, or simply that the captain had lost his bearings in the storm. The ship was standing inshore, the captain wondering if somehow he had missed the light in the dirty weather, when suddenly he saw it, a glimmer of green blinking through the rain.

The captain pointed the *Marysburgh* toward the green light... and ran her right onto some rocks. The bottom was ripped out and the *Marysburg* was a total loss. When captain and crew dragged themselves ashore, they found that they were not at Frenchman's Bay at all. What then, was that

green light the captain was certain he had seen?

The *Marysburgh*'s owners thought that the captain had seen a green semaphore light (a type of railway signal) at the Port Union Railway station, which was quite close to the lakeshore. The Grand Trunk Railway said that there was no green semaphore light at Port Union. What the captain had most likely seen was the green light on a train that was taking on water at the tower. The ship owners tried to sue the Grand Trunk for damages, but got nothing. For a long time after that Halloween night, the wreck of the *Marysburgh* lay in the shallows, gradually being picked apart by the surf.

PRESQU'ILE LIGHT: CHANGING THE COURSE OF HISTORY

The presence of a single man-made structure at a strategic site, or the lack of one, can be a catalyst in the course of human events. Cities have grown at locations where, long ago, someone built a bridge or a trading post. The arbitrary selection of a route for a railway causes one community to flourish while half a dozen others die. The Presqu'ile Lighthouse on Lake Ontario had an effect not only on the direction settle-

The Presqu'ile Lighthouse not only helped save ships, but it also helped save the very land upon which it stands. Here, the stone tower is shingled to protect against erosion.

John Graves Simcoe planned to establish a colonial centre called Newcastle at Presqu'ile.

ment took in that part of eastern Ontario, but also on the fate of the very peninsula upon which it stands.

The small Presqu'ile Peninsula juts out into Lake Ontario just to the west of the much larger Prince Edward Peninsula, about 100 miles (161km) east of Toronto. It is separated from the Bay of Quinte by the narrow isthmus that connects the Prince Edward Peninsula to the mainland. Part of the Presqu'ile Peninsula hooks around to the east, so that a small protected bay is enclosed between it and the mainland.

In 1797, John Graves Simcoe, the Lieutenant Governor of Upper Canada, had plans drawn up for a townsite at Presqu'ile. There was a good harbour there, the site was defensible, and if a canal was cut through the isthmus to the Bay of Quinte, the town would be at the western end of a valuable shortcut on the water route between Kingston and York (Toronto). Shipping would be safe from the unpredictable crosswinds of the open lake, and from American attack in the event of war. The proposed settlement was to be called Newcastle, and Simcoe planned to make it a regional administrative centre. But settlement had barely begun when, in 1804, a major disaster doomed the town.

On October 7 of that year, the Provincial Marine schooner HMS *Speedy* was en route to Newcastle from York. On board was Robert I.D. Gray, the Solicitor General for Upper Canada, along with several other important officials. They were going to Newcastle to conduct a murder trial. Just off Presqu'ile, the *Speedy* was caught in a squall and sank, taking about twenty people to their deaths. Now the government deemed the site "inconvenient", and the proposed town was never developed. Had there been a lighthouse on the peninsula, the *Speedy* might have been saved. There is a legend that a Captain Selleck lit a bonfire in an attempt to guide the ship to safety, but to no avail.

The loss of the schooner HMS Speedy *doomed the fledgling settlement of Newcastle. A lighthouse might have prevented the disaster. (Inset) Nicol Hugh Baird, builder of the Presqu'ile Lighthouse, was beset by financial problems.*

Still, the natural harbour at Presqu'ile was seen as a safe refuge for ships caught by storms. In 1837, the House of Assembly for Upper Canada passed legislation for the construction of lighthouses at Port Colborne, Port Burwell, Oakville, Lake St. Clair and Presqu'ile. There were still plans to dig a canal across the Prince Edward isthmus, and another canal to connect Lake Ontario with the Trent River. The Presqu'ile Light would be a key beacon on that water network. However, though the lighthouse was completed in 1840, it would be many years before either canal was constructed.

Work on the Presqu'ile lighthouse actually began in 1837, under the supervision of Nicol Hugh Baird, a Scottish engineer who had worked on the Rideau Canal. The 69-foot (21-m) stone tower rose slowly due to shortages of funds. One workman complained to the government for five years that he had not been fully paid.

If the town of Newcastle failed because there was no lighthouse on Presqu'ile, the town of Brighton, at the head of the small bay between Presqu'ile and the Prince Edward Peninsula, prospered because of the light. The lighthouse made the approach to Brighton safe, so the town developed as a thriving export port and fisheries centre. Other developments, however, were to change the direction of shipping on Lake Ontario, and the role of the Presqu'ile Light.

By the time the Murray Canal was finally dug through the Prince Edward isthmus in 1889, the concentration of shipping on Lake Ontario had shifted. There was no longer concern about war with the United States. The Erie Canal linked Buffalo to the Atlantic seaboard, and the Welland Canal connected Lake Ontario to Lake Erie. The heaviest traffic had been drawn to the western end of the lake. Moreover, the Murray Canal was too shallow for the big steamers that were rapidly replacing schooners. The Presqu'ile light would be a beacon operating mostly for fishermen and pleasure boaters.

The building of the Erie Canal and other developments drew major shipping away from Presqu'ile.

Though major commercial navigation had passed it by, the Presqu'ile Light still stood watch over a harbour that was a port of refuge, as well as home port to many fishermen and recreational boaters. It was also an increasingly popular tourist destination. Range lights and a foghorn were installed as further safety measures, making the harbour all the more attractive to small boats. This would have a definite impact on the region, and the Presqu'ile lightkeepers would play a significant role, not only in being the tenders of the light, but also as guardians of the peninsula itself.

The first lightkeeper at Presqu'ile was William Swetman, a 55-year-old Englishman who had arrived in Canada in 1821. His younger brother, Jerome, had been the lightkeeper at False Duck Island since 1828. It was probably through Jerome's influence that William was hired. William was lucky he took the position when he did, because in 1844 the government passed legislation that gave preference to the hiring of experienced Great Lakes mariners as lightkeepers, and he was not a sailor. Nonetheless, he evidently did the job well, because he was at the Presqu'ile Light for 31 years.

Unlike the British government, which assigned three or four trained, uniformed and reasonably well paid men to a lighthouse, the colonial government in Canada was very stingy with lightkeepers. Swetman was paid a paltry 65 pounds a year at the start of his lightkeeping career. He had to supplement his income by raising cattle. No house was provided for him and his family until 1846, and only after he had petitioned the government for a place to live, and a raise in salary.

Early colonial planners wanted to dig a canal across the isthmus of the Prince Edward Peninsula as part of a waterway that would be safe from storms and American attack. The Murray Canal was constructed in 1889, too late and too shallow for large-scale commercial shipping.

Swetman fortunately had a wife, son and grandchildren to help with the many duties at the light station, as well as with the cattle. In fact, he founded something of a lightkeeping dynasty. His son, William Jr., kept the range lights at Presqu'ile until he went to be the Pelee Island lightkeeper. (He was killed there in an accident in 1866). When the elder Swetman died at Presqu'ile at the age of 86 in 1871, his grandson, also William Swetman, became the keeper for a short time. He was followed by his brother-in-law, G.B. Simpson, who was the keeper until 1874.

From 1863, the Swetmans (and later Simpson) had an assistant, James Cummins, whose duty was to tend to the range lights. A former Pelee Island lightkeeper, Cummins was well acquainted with the frugal ways of the government. At Pelee he'd had to sleep on the beach or on the lighthouse steps, because no house had been provided for him. Things weren't much better when he arrived at Presqu'ile.

> I found a miserable dwelling, an old log house, a part of it weatherboard, the principal part of it is neither lathed or plastered. I have, being compelled this past winter to sit up all night in cold weather, to make fires to keep my family from freezing. The dwelling is built in a very low spot. The storms roll down from the hills and takes its abode around this old fabric. Water and ice is our companion.

The superintendent of lighthouses eventually wrote to the Secretary of Public Works, requesting a new dwelling for Cummins. The government loosened the purse strings enough to provide a decent place for the Cummins family to live.

While Cummins was fighting to get a roof over his head, other people were making themselves comfortable—illegally—on Presqu'ile. Because of its popularity as a vacation spot, Presqu'ile was being invaded by squatters, people who held no title to any land, but simply moved in, setting up campsites and even building cottages. These people cut down a lot of trees, which alarmed the provincial government. There was concern that deforestation would ruin the harbour. As early as 1868, the harbourmaster at Brighton had complained about the uncontrolled cutting of trees. In 1871 Ontario transferred the Presqu'ile Peninsula to the Dominion of Canada, thus placing it under federal protection. The government leased over 80 acres (32h) to the Swetman family, and 44 acres (18h) to James Cummins. It was the keepers' duty to protect this property. Nineteen squatters were granted leases, on the condition that they not cut down any green timber. This would be the first step toward the establishment of a major provincial park, but it also set the stage for conflict.

Looking after the lighthouse, the foghorn, and chasing away squatters was too much for Simpson. In 1874 he resigned as lightkeeper and took over the range lights from Cummins. Captain William Henry Sherwood was appointed lightkeeper at Presqu'ile. Sherwood soon found himself in confrontation with squatters who erected temporary cottages, or simply trespassed by picnicking and camping on lands under his guardianship.

In trying to do his job, Sherwood evidently had some unpleasant moments, and for a long time was getting no support from the government. This is indicated in a letter he wrote to federal authorities twenty years after the squatter problem started: "Should it be found necessary to order the removal of the cottages at the close of the season, will you be kind enough to do so from the Department as they will take it very ill from me". Apparently eviction notices were served, but then were rescinded through the influence of the local member of parliament, which further suggests that Sherwood had been caught in an exasperating situation.

In 1898, Herbert E. Smith became the Presqu'ile lightkeeper, and inherited Sherwood's "squatter" headaches. The government warned Smith at the outset that he would be held responsible if anymore squatters moved onto federally protected lands. At the same time, the government was making "exceptions" in the cases of some squatters. Smith may well have wished that he'd drawn lighthouse duty on some remote island.

In 1904, the legitimate cottagers at Presqu'ile complained to the government that they had to pay municipal taxes, while the squatters got away

The Presqu'ile lightkeepers protected the peninsula from squatters. Their efforts led to the creation of Presqu'ile Provincial Park.

with paying nothing. There was even a rumour that one cottager tried to get Smith fired so he could take over the lightkeeper's job. In 1905, the federal government gave in to the squatters and issued new leases. The lightkeeper now became, in effect, an agent for the landlord—the government. In addition to his lightkeeping duties, he was responsible for handing out leases, collecting rents, keeping detailed accounts and approving building plans for cottages. He was compensated for this extra work by receiving a commission on the leases.

The squatter problem was solved. One of the most important outcomes of all this, was that even though the squatters had been a nuisance, the peninsula had been protected from excessive farming, logging or settlement. The forest was still largely intact. This quite likely would not have been the case had it not been for the presence of the lighthouse and its keepers. The lighthouse had been instrumental in making Presqu'ile a popular tourist and vacation site. The keepers, though at times they must have felt abandoned by the government, had done their best to preserve the natural beauty of the peninsula.

Most of Presqu'ile was transferred back to the province of Ontario in 1921. The lighthouse reserve of 125 acres (50.5h) followed in 1928. Enough of the land had been preserved in its natural state to make the foundation of Presqu'ile Provincial Park.

The Presqu'ile Lighthouse is still in operation (automated), making it one of the oldest active aids to navigation on the Great Lakes. Its exterior has been shingled to protect the stonework from erosion, but it nonetheless remains an imposing structure. Though the interior is currently closed to the public, the lighthouse is still a central attraction in the park it helped to create.

MAIN DUCK ISLAND

A SANCTURAY FROM STORMS

Scattered like stepping stones across the eastern end of Lake Ontario are several islands, the largest of which is Main Duck, about 25 miles (40km) south of Kingston. Since the earliest colonial times this has been one of the most well travelled regions of the Great Lakes, because this is where Lake Ontario empties into the St. Lawrence River. Like the Soo, the Detroit River, and the Welland Canal, it is a primary link for the entire inland seaway. But deadly shoals lurk in the waters here. Many a ship has been wrecked on hidden rocks or on the islands themselves, making this one more region with the nickname "graveyard". The Main Duck Light, an 80-foot (24.3-m) concrete tower, was built in 1914 to warn vessels of the dangerous waters and to guide them into the St. Lawrence. Near the tower a small house was built for the keeper. On several occasions, men who had encountered trouble out on the lake were fortunate that the Main Duck lightkeeper was on hand to provide food, warmth and shelter.

THE *JOHN RANDALL*: A CAPTAIN'S FATE

Fred Bongard, keeper of the Main Duck Island Light in 1920 (he'd been there since 1915), liked to keep his larder well stocked. It was the age of Prohibition, and Main Duck Island was a favourite stopover for rum-runners smuggling booze into the United States. Sometimes the bootleggers would be Bongard's guests for days, and those gentlemen liked good food and comfort while they waited out the weather or the United States Coast Guard. There was one time, however, when guests of a different nature were grateful for Bongard's hospitality.

"It is feared that the steambarge *John Randall*, well known in this port, has been lost on Lake Ontario", the Kingston *Whig* reported on November 17, 1920. A day earlier the *John Randall* had cleared Oswego, New York, with a cargo of coal for Belleville. The weather had been foul for several days, and the *John Randall* was a leaky old ship whose pumps had to be in constant operation. But Captain Harry Randall (whose father, Captain John Randall, had built the ship and was the owner) decided that he could make the 12-hour crossing. He had a crew of four good men, two of whom were his cousins.

Daily British W

KINGSTON, ONTARIO, FRIDAY, NOVEMBER 26, 1920.

CAPT. RANDALL AND HIS CREW EIGHT DAYS ON DUCK ISLAND

Steambarge John Randall Foundered Half a Mile From Island At 1:30 a.m. of 17th--Crew Swam to Shore--Stormy Weather Held Them on Island With Lighthouse Keeper--Reached Kingston on Friday.

After having practically been given up as lost, the crew of the steambarge John Randall, of Kingston, which has been missing since a week ago last Tuesday, were located on Thursday afternoon. The first intimation received in the city was a message sent from Picton by Captain Harry Randall, who was in command of the vessel. Captain Randall, stated that his steamer foundered on Wednesday morning, November 17th, at 1.30 o'clock, about a half a mile from the Main Ducks, but he and the other three members of the crew were able to swim to the island, where they remained ever since.

Shortly after this message was received in the city, the Whig- was fortunate in being able to speak to Captain Randall over the long distance telephone at Picton. The captain stated that on Wednesday morning, November 17th, the steamer, which carried 260 tons of coal from Oswego for Belleville, was caught in the storm, and when about half a mile from the Main Ducks, she broke in two and foundered. The captain and members of the crew were thrown into the cold water, and had to swim a distance of half a mile to shore. Capt. Randall stated that he thought they were in the water for about an hour. The men were so fatigued when

walk. On the island they met Fred Bongard, the lighthouse keeper, who cared for them during the eight days that they were shipwrecked. There was no shortage of food, as the light keeper had a considerable quantity of provisions on hand.

Captain Randall stated that a great deal of praise was due Mr. Bongard, who had cared for them.

Couldn't Send a Message.

As much as they tried to get in touch with the mainland, it was impossible until Thursday afternoon, when the lighthouse keeper took them to South Bay, and then they drove to Picton and immediately got in communication with Kingston and Seeley's Bay.

The captain stated that at the time the ship foundered, there was a very heavy gale blowing from the east, and many times he thought he would never reach a point near the Ducks. The Ducks islands are located about twenty-three miles from Kingston and are divided into two islands known as the Main and False Ducks.

The captain when asked about the condition of his ship, stated that if there was mild weather he believed it might be possible to salvage the boiler and the engine, as they were not so far under water that they could not be reached by hooks. He

Captain John Randall, father of Captain Harry Randall, never gave up hope that his son would be saved. On Tuesday, when speaking to the Whig, he stated that he had every hope that his boy and the members of the crew were safe on the Ducks. When told that a captain of a steamer, who passed the Ducks, stated that he did not see the steamer, it did not dampen his hopes, as he felt his son had taken shelter in a hollow in the island.

On Wednesday afternoon, Captain Randall, Sr., went up to the Ducks on the steamer Brockville, thinking that he might get trace of his son. One can imagine how he felt on Thursday afternoon, after arriving back in the city, to be informed that his son and the members of the crew were safe and sound.

He had only left for home about half an hour when his son and the three members of the crew arrived at South Bay. He had been up to South Bay and Timber Island, but had been unable to get any word of the missing boat. When he returned home, he was not discouraged as he was confident that the missing men would be found.

On Monday night, Marjah, the mystic, who was playing at the Grand Opera House, stated that the Randall was at the Ducks and the

Captain Harry Randall and his crew found refuge in the Main Duck Lighthouse when the steambarge Randall *went down. A year later, Captain Randall was not so lucky.*

Another steamer, the *Jeska*, cleared Oswego harbour after the *Randall*. After a difficult crossing she docked in Kingston, where the skipper said that he had passed the *Randall* in the night. The old ship had been bucking heavy seas, he said, and appeared to be headed for the Bay of Quinte. Hours passed, and the *Randall* did not arrive at Belleville, or at any other port.

Then came reports from Sackets Harbor, New York, that people near the lakeshore there had heard the distress whistle of a ship and cries of men coming from out of the black night over Lake Ontario. A lifejacket was found floating in the harbour. The Americans said there was little doubt that the *Randall* was "lost".

But Captain John Randall wasn't about to give up hope. He was certain that his son had taken the ship into the shelter of the "Ducks"—Main Duck and False Duck Islands—whose lighthouses had guided many a beleaguered sailor. But there was no telephone or radio communication with the islands. Moreover, the captains of other ships arriving at Kingston said that they had passed the Ducks and seen no trace of the *Randall*.

John Randall remained optimistic. He said that the ship could have been hidden from view in one of the islands' inlets, and that as soon as the weather cleared he was going out to look for himself. A mystic who went by the stage name Marjah was performing at Kingston's Grand Opera House, and Captain Randall asked him about the missing vessel. Marjah said that the ship was at the Ducks and that the crew was safe. Whatever spirit Marjah consulted with was only partly right.

Soon after leaving Oswego, Captain Harry Randall had second thoughts about his decision to cross the lake in such hostile weather. Engineer Jack O'Grady reported no water in the hold, but the wind and seas were rising, snow was making visibility poor, and the ship was taking a pounding. With huge waves breaking over the bow, the *John Randall* altered course for the Ducks, where the skipper hoped to ride out the storm in the lee of one of the islands.

But the *John Randall*'s fate had already been decided. Just half a mile (.8km) off Main Duck Island, a monstrous wave swept away the pilothouse and the lifeboats. Then the ship broke in two. Captain and crew were hurled into the water. Somehow, they managed to stay in a group as they swam for shore.

It took an hour of fighting the lake for the men to cover that half mile. They were tossed by giant waves, and the November water was freezing. They had lifejackets, but these tended to have a strangling effect once they became sodden. Randall later said that they were "man-killers". His crew agreed. At last the men dragged themselves onto Main Duck Island, so fatigued that they could hardly stand. They might still have perished there in in the cold had it not been for the lighthouse and keeper Fred Bongard.

Left) Ticket to a show featuring the mystic called Marjah, who told Captain Randall, Sr. that the ship and crew were safe. Marjah was only partly correct. (Above) Main Duck Light stands watch over the "graveyard" of Lake Ontario.

Bongard was startled to hear someone pounding on his door in the dead of night, and when he opened it, the shipwrecked men practically collapsed at the threshold. Bongard took them in and gave them food, hot drinks and dry clothes. They would be his guests for the next eight days, while on the mainland the men's families and the public in general had no clue as to their fate. Most people had given up hope of seeing any of them alive—except Captain John Randall and Marjah. Oddly enough, the younger Randall himself had been fearful that something terrible would happen. He told lightkeeper Bongard that for weeks before that last voyage he'd had feelings of foreboding.

After a stormy week, the weather finally cleared and Bongard took the men to South Bay. There they got a ride to Picton, where they could use a telephone. There was relief all around as families received the news that all of the *Randall*'s crew was safe. The men had no shortage of praise for light-keeper Bongard. He'd only had to let them in, of course, but for men in their desperate situation he must have seemed a godsend.

If Marjah really could see whatever it was Destiny had in store for mere mortals, he might have advised Harry Randall to seek a different calling, something on dry land. Early on the morning of November 24, 1921—a year almost to the day of the sinking of the *Randall*—the steamer *City of New York* left Oswego bound for Trenton, Ontario. Captain Harry Randall was commanding, and his wife and two small sons were aboard. The *City of New York* went down in a storm, it was believed about 10 miles (16km) off Stoney Point, New York. At five p.m. the next day, the freighter *Isabella* found a yawl adrift on the lake near the entrance to the St. Lawrence River. In it were the bodies of Mrs. Randall, three members of Randall's crew, and an unidentified teenaged boy. All had died of exposure. Nearby was another yawl, floating upside down. The bodies of Captain Randall, his two sons, and another crewmember were never found.

THE *CONCRETIA*: TENDER IN TROUBLE

The next vessel to run into trouble at Main Duck Island was the very boat that was supposed to take the lightkeepers home for the winter. On December 16, 1921, the Canadian lighthouse tender *Concretia*, described as being "of corvette construction", set out from Kingston to retrieve some navigational buoys and to pick up lightkeeper Wesley Thomas and his assistant Garfield Thomas from Main Duck. The *Concretia* had a crew of 16, including Captain Daniel Mills.

Two days after the *Concretia* left port, a severe storm struck Lake Ontario. The gale was violent enough to draw a comment from a veteran saltwater captain named R. Kendall of the steamer *Clyde*, who was making his first voyage on the Great Lakes. "After Sunday morning on Lake Ontario, I have every respect for freshwater mariners", he said. Kendall had been forced to run his ship into Port Dalhousie for shelter.

When the storm abated, there was no word from the *Concretia*, and searchers could find no sign of the tender. Marine men in Cape Vincent, New York, said that on the night of the 18th, while looking across the water with a telescope, they had seen a light far out on the lake; a light that subsequently disappeared. They believed it must have been the missing Canadian ship. Word quickly spread from one Ontario lakeshore community to another that the *Concretia* had gone down with all hands. This was particularly bad news for Kingston, home for many of the *Concretia*'s crew.

Concrete was actually used in the construction of the Concretia, *an experimental vessel that saw service as a tender. In 1935 the* Concretia *was sunk to form a wharf at Kingston. In this photo the ship has evidently been stripped down for that purpose.*

Then, on the afternoon of December 20, the tug *Mary P Hall* chugged into Kingston harbour with the crew of the *Concretia* and the two light-keepers aboard. Captain Mills explained to a relieved city that the storm had been so strong, the *Concretia* could not ride at anchor. He'd been forced to beach the ship on Main Duck Island. He and his crew had to stay there with the lightkeepers they'd been sent to pick up. The *Concretia*, it was reported, was not damaged, and presumably the crew was able to sleep aboard the grounded ship. Sixteen men would have been quite a crowd for the light-keeper's small house. The light that had been seen from the American shore was the Main Duck beacon. The keepers had shut it down for the season, but after the *Concretia* ran aground, they'd lit it again to signal for help. The *Concretia* was left on the Main Duck beach for the winter, and refloated the following spring. For lightkeeper Wesley Thomas (who tended the light until 1953), the *Concretia* would not be the last ship to run into trouble at Main Duck during his watch.

THE *SARNIADOC*: FINAL RUN

A Canadian maritime insurance expert named Captain J.B. Foote said in 1929, "Every fall seems to bring its stories of wrecks on the Great Lakes, and pluck and sacrifice by officers and crew". Great Lakes mariners often

referred to the closing days of navigation as "the gambling season". Those were the dangerous days when shipping tycoons gambled with ships, cargoes—and lives—and ordered their captains to make one last run on the lakes before the gales of late November and early December roared across the lakes. It was during "the gambling season" that lightkeepers saw the most potentially deadly dramas on the water.

(Above) The Sarniadoc *was wrecked on her maiden voyage on the Great Lakes, a victim of what sailors called "the gambling season". (Left) The ice-coated hulk of the* Sarniadoc, *aground on Main Duck Island.*

On November 30, 1929, a blizzard swept across the Great Lakes, sending ships everywhere scurrying for cover. Some were forced to ride out the gale for three terrifying days. The steamer *City of Hamilton*, sheathed in ice, barely made it into Cobourg, Ontario. The captain declared that the ordeal he'd just been through was the worst experience he'd had in 16 years on the water.

The 253-foot (77.1-m) *Sarniadoc*, a steel freighter built in Scotland just the year before, was making her maiden voyage on the Great Lakes. Captain R.B. Angus was steaming down Lake Ontario from Cobourg, bound for Montreal, when the storm hit. Blinded by driving snow, and with his ship at the mercy of winds that hit up to 60 miles (96km) an hour, the skipper was startled to see the Main Duck Light suddenly appear in front of him. Captain Angus desperately tried to swing his vessel past the island. The manoeuvre failed. The captain later said that the ship "didn't have the pep". The *Sarniadoc* ran onto the rocks about 800 feet (244m) from the lighthouse and was held fast. Angus sounded the danger signal, five sharp blasts on the ship's whistle. He didn't know it at the time, but that signal saved another ship from following in the *Sarniadoc*'s wake.

All night waves washed over the freighter, coating the ship with ice. Water surged into the engine room and put out the fires in the boilers, which meant that the ship had no heat. The vessel remained firmly lodged on the rocks. The great danger was that the pounding surf would break the vessel up before the crew of twenty could be removed. With the grey light of dawn, lightkeeper Wesley Thomas could see the stranded ship through the still howling gale, but it was impossible for him to be of assistance. The ship was tantalizingly close to the lighthouse, but surrounded by a boiling sea that made a metre as good as a mile.

With the huge waves washing over the ship, and every inch of the exterior coated in ice, Captain Angus did not dare try to launch a lifeboat for a dash to the lighthouse. He and his crew could do nothing but stay inside and try to keep warm. He must have radioed Kingston, because two tugs tried to go to his assistance. The storm drove them back into port. Canadian officials called the American Coast Guard. Two cutters came out of Oswego and another from Rochester, but they too were forced to retreat to safe harbour.

For 36 cold, tension-filled hours, the men on the *Sarniadoc* endured the beating Lake Ontario was giving their ship. Then, during a lull in the tempest, the freighter *Valley Camp* managed to come alongside the ship and take off the half-frozen men. All were safely taken to Prescott. Over the next several days as Wesley Thomas looked on from his tower, Lake Ontario gradually pulled the *Sarniadoc* under. Another loss to "the gambling season".

EAST CHARITY SHOAL: ONE LIGHT IN THE DARKNESS

Dr. Joseph Reidel, 37, of Syracuse, New York, owed his life to a single beam of light. On August 5, 1955, Reidel, his wife, and another couple were out on the eastern end of Lake Ontario, enjoying a late afternoon cruise in a sailing sloop. One of the sudden squalls for which the lake is notorious blew up, and a 70-mile (113-km) -per-hour gust of wind caught the Dragon-class sailboat. The vessel went over on the beam, and Dr. Reidel was thrown overboard. Within seconds the boat was carried far from him. The people still on board lost sight of him, and thought that he had gone under.

But Reidel was still very much alive, and was determined to stay that way. Darkness fell, and with the waters heaving around him, he had no sense of direction. Then he saw a beacon in the distance. It was the East Charity Shoal Light, about eight miles (13km) away. He started to swim toward it.

It was an exhausting ordeal, and the waters of Lake Ontario are never really warm. But Reidel refused to let himself be overcome by fatigue or cold. He kept his arms moving, and never took his eyes off that light. He lost all sense of time, but every stroke took him closer to the beacon. Finally, exhausted and chilled to the bone, he crawled onto a shoal not far from the lighthouse. Then fatigue overcame him and he fell asleep, alone on a bare rock in the middle of Lake Ontario.

Reidel awoke before dawn, cold and

Dr. Joseph Reidel (inset) spent a long, cold night in Lake Ontario. He owed his life to the East Charity Shoal Light.

well aware that he was still in danger. A storm might blow up and, as a doctor, he was quite familiar with the effects of exposure. In the distance he saw two Coast Guard vessels moving along the shore (quite possibly searching for his body). He shouted and waved, but failed to attract their attention.

At 5:30 a.m., the crew of a fishing boat heading out into the lake were surprised to see a man standing on a rock in the middle of nowhere. They picked Dr. Reidel up and took him to the mainland. There he was reunited with his wife, who for over 12 hours had thought him dead. All that had guided him during his hours in the dark water, he told the press, was the beam of light from the East Charity Lighthouse.

THE OSWEGO LIGHT: SIX MEN DOWN

December 4, 1942. Another three days and the United States would mark the first anniversary of its entry into the maelstrom of the Second World War. The movement of shipping down the Great Lakes had become more important than it ever had been. For even though the battle zone of the North Atlantic was half a continent away, the ore, grain and industrial output of hundreds of factories had to be moved in record volumes and at record speeds through the Inland Seas to replace the millions of tons of Allied cargoes destroyed by German U-boats. That meant stretching the navigation season into the most dangerous days of winter. And that in turn meant lightkeepers staying on the job until, or beyond, the last possible moment. For the men of the United States Coast Guard on the Great Lakes, this was the front line of the war. On this day, at Oswego, New York, six of them would die with their boots on in the line of duty.

Boatswain's Mate First Class Karl A. Jackson, 42, was on lightkeeper duty at the Oswego West Pierhead Light that morning. He was supposed to have been relieved three days earlier, but a gale-force storm with winds of over sixty mph (96.5kph)—the worst in almost thirty years—had been raging on Lake Ontario, wreaking havoc on land and water alike. Marooned in his station half a mile (.8km) offshore at the end of a pier, Jackson might as well have been on a rock in the middle of the lake. No boat could get to him in that tempest. For him to try to make his way back along the breakwater would have been suicide. If the shrieking wind didn't carry him off, the huge walls of water that crashed over it would have. With his supplies of food almost gone, all Jackson could do was blow the lighthouse

The Oswego Lighthouse. Six Coastguardsmen died trying to rescue the stranded lightkeeper in one of the worst disasters in the history of the U.S. Coast Guard.

foghorn to remind those ashore that he was still there, peer through the driving snow in anticipation of rescue, and wait.

Finally, shortly after ten a.m., the winds dropped to about thirty mph (48kph) and Lake Ontario seemed to draw in her horns. Lieutenant A.J. Wilson, 54, commander of the Coast Guard station at Oswego, decided to take advantage of the lull in the storm to rescue Jackson and deliver the two men who were to replace him in the lighthouse: Bert Egelston and Carl Sprague. Into a 38-foot (11.5-m) wooden picket boat went Machinist's Mate First Class Fred Ruff, Second Class Seaman Irving Ginsberg, Second Class Bos'un's Mate Eugene Sisson, First Class Seaman Leslie Holdsworth, Second Class Machinist's Mate Ralph Sprau, and Chief Boatswain's Mate John Mixon, Wilson's second-in-command. The water was still extremely rough, and it would take all those hands to keep the boat from being dashed against the ten-foot-high (3-m) concrete structure that supported the lighthouse, while Jackson came down the ladder and his replacements went up. Because he was not the kind of officer to send his men on a dangerous assignment he would not tackle himself, Lieutenant Wilson took personal command of the operation.

The picket boat cut through the heaving waters of Oswego's harbour, headed for the West Pierhead Light off the port bow. Off to the starboard, on the other side of the harbour entrance, was a smaller beacon called the East Light, also at the end of a long seawall.

Wilson skillfully took the boat up to the ladder on the leeward side of the lighthouse foundation. Egelston and Sprague nimbly hopped from the pitching boat to the ladder and scurried up. Then, while the crewmen kept the little craft from being crushed against the concrete, Jackson shinnied down the ladder and dropped into the boat. He was one hungry man and all that stood between him and a hearty meal ashore was a quick run back to the base. That, at least, was how it should have been.

The boat, with its company of eight, reversed away from the lighthouse. Then, as it was shifted into forward, the engine stalled and quit. The boat was immediately at the mercy of the wind, the waves, and the current surging outward from the mouth of the Oswego River. It was rapidly drifting across the harbour mouth toward the rocky pier of the East Light. Twice, Fred Ruff managed to restart the engine, and both times the machine sputtered and died. Without power, the picket boat was a toy in the rough hands of the elements. Lieutenant Wilson, a survivor later reported, was absolutely cool and calm.

The skipper ordered the anchor dropped to stop the boat from drifting. The bow was icy and pitching, but Ginsberg and Sisson crawled out and released the 125-pound iron. The big weight sank to the bottom, and the boat was held secure. It could ride the swells safely enough until Ruff got the motor going or until another boat came out from the base to pick the men up. But fortune was not smiling that day.

Less than two minutes after the anchor had been dropped, the line snapped! Once again the picket boat was helpless. Still, all was not necessarily lost for the hapless men on board. Lieutenant Wilson left the now useless helm to Mixon, and went out on deck to join Jackson, Holdsworth, Sprau, Ginsberg and Sisson. Ruff was still in the engine room, valiantly trying to coax the motor back to life. Wilson could see that they had a good chance of getting out of the fix alive. If the wind and current carried the boat to calmer water, they could buy some time and most likely be rescued. If they fetched up along the east breakwater at a spot that was in the lee of the west breakwater, they could scramble onto the rocky wall and wait to be picked up. The one danger point was the East Light itself, which was surrounded by jagged rocks.

And that's exactly where the wind and current joined forces to take them! Not by means of a gentle drift, but on the crest of a wave that carried the boat like a predator its victim, and smashed the wooden craft onto the rocks with a fury. Lieutenant Wilson cried out a warning an instant before impact. Then the men were in the frigid, turbulent water and their boat was a shattered wreck, belly-up in the water and floating out to the open lake.

"Save your own life, John" were Lieutenant A.J. Wilson's last words.

John Mixon escaped from the pilothouse by smashing a window and squeezing out into the grey water. He would never remember just how he managed to drag himself up onto the slimy rocks of the breakwater. Fred Ruff, finding the engine room suddenly awash, lunged through the hatch onto deck and dived into the water. He was only ten feet (3m) from the breakwater, and reached it in a few frantic strokes. That was as much luck as would be granted to the men of the Coast Guard that morning.

The veterans Wilson and Jackson, as well as Holdsworth and Ginsberg, both 21; Sprau, 27; and Sisson, 29, were in the water and losing the fight to survive. Jackson was clinging to the anchor rope trailing behind the smashed boat. Perhaps he thought he could pull himself onto the wreck and stay afloat until help came. No one would ever know. Succumbing to the cold, he released his grip and sank into the frigid water.

Ginsberg, too, after a desperate attempt to swim to the breakwater, slid beneath the surface and was gone. Sisson and Sprau were both caught in the current and in spite of their efforts to fight against it, were swept out into the open lake. There was no hope for them. Holdsworth was nowhere to be seen.

Lieutenant Wilson was still afloat, and a wave pushed him closer to the breakwater. But the cold had drained every ounce of strength from his body and he could not save himself. When Mixon saw Wilson, he stumbled down to the edge of the rocks and was about to dive in. Exhausted and chilled to the bone himself, he was nonetheless going to risk his life to save his commanding officer. But the selfless lieutenant wouldn't allow it. "Don't try it", he told Mixon. "Save your own life, John". They were his last words.

Ruff and Mixon started to crawl along the breakwater toward the shore. Many times they fell on the sharp, slippery rocks, but they kept going. The breakwater was 2,100 feet (640m) long and did not reach all the way to shore. Between its opposite end and the land there was a 250-foot (76-m) gap of churning water. The men's only hope lay in being picked up by a boat, but in the meantime they knew that to stop moving was to surrender to a cold, wet death.

Back at the base, other Coast Guard men had gone into action as soon as they saw the picket boat in danger. Second Class Boatswain's Mate

Robert Burnet, now in charge at the base, ordered a 36-foot (11-m) lifeboat into the water. The boat had been cradled for winter storage, but in less than twenty minutes Burnet and six other guardsmen were crashing through the waves at full speed. Burnet headed for the men who were inching along the breakwater. But plucking them from that rocky spine wasn't going to be easy.

If Burnet took his boat too close to the rocks, it could be dashed to pieces just as the picket boat had been. Instead, he sent out two men in a skiff with a line attached. The idea was to have the smaller boat manoeuvre in close enough to pick up Ruff and Mixon, and then pull it back to the larger boat. But the storm had its own hand to play. It swept up the little boat like a bathtub toy and smashed it to splinters against the rocks. Now there were four men shivering on the breakwater.

Believing there might still be somebody from the picket boat alive in the water, Burnet left the men on the rocks for the moment and sped toward the wreck. All he could see was Lieutenant Wilson's body, the only one still afloat. He asked for a volunteer to recover it, and Second Class Seaman Andrew Cisterino responded. He tied a rope around his waist and dove into the icy, heaving water.

Cisterino grabbed hold of the body, but became so numb with the cold that he couldn't hang onto it. It was all his shipmates could do to get him back into the boat alive. The corpse of Lieutenant Wilson disappeared from sight.

Now Burnet turned back for the men on the breakwater. He had no choice but to risk everything if he was going to save them. One wrong move, and it could be the end of the line for everyone involved. Using every bit of seamanship at his command, Burnet brought the lifeboat up to the break-water while witnesses ashore watched with heart-stopping anticipation.

It was difficult for those on shore to see just what was happening, with the lifeboat rising and falling on the waves, and the snow drastically reducing visibility. Then the boat was racing for shore, and in it were the survivors from the picket boat and all of the men who had gone out with Burnet. The disaster, at least, had not been total.

The bodies of the six drowned men were never recovered, in spite of a thorough search of lake and shoreline. They lay in the cold, dark depths of Lake Ontario, while above the Oswego Light kept shining, helping to guide the ships whose cargoes were so vital to the victorious end of the war. However distant that war might have been, it had reached all the way to an American port on Lake Ontario and snatched the lives of six men of the United States Coast Guard.

THE BURLINGTON BAY LIGHT: YESTERDAY IN THE SHADOW OF TODAY

The old Burlington Bay Lighthouse stands in the shadow of the huge Burlington Skyway Bridge that spans the western end of Lake Ontario, with the open lake on one side, and the harbour and city of Hamilton on the other. The lighthouse overlooks the canal that connects the harbour to the lake. Not only is the lighthouse dwarfed by the massive Skyway, but its nineteenth-century limestone masonry also looks decidedly out of place alongside a steel-and-concrete wonder of twentieth-century technology. Yet, the lighthouse was itself once considered a marvel of its time. It contributed, merely by its presence, to the development of one of the principal cities of the Great Lakes.

A narrow bar of land stretches across the western extremity of Lake Ontario between the present day cities of Burlington and Hamilton. Early colonial navigators called the body of water on the western side of this spit Little Lake (later renamed Burlington Bay, then Hamilton Harbour). They realized that it had tremendous possibilities as a harbour. There was good anchorage, protection from

Burlington Bay, originally called Little Lake, held tremendous potential as a harbour. A small creek called The Outlet was deepened and widened to make a canal out to the main body of Lake Ontario. (Inset) John Chisholm, patriarch of an influential family, was caught up in a scandal involving the collection of customs duties and lighthouse tolls.

George Thompson, Burlington Bay lightkeeper, was a complex man who growled at people but was kind to animals. He claimed the lighthouse was haunted.

the wind and heavy seas, and the place was easily defensible militarily. However, the only access for vessels between the bay and the lake was through a shallow creek called The Outlet, which only the smallest craft could navigate. The Outlet was dredged and widened, and the Burlington Bay Canal opened in July 1826.

The first light marking the entrance to the canal was just a lantern on a pole, but the frequency of storms and shipwrecks made it clear that a proper lighthouse was needed. There were also dark rumours that the western end of Lake Ontario was the haunt of "wreckers"—criminals who used false lights to lure ships to destruction so they could be looted.

In 1837, a 54-foot (16.4-m) wooden lighthouse was built on the south side of the canal. John Chisholm, the Collector of the Customs, appointed William Nicholson as lightkeeper. Tolls were collected from ships using the canal to pay for the upkeep of the lighthouse. In one year the lighthouse required 213 gallons (977L) of whale oil, 12 dozen wicks, 20 pounds (9kg) of soap for the windows, two chamois skins for polishing its reflectors, and 10 pounds (4.5kg) of whiting for its exterior.

The new lighthouse made the western end of Lake Ontario safer for shipping, but it was also connected to a scandal that rocked the area in 1841. The law stated that no more than one person from any given family could be a collector of tolls and customs. The prominent Chisholm family, solid Tories whose patriarch John, Sr. had hired lightkeeper Nicholson, had the collection of tolls and customs locked up solid. Members of the Chisholm family collected the lighthouse and canal tolls, as well as the customs duties at Hamilton, Wellington Square, and Oakville, a port town a few miles to the east. The family kept their records private, and mixed funds from the tolls and customs together, so that it was impossible to tell just how much money was involved.

The Chisholms were relieved of their plum positions, and their influence and prestige diminished. But no one could say how much lighthouse money had gone into their coffers. One thing was certain: within a year of replacing them, the community could afford to deepen and widen the canal, and add a range light to the end of the pier that extended out into the lake.

In 1846, George Thompson became the Burlington Bay lightkeeper as well as the ferryman at the canal. He had been a sailor, and after some close calls out on the lakes he'd decided that he preferred to stay on dry land. He would learn soon enough that lightkeeping had challenges of its own.

During storms, when the light was most needed, Thompson had a difficult time keeping the temperamental oil lamp lit. Waves breaking over the pier made it dangerous to go out to light (or relight) the beacon at the end of the pier. But keeping those lights lit was important, because if a nor'easter blew up, the western end of Lake Ontario became a trap for sailing ships, and Burlington Bay was one of the few harbours of refuge. In the fall of 1848, the barquentine *Ellenora* was wrecked on the pier when the skipper lost sight of the pier-end light.

Steamships brought their own problems. Sparks from their smokestacks often set the wooden pier on fire, and Thompson would have to run out to tear up the burning planks and throw them in the water. On July 18, 1856, the steamer *Ranger*, which was delivering a supply of whale oil, set the pier on fire, and this time Thompson could not put it out. Everything was destroyed: the lighthouse, the pier, the pier light, the ferry house, and Thompson's living quarters along with all of his belongings.
The pier and range light were quickly replaced, but the Public Works Commission decided that the main lighthouse and the lightkeeper's dwelling would have to be of more substantial materials than wood. While a fine, two-storey brick house was being built for George Thompson, the commissioners hired John Brown, of Imperial Tower fame, to build a new Burlington Bay Lighthouse.

Construction began on April 1, 1858, and was completed in October. Burlington Bay now had a 55-foot (16.7-m), gleaming white Imperial Tower. Not only was this limestone monument fireproof, it was also, John Brown said, impervious to storms. Brown considered it his best work.

George Thompson was undoubtedly thrilled with his new lighthouse. But there was one thing he was not at all happy with. Like many other keepers, he had trouble adjusting to the new fuel (at least, he said he did). He said the coal oil lamps were too smokey, and choked themselves out. He grumbled that the coal oil froze. "I had much trouble in warming the coal oil in the pier and lighthouse", Thompson wrote. "I wrapped the oil lamps all round with flannel and rope yarn. I was wearing mittens with the earflaps of the cap down. I kept the large lighthouse burning, but the coal oil partially froze". Coal oil did prove to be superior to whale oil, and eventually Thompson gave the new fuel his grudging endorsement, especially since whale oil was becoming more and more expensive, and its supply less and less reliable.

The marvelous new lighthouse did not end the peril Thompson faced when he had to go down the long pier to tend to the range light on stormy nights. On several occasions he was almost swept away by crashing waves. Two of his assistants who worked on the ferry were drowned. One might wonder if Thompson, who had given up a sailor's life to work on "dry land", had second thoughts about his choice of jobs.

From his vantage point atop the tower, Thompson was the first to spot ships approaching the canal. In his lightkeeper's diary, he wrote down the name of each passing ship. Thompson also had a clear view in the other direction, across the harbour toward Hamilton, a bustling city with the smoke of industry hanging over it.

George Thompson seems to have been a rather complex man. He would growl at ferry passengers and at his neighbours, but he nursed back to health birds that had injured themselves by crashing into the lighthouse windows. He was an amateur naturalist who studied the habits of tortoises and turtles in the area. But he was also a spiritualist who insisted that the lighthouse was haunted. He claimed to have heard voices and other strange noises in the tower. (Later lightkeepers also said they heard footsteps and saw unusual lights.)

After 29 years as the Burlington Bay lightkeeper, George Thompson retired in 1875. His health was poor, and he died only four years later. During his tenure at the light, Hamilton had become one of Lake Ontario's busiest ports, second only to Toronto. Steam power had largely replaced sail, and railways now competed with ships for freight and passengers. The spit of land that separated lake and harbour was now

The spit of land called Burlington Beach shelters the bay (Hamilton Harbour) from the storms of Lake Ontario. (Inset) A ship passing through the Burlington Canal. The lightkeeper operated a ferry here.

(Top) Burlington Beach became a popular vacation spot. Lightkeepers like Thomas Campbell had to do extra duty as lifesavers when there were swimming or boating accidents. (Bottom) Before the Burlington Skyway was built, a drawbridge spanned the canal. It caused backups in highway traffic, and was once badly damaged when a ship rammed it. (Page right) The old Burlington Bay Lighthouse now looks out of place, surrounded by twentieth-century structures.

called Burlington Beach, and it was an important tourist destination. Marinas, resorts and cottages sprang up as people flocked to Burlington to enjoy boating and the increasingly popular sport of recreational swimming. These activities were to provide plenty of extra-curricular work for the new lightkeeper, Thomas Campbell.

In addition to his regular lighthouse duties, Campbell kept an eye open for illegal fishing. (Taking fish with nets had been banned by this time.) He also kept watch over the crowds of picnickers, swimmers and boaters. There were a lot of amateurs handling those skiffs and dinghies, and many times Campbell had to rush to somebody's aid. In one rescue he did not have room in his small boat for two men who were in the water, so he dragged one into the boat, and tied the other to the back and towed him to shore. On Dominion Day, 1891, Campbell dove into the canal to save a woman who had fallen out of a rowboat. In her panic, the woman struggled, and Campbell had a difficult time holding her until help arrived. The lightkeeper, who was by then 60 years old, said that only the lifesaving chains that lined the walls of the pier enabled him to keep both their heads above the water.

One year later, Campbell himself was washed into the canal while try-ing to light the pier light during a storm. Some people saw him in the water, threw him a rope, and managed to pull him out. But it was usually he who did the rescuing. Campbell was credited with saving at least 16 lives, and before he retired in 1905, he was awarded the Canadian Humane Association's medal for lifesaving.

Other lightkeepers came and went, keeping the lamp burning for ships entering the port of booming Hamilton, now a centre of the steel industry. But as much as shipping on the water was growing by leaps and bounds, so was the movement of people and material by land, with the coming of the automobile. The bascule bridge (a type of drawbridge) that had replaced ferry barges at the canal, was inadequate for the volume of traffic, and was creating a highway bottleneck. The need for a new super-bridge became glaringly evident in 1952 when the freighter *W.E. Fitzgerald* rammed the bridge and demolished it.

Work began on the new bridge in 1954, and by the time it was completed in 1958, it had totally altered the lake-view of the Hamilton–Burlington skyline. The Burlington Bay Lighthouse, once a prominent feature, now looked like an insignificant little white finger beneath the 8,400-foot-long (2,560-m) bridge that filled the sky 120 feet (36.5m) above the canal. That same year, a powerful storm raged across Lake Ontario, and the old lighthouse sustained interior water damage, no longer as watertight as it had been in its glory days. In 1961, an automated light was placed on the canal pier. The old lighthouse was deactivated. Fortunately, due to the costs involved, it was not torn down. The old Burlington Bay Light certainly does appear overwhelmed by the immensity of the modern structures around it. Quite likely, few of the thousands of people who drive across the Skyway everyday even notice it. It remains, nonetheless, a reminder of another era, when sailors out on the dark waters looked for the single beacon that would guide them safely into harbour.

LAKE ONTARIO:

FIRE FROM HEAVEN

In order for the beacon to be visible for a long distance, a lighthouse usually had to be higher than other objects around it. Because they were prominent and exposed, the towers were very frequently struck by lightning during storms. Browse through late-nineteenth and early-twentieth -century newspaper archives, and the articles about lightning strikes on lighthouses appear with considerable regularity. Though the towers were equipped with lightning rods to carry the charge down to the ground, there were times when this safety device did not work.

FIRE AT PORT DALHOUSIE

Port Dalhousie pier-end lighthouse, built in 1856. The exposed towers frequently drew lightning strikes.

Captain Hunter was proud of his 40-foot (12.1-m), white wooden lighthouse. The government had completely rebuilt the East Pier Light at Port Dalhousie, at that time the Lake Ontario entrance to the Welland Canal. Hunter was also the keeper for the town's other tower, the Front Range Light, but he spent almost all of his time at the new lighthouse. Shortly before eight o'clock on the morning of August 12, 1898, with a severe lightning storm crackling in the skies over much of Southern Ontario, Hunter decided to tear himself away from his spanking new lighthouse long enough to go home for breakfast. As the lightkeeper left the building he passed John Adie, who was fishing from the pier. The passenger steamer *Lakeside* was coming down the locks, heading for Lake Ontario. As he strolled up the street, Captain Hunter could hardly have known that he had just saved his own life.

Port Dalhousie, at one time the Lake Ontario gateway to the Welland Canal.

At 8:06, fire from the sky ripped into Hunter's beloved lighthouse with a blinding flash. John Adie, momentarily blinded, heard a tremendous *crack* and felt a powerful shock. He turned around, and when his vision returned after a few seconds, he saw the lighthouse in flames. The lightning bolt had smashed the revolving lamp, split open the entire top of the tower, and set the fuel oil on fire. Adie dashed for safety.

On the *Lakeside*, Captain Wigle ordered his crew to man the ship's fire hoses. His ship would pass right by the lighthouse, and he thought he could quickly put out the fire. But as the steamer came alongside the burning tower, the captain remembered that there would be a large quantity of fuel oil stored in the building. Fearful of an explosion, he pulled the *Lakeside* away. Harbour tugs that might have fought the fire kept their distance for the same reason.

There was no explosion. The lightning strike had ruptured the fuel storage tank, and the oil burned away as it leaked out. Captain Hunter's beautiful new lighthouse was destroyed.

Port Dalhousie Lighthouse. In 1898 the brand new Port Dalhousie East Pier Light was destroyed by a lightning strike.

STRIKE AT FALSE DUCK ISLAND

On the night of November 26, 1905, a lightning storm was again raging over Lake Ontario. In the lightkeeper's house on False Duck Island in eastern Lake Ontario, Dorland Dulmage and his family huddled in nervous anticipation. The 30-foot (9.1-m) stone tower and adjacent buildings on the small, low-lying island were the only vertical objects for miles around. Dulmage had a bad feeling about the situation. He wasn't sure if the house was safe, and he felt that the building that housed the fog signal would be a better place in which to wait out the storm. The family left the house and took shelter in the other building.

Dulmage's hunch was right. A thunderbolt flashed down from the heavens and struck the False Duck Light Station like an artillery shell. The house, the oil storage room, and the lantern room on the lighthouse were all destroyed. The only building untouched, fortunately, was the one that housed the fog signal.

Smoke from the burning buildings must have been seen from the mainland the next morning, because newspapers reported the fire and expressed concern that the lightkeeper might be injured or even dead. "A family named Scott [sic] made their home at the lighthouse", said the Toronto Globe, "and it is feared that they have perished in the fire".

Because of the storm, no one could go out to False Duck to investigate. When the weather finally cleared a day or two later, a boat went out from Kingston. The crew found most of the light station a smoking ruin. But the Dulmage family, safely sheltered in the fog signal building, was alive and well.

GULL LIGHTHOUSE ELECTRIFIED

On July 19, 1906, less than a year after the lightning strike at False Duck Island, a group of 16 young men from Port Hope were travelling in a motor launch to Cobourg. Among them were Sam Welsh (or Welch) and his brother, W. Welsh, known to friends as "General". Shortly before four p.m., dark clouds rolled across the sky and lightning forked in a menacing display above Lake Ontario. Open water was no place to be during a lightning storm, so the youths raced at full speed for the nearest shelter: the Gull Lighthouse, halfway between Port Hope and Cobourg. When they reached the shore they piled into the building, sitting on the stairway that wound to

False Duck Lighthouse. The light-keeper and his family escaped death from a lightning strike by taking shelter in the fog signal building.

the top. They were undoubtedly relieved to be inside and safe.

Then, just after four o'clock, a bolt of lightning struck the lighthouse. "ENTIRE PARTY STUNNED", said the Toronto *Globe* the following day. "Stunned" indeed! The lightning hit the tower with a terrible crash, and "electric fluid", as the paper called it, coursed through the building. Every watch was stopped. No one escaped injury from flying glass or splinters. Almost everyone received at least minor burns. The worst injured were the Welsh brothers, who seem to have been sitting higher up in the tower. "General" had severe burns to his lower legs and feet. Two of his toes were completely burned off. Sam Welsh had badly burned feet. A young man named Charlie McMahon had a broken nose. He had probably been thrown by the electric shock. The lighthouse itself was "shattered" according to the press, but fortunately no fire broke out. The injured youths were rushed back to Port Hope for medical care.

Lighthouses, tall against the sky in their time, continued to attract lightning like magnets until modern technology devised better means by which tall buildings could be grounded. As late as June 1931, a lightning strike on the lighthouse at Corbeil Point near Batchawana Bay on Lake Superior started a fire that almost claimed the lives of lightkeeper William Rell and his daughter Philomen. The young woman was apparently trapped by flames, but her father burst through the blaze and carried her to safety. They escaped with nothing but the clothes on their backs, but like Captain Hunter at Port Dalhousie 33 years earlier, they were thankful that they had not been taken by fire from heaven.

Port Huron
Sarnia
MICHIGAN
St. Clair River
(to Lake Huron)
St. Clair
ONTARIO
Lake
St. Clair
Windsor
Detroit
Amhertsburg
Detroit River
Colchester
Kingsville
Grosse Ile
Leamington
Colchester
Reef Light
Point Pelee
Southeast Shoal Light
Pelee Island
Light
Toledo
Pelee Island
Sandusky
OHIO
Vermilion
Lorain
Cleveland

Old Cut Lighthouse
Port Burwell
Mohawk Island Light
Long Point

Horseshoe Reef
Lighthouse
Niagra River
Welland Canal
(to Lake Ontario)
Erie
Canal
Dunnville
Port Maitland
Buffalo
Port Colborne
Light
NEW YORK

LAKE ERIE

Erie

PENNSYLVANIA

PART THREE
LAKE ERIE &
THE DETROIT RIVER

FEBRUARY 1, 1896

LIGHTKEEPER'S STORY.

His Wife Was a Fearful Sufferer From Rheumatism.

AN INVALID FOR YEARS.

Her Joints Were Swollen and Distorted.

Her Nights Were Almost Sleepless and Her Appetite Gone—How She Found Relief at Last.

(From The Kingston News.)

Mr. Hugh McLaren, lighthouse keeper on Wolfe Island, is one of the best known men in this section, and to his vigilance in the performance of his duties is due the safety of the many craft sailing in that part of the St. Lawrence. Mrs. McLaren, his wife, has been an invalid for a number of years, and in conversation with a reporter recently, Mr. McLaren stated that she was rapidly regaining her old-time health under the treatment of that most marvellous of modern medicines—Dr. Williams' Pink Pills. Asked if he had any objections to giving the particulars, Mr. McLaren replied that emphatically he had not if such publication was likely to benefit any other sufferer. He said: "A number of years ago my wife contracted rheuma- tism, and for a considerable time was a helpless invalid. Her joints were swollen and distorted; her nights were sleepless and her appetite poor and very fickle. During those years she experienced excruciating tortures, the pain never ceasing day or night. She had the benefit of skilled medical advice, but the treatment afforded no relief, and we began to fear that her trouble had gone beyond human aid. On a number of occasions I had read in the papers of cases of rheumatism being cured by the use of Dr. Williams' Pink Pills, and this at last determined us to give them a trial. She had used some three boxes before any improvement was noticed; and then we began to note that she slept better and that her appetite was improved. Then the pains gradually began to subside, and after using about a dozen boxes she was able to get up and walk about. She continued the use of the pills for a while longer, and although occasionally she feels twinges of the trouble in changeable weather, she now enjoys better health than she has done for years, and can sleep as soundly as ever she did in her life, while her appetite never was better. I look upon Dr. Williams' Pink Pills as a wonderful medicine, for I know they have done wonders in my wife's case, and I feel certain that if any who are afflicted as she was will give them a good trial, equally happy results will follow, and I therefore give this testimony freely, hoping that it will benefit some other suffer- er."

Mr. McLaren's strong testimony proves the claim made that Dr. Williams' Pink Pills cure when other medicines fail, and that they deserve to rank as the greatest discovery of modern medical science. The public should always be on their guard against imitations and substitutes, which some unscrupulous dealers for the sake of extra profit, urge upon purchasers. There is no other remedy "just the same as" or "just as good" as Dr. Williams' Pink Pills and the genuine always have the full trade mark, "Dr. Williams' Pink Pills for Pale People" on the wrapper around every box.

This nineteenth-century advertisement explains how a lightkeeper's wife found relief from rheumatism by taking "Dr. Williams' Pink Pills". If the pills could help a sufferer in a clammy environment, the advertisement suggested, they could help anyone.

In its early days, Buffalo was in stiff competition with the settlement of Black Rock, at the entrance to the Niagara River. Having a lighthouse gave Buffalo an edge.

THE LIGHTS OF BUFFALO:

TOWERS, SHIPS, AND A PIECE OF THE BRITISH EMPIRE

Lighthouses have played a colourful role in the history of Buffalo, New York. The community has peculiar examples of lighthouse lore that can be found nowhere else on the Great Lakes. One little-known story concerning a Buffalo lighthouse actually involves a small piece of British Canada, just across the water.

Buffalo was still just a raw frontier settlement at the mouth of Buffalo Creek at the eastern end of Lake Erie when its potential as a port was recognized in the early 1800s. There were plans for a lighthouse as far back as 1811, but construction was delayed by the outbreak of the War of 1812. The project was set further back when the British and Canadians burned the village to the ground in December 1813.

The first Buffalo lighthouse, a 30-foot (9.1-m) stone tower, was finally built in 1818, and helped give Buffalo an edge over its nearby rival, Black Rock, a settlement at the entrance to the Niagara River. But right from the start there were problems. The lightkeeper, John G. Skaats, was, according to the good citizens of Buffalo, "a man of dissolute morals and whose manners are singularly obnoxious to the public". Skaats was undoubtedly the first Great Lakes lightkeeper to inspire his neighbours to demand his removal, though it seems such action was not taken. Another problem was the tower's location. It was built on a spit of land between the lake and Buffalo Creek, and the smoke from the wood fires of the town obscured the light. This may have been a factor in the demise of one of the most famous ships in the early days of Great Lakes navigation.

The busy harbour in 1825.

The Walk-in-the-Water, *the first steamship on Lake Erie. The steamer was wrecked when the skipper could not find the Buffalo Light.*

As the American Midwest opened up, port towns like Buffalo grew into cities, and more light-houses were needed to aid the steadily increasing maritime traffic.

WALK-IN-THE-WATER: FIRST STEAMER ON LAKE ERIE

The *Walk-in-the-Water*, launched at Black Rock in 1818, was the first steamship on Lake Erie. (The British and Americans already had one each on Lake Ontario.) The vessel received its unusual name after an Indian who had seen a sidewheel steamer commented that the boat "walks in the water". To the people of Buffalo and other Lake Erie communities, she was simply "the steamboat". The *Walk-in-the-Water* carried freight and passengers between Detroit and Buffalo, and was a popular sight all along the American shore. But her career was a short one.

At four p.m. on October 31, 1821, the *Walk-in-the-Water* left Black Rock for her regular run to Detroit. It was raining, but the skipper, a Captain Rogers, was not expecting any problems. That evening, however, one of the sudden storms for which Lake Erie is notorious, rose up. A passenger aboard the ship wrote later: "The lake became rough to a terrifying degree, and every wave seemed to threaten destruction to the boat and passengers. To proceed up the lake was impossible. To attempt to return to Black Rock amid darkness and howling tempest would be certain destruction".

Captain Rogers turned back, but evidently was unable to find the Buffalo Light, though he was very near it. He cast anchor and tried to ride out the gale. One passenger, Mrs. Alanson W. Welton, recalled: "During all this time the creaking of her timbers throughout her whole length warned us of the probable fate in store for us all. The joints in her timbers opened in a most frightful manner".

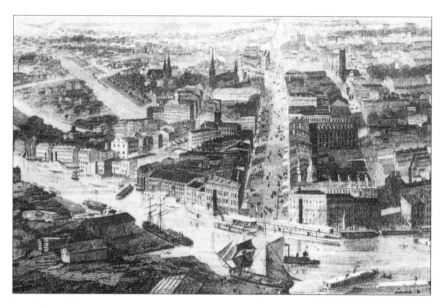

Buffalo, 1852: one of the busiest ports on the Great Lakes.

dragging her anchors. Captain Rogers ordered the cables cut so that the ship would drift, and warned the passengers of the "possible fatal result". Mrs. Welton wrote, "I will not attempt to describe the anxious, prayerful, tearful, upturned faces that were grouped together in the cabin of the 'Walk-in-the-Water' on that terrible, cold morning as we looked into each other's faces for probably the last time."

At the height of that terrifying battle with the lake, it must have seemed that Captain Rogers's dire warning would come true, because the *Walk-in-the-Water* did run aground. It was, in fact, thrown entirely onto the beach. But by some miracle, there were no serious injuries. "The boat struck the beach in a fortunate spot for the safety of the passengers and crew—near the lighthouse—and all were saved", Mrs. Welton wrote. "The warm fireside we gathered around at the lighthouse was comfortable to our chilled bones, and our hearts warmed with gratitude to God for deliverance from our peril".

The Erie shore at that time would still have been pretty rugged, and the temperature at the end of October would not have been warm. The ship-wrecked people of the *Walk-in-the-Water* could have been in a much more serious situation had it not been for the lighthouse and its keeper. According to a Buffalo newspaper, the ship was wrecked "about 100 rods above the lighthouse". One source says she actually went ashore at Point Abino, on the Canadian side. Whatever the case, the Buffalo lighthouse had played a significant role in the first steamship wreck on Lake Erie.

THE ERIE CANAL: BOOM YEARS FOR BUFFALO

In 1825, Buffalo became the principal American port on Lake Erie—indeed, on the Great Lakes—with the opening of the Erie Canal. This vital 360-mile (580-km) barge canal connecting Lake Erie to the Hudson River and the Atlantic Seaboard has been referred to by historians as "the super-highway of pre-Civil War America". It transformed Buffalo from a backwater lake port to a link in international trade. No longer did cargoes have to be shuttled overland to Lake Ontario, where ships took them to the Upper St. Lawrence, there to be shuttled again past the rapids above Montreal, to the Lower St. Lawrence, where they were loaded onto ships for the long voyage to the sea. Grain, ore and timber from the rapidly developing Great Lakes region could take the Erie Canal shortcut, a saving of much time and well over a thousand miles. Likewise, manufactured goods from Europe and eastern American cities, as well as imported sugar, coffee and other "necessities" to which North Americans had become accustomed were barged up the canal to Buffalo.

The town boomed, and as it did, the harbour became more and more congested. The traffic in and out was far beyond what anyone would have imagined before the construction of the canal. A new, more efficient lighthouse was obviously needed. In 1832–33, a 46-foot (14-m) octagonal, limestone tower was built at the end of a long pier. The local

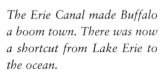

The Erie Canal made Buffalo a boom town. There was now a shortcut from Lake Erie to the ocean.

press proudly described the new lighthouse as the "most perfect work of its kind on this side of the ocean and perhaps in the world". An exaggeration, perhaps, but the kind of crowing that was typical of the time.

Yet, within five years, captains were complaining that Buffalo's harbour was becoming so crowded with schooners, steamers, barges, scows and anything else that sailed, paddled or chugged, that the single light was inadequate. Additional lights were recommended, but it took the government a long time to act. There was more than just one trouble spot off Buffalo's shore.

Black Rock Reef had been recognized as a hazard since 1832 when the schooner *Jesse Smith* struck it and sank. A range light was finally placed there in 1853. It was simply a matter of badgering the government into spending the money. The situation with Horseshoe Reef was not so straightforward. It would lead to a most peculiar solution.

Horseshoe Reef lay at the very eastern extremity of Lake Erie, right where it drains into the Niagara River. Only inches beneath the surface, it was a dangerous obstacle to traffic on the very busy Upper Niagara, and to vessels approaching Buffalo from that quarter. The Americans desperately wanted to establish a lighthouse to warn ships away from it. But according to the International Boundary drawn after the Revolutionary War, Horseshoe Reef was on the Canadian side of the line.

During Prohibition, Buffalo's lighthouse was used as a lookout tower to watch for rum-runners crossing the Lake Erie from Canada.

The destruction of the Caroline. *Canadian militia burned the American ship that had been supplying William Lyon Mackenzie's rebels on Navy Island in the Niagara River. Such incidents strained international relations when it came to negotiations over matters such as lighthouse building.*

In 1849, the Commissioner of the American Lighthouse Service, Stephen Pleasonton, recommended that the American government ask permission from the British government to build a lighthouse on Canadian territory. He was sure the request would be refused. The British had already turned down an American request to build a lighthouse in the Bahamas, and even though the War of 1812 had been over for a long time, there were still tensions along the border. It had not been all that long since the Hunter invasion of Canada (see p.33) and just prior to that event Canadian militia had destroyed the American ship *Caroline* for supplying William Lyon Mackenzie's rebels on Navy Island in the Niagara River. Moreover, the American press, and American playwrights and pulp novelists still delighted in "bashing" all things British. Why then, should John Bull do any favours for Uncle Sam?

However, the British realized that a lighthouse marking Horseshoe Reef would be beneficial to Canadian shipping, too. If the Yanks wanted to spend the money to build a lighthouse there, why not let them? To Pleasonton's surprise, they said yes.

But the transfer of territory from one nation to another involves a lot of diplomatic protocol. The long chain of negotiations and protocol involved U.S. Minister to London Abbott Lawrence, British Foreign Secretary Viscount Palmerston, British Colonial Secretary Earl Grey, Governor General of Canada Lord Elgin, Queen Victoria and President Millard Fillmore (a native of Buffalo). When all the documents were signed and stamped, the British Crown gave the United States of America an acre (.4ha) of underwater reef 1,150 feet (350m) inside the Canadian border, on the condition that the Americans build a lighthouse but not construct any fortification; a tiny patch of America surrounded by British Empire!

The lighthouse the Americans built was not on Horseshoe Reef itself, but on nearby Middle Reef. They constructed a crib, upon which was a

The 1833 Buffalo Lighthouse, the oldest historic Buffalo building still at its original location, as it appeared in 1859.

spider-like support for a platform for the lighthouse, fifty feet (15m) above the water. Horseshoe Reef Lighthouse went into operation in 1856.

It quickly became one of the most unpopular stations among American lightkeepers. To begin with, they didn't like being in foreign territory, even if the spot was officially American and they were within shouting distance of the American shore. Moreover, even the Lighthouse Service said that the Horseshoe Reef Light was "one of the most comfortless and unattractive stations in the district". Two lightkeepers did alternate duty, and had to arrange their own lodgings ashore. The trip by rowboat was only a mile and a half (2.4km), but the crossing could be dangerous. Bad weather could leave a man stuck there for days, and the accommodations were Spartan.

In 1913, a new treaty between Canada and the United States moved the border so that the lighthouse was 100 feet (30m) inside American territory, but by then the Horseshoe Reef Light had become obsolete. A new channel and a new light had moved traffic away from the deadly reef. The Horseshoe Reef Light was abandoned in 1920. It fell into disrepair, until only the iron framework remained as a reminder of the deal that saw Queen Victoria sign away a tiny piece of Canada in return for an aid to the shipping of both countries.

In the second half of the nineteenth century, the volume of shipping passing through Buffalo's harbour made it one of the busiest ports in North America. Extra storeys were added to the 1833 lighthouse, increasing its height to sixty feet (18.2m). During the Civil War the lightkeeper no doubt kept an eye peeled for something besides commercial traffic: Confederate raiders! Confederate agents operating in Canada tried desperately to obtain ships they could use as privateers to harass Union shipping on the Lakes and possibly bombard port cities like Buffalo. It was a hare-brained scheme, but one that posed a threat nonetheless. In 1864, the rebels actually did purchase

(Right) The British Crown gave the United States an acre (.4ha) of reef in Canadian territory so the Americans could build the Horseshoe Reef Lighthouse. It was an unpopular posting with American lightkeepers.

(Left) The second Buffalo Breakwater lighthouse, built in 1914, was rammed by the freighter Frontenac *in 1958, and had to be demolished.*

a Canadian ship, the steamer *Georgian*, but it was subsequently seized by authorities at Collingwood. Canadians were divided over issues of the American conflict, and the Canadian government did not want to give Washington an excuse to invade.

After the war, Buffalo added two more lights by 1872: a harbour light; and a pagoda-shaped wooden tower that was called Chinaman's Light. This was not only because of its design, but also because it was used as a lookout from which to spot illegal Chinese immigrants crossing over from Canada. When it was eventually torn down, the old 1833 lighthouse inherited the colourful nickname. During Prohibition, the old tower would also do duty as a vantage point from which to watch for rum-runners smuggling Canadian liquor across the border.

The other noteworthy structure was an impressive pier light that would meet a most ignoble end. For some inexplicable reason, Buffalo's harbour had a history of run-ins between ships and lighthouses. There were collisions in 1899 (a tug), 1900 (a barge), 1909 (a freighter), and 1910 (a steamer). The harbour was free of this sort of accident for almost half a century. Then on July 26, 1958, the huge freighter *Frontenac* made too wide a swing in leaving the harbour for open water, and put itself on a direct collision course with the pier light. Coastguardsmen on duty in the lighthouse shouted a warning, but it was too late. The *Frontenac* hit the lighthouse like an ancient Roman galley ramming an enemy vessel. The impact drove the lighthouse back twenty feet (6m) and caused a tilt of 15 degrees! Fortunately, there were no serious injuries on the ship or in the lighthouse. The disabled light station had to be replaced by a temporary light, and was now called The Leaning Lighthouse. It was demolished in 1961.

LOSS OF THE L.V. 82

The most tragic story of the Buffalo Lights involved not a lighthouse, but a lightship. The Lighthouse Service used many of these specially constructed and equipped vessels to mark danger spots along American seacoasts and on the Great Lakes. Light Vessel 82, a brand new ship, was sent out in 1912 to warn shipping away from deadly Waverly Shoal, an extension of Port Abino on the Canadian shore of Lake Erie, just a few miles from Buffalo. The navigable passage in this part of the lake was very narrow, and the submerged wreck of the steamship *W.C. Richardson*, which had gone down in a storm in 1909 with a loss of five lives, made the shallows off Port Abino all the more hazardous.

L.V. 82 was built to handle stormy seas, it being her duty after all to remain at her post in the very worst weather, as a beacon for other ships. She was 95 feet (29m) long, 21 feet (6.4m) in the beam, and had a steel hull. Her design was "whaleback": a cylindrical-hulled construction unique to the Great Lakes that was supposed to make a ship almost unsinkable. For a year L.V. 82 did her job, stationed at a point about 13 miles (21km) from Buffalo, and the lights on her forward mast were a welcome sight to mariners navigating those treacherous waters. But nobody could have predicted the monstrous storm that would sweep across the Great Lakes like a juggernaut on November 9, 1913, and rage for four days.

In that era before reliable weather forecasts and ship's radios, many a vessel was caught out on the open lakes by storms that materialized without warning. They would run for shelter, and if luck was with them they would make it. Often there would be a ship whose luck had run out, and all that would be left would be some debris. But the storm that came to be known as The Big Blow would claim no fewer than a dozen ships and take from 250 to 300 lives. Among the victims were L.V. 82 and a crew of six.

L.V. 82 kept to her post as Lake Erie's turn came to be slammed by the gale that had already savaged Lakes Superior, Michigan and Huron. The lightship's beacon was last sighted about 4:45 a.m. on Monday, November

(Right) Lightships, literally floating lighthouses, were often used at danger spots. In the "Big Blow" of November 1913, LV 82 went down with all hands off Buffalo. (Below) Crew of L.V. No. 82 Capt. Hugh M. Willimas at far right.

10. Twenty-four hours later the freighter *Champlain*, running for safety, steamed into harbour at Buffalo and reported that L.V. 82 was gone. Just what had befallen her, no one knew, because the storm had carried with it a record-breaking blizzard. Driving snow had made it impossible for anyone on either the Canadian or American shores to see what was happening out on the lake.

After the worst of the storm had passed, an initial search turned up some wreckage—lifejackets, pieces of railing and other debris. But those could have been torn from the ship by the violence of the gale. Surely, a craft as seaworthy as L.V. 82 had not sunk! She might have been forced to seek shelter in some port. But there was no sign of the lightship anywhere. It just did not seem possible that L.V. 82 could have gone down with all hands.

Then a piece of wreckage was fished out of the water that added mystery to the tragedy. It was a board with a message written on it in pencil, apparently a last farewell from Captain Williams to his wife. "Goodbye, Nellie, ship is breaking up fast. Williams". It was perplexing. Captain Williams's wife was named Mary. Some people said they had heard him call her Nellie, but Mrs. Williams claimed that he had never called her that. But he *had* told her that he would try to leave some sort of message if he were ever facing certain death. But would he sign so poignant a message with only his last name?

Mary Williams had no doubt that the message was from her husband, even though the handwriting was not his. Perhaps he had been badly hurt, and had asked one of his crew to write it, and that person had mistakenly addressed it to "Nellie". The "s" in Williams was just an awkward scrawl, as though the hand of the writer had been jolted. Was the message really from the captain, or had someone used a scrap of wood from the vanished ship to play a cruel hoax, and included the misshapen "s" only for effect?

The wreck of L.V. 82 was found the following May in 63 feet (19m) of water, almost two miles (3.2km) from her station. The hull was intact, but the windows, doors and hatches had been smashed by the incessant pounding of the waves during the storm, allowing the water to pour in. There were no bodies on the sunken ship. The only body ever recovered was that of engineer Charles Butler, which was found in the Niagara River in October 1914, 13 miles (21km) from where L.V. 82 had sunk.

One of the oddly shaped "Buffalo Bottle" lights. Its twin is in a museum in nearby Dunkirk.

L.V. 82 was raised, repaired and refitted, and served as a relief lightship for many years, though not at Buffalo. Other lightships marked Waverly Shoal until 1917 when the new Point Abino Lighthouse built by the Canadian government became operational.

The harbour at Buffalo today is graced by a unique collection of lighthouses, including one oddly shaped "Buffalo-Bottle Light", a 29-foot (8.8-m) iron breakwater light that greatly resembles a decanter. (Its twin is now part of a maritime museum at nearby Dunkirk.) And still standing—in fact, the oldest historic Buffalo building to remain in its original location—is the old 1833 Buffalo Main Light. It is no longer operational, but stands a silent witness to the history of one of the first major ports on the Inland Seas.

LONG POINT: GRAVEYARD OF LAKE ERIE

Lake Erie is the second smallest of the Great Lakes, and the most shallow. Yet, its reputation as a sailor's nightmare almost equals that of mighty Superior. Tricky winds and currents have bedeviled mariners from the earliest times, and the speed with which storms and waves can build up over the lake and lash out at hapless vessels is truly phenomenal. As if these hazards to

(Above) The collision between the Atlantic *and the* Ogdensburg *off Long Point. It is thought that the disaster cost up to 350 lives. (Right) The Americans threatened to annex Long Point and build their own lighthouse if the British did not build one.*

ships and the stalwart souls who venture out in them were not enough, Nature provided Erie with a weapon as deadly to marine traffic as any to be found on a treacherous coast of the high seas: Long Point!

"Long Point" is a geographically accurate but deceptively passive name for this deadly peninsula. Perhaps "The Talon" or "The Claw" would be more appropriate, because it reaches out for prey with such terrifying efficiency as to give the waters around it the name applied to so many dread places on sea captains' charts—"graveyard"! There are literally hundreds of wrecks in the sandbar-strewn waters around Long Point, dating back to the Canadian sloop *Annette*, which came to grief there in 1789. How many people died in those shipwrecks, or were swept away from other vessels that managed, by the grace of God and a seasoned captain to escape the trap, one can only guess at.

Long Point extends some twenty miles (32km) from the Canadian shore into the eastern part of Lake Erie, reaching halfway into the lake. Though it is another twenty miles to the American shore, because of the shallowness of the lake, the navigable channel is relatively narrow. Long Point thus

(Left) The second Long Point Lighthouse, built in 1843. (Above) Long Point's third tower, constructed in 1916. Sand provided a very unstable base upon which to build.

extends its threat well beyond its own shifting dunes and sandbars, making collisions in the heavily travelled channel an ever-present danger. The worst such accident occurred in August 1852, when the passenger steamer *Atlantic* collided with the propeller *Ogdensburg*. It is uncertain how many passengers were aboard the *Atlantic* when she went down, but as many as 350 lives might have been lost.

In earlier years, Native people, explorers and fur traders avoided the hazards of navigating around Long Point by portaging canoes and small craft across the peninsula. But with the coming of naval vessels and larger commercial transports, this was not an option. And so Long Point began to reap its grim harvest.

As the list of wrecked ships and drowned sailors grew, the American government demanded that the British government build a lighthouse on Long Point. The British had actually taken the initiative in lighthouse building on the freshwater seas when they erected lighthouses at Point Mississauga and Gibraltar Point in 1804 and 1808. But by the 1820s, the tight-fisted colonial government in Upper Canada had fallen behind the Americans. Voices in the Legislative Assembly had been calling for a light on Long Point, but

The Old Cut Lighthouse. A storm cut a natural channel across the neck of the peninsula, making Long Point temporarily an island. This lighthouse guided vessels to the shortcut.

no action had been taken. Finally, the Americans delivered an ultimatum. If the British wouldn't build the much-needed light, they would build one themselves, and annex the ground it stood on. The threat worked, and on November 3, 1830, the first beam of light shone forth from Long Point's 52-foot (15.8-m) beacon.

Even though the tower was solidly built of masonry, the base upon which it stood was not very stable. Long Point is composed primarily of sand, and sand does not stay in one place. Wind and water move it around, sometimes gradually, sometimes—as in a violent storm—with dramatic suddenness. The physical outline of Long Point is constantly being altered. This means that a fixed structure like a lighthouse can have the very ground upon which it stands eroded from under it. Also, the surrounding topography can shift in such a way that the light is no longer located in the best place to do the job for which it was intended. For these reasons, the first light at Long Point had to be abandoned in 1843 after only 13 years of service, and a new one built nearby. This second lighthouse stayed in operation until 1916, when it was replaced by a third. That light, a 68-foot (26.2-m) white, concrete tower, is still in operation (automated) but is no longer right at the tip of the peninsula, as it once was.

In 1833, a storm opened a "cut"—a natural canal—across the neck of Long Point, temporarily making much of the peninsula an island. The cut was a boon to navigation, as it spared mariners the trip around the point. For many years a lightship guided vessels to the Cut. Then, in 1879, a 50-foot (15.2-m) wooden lighthouse was built as a permanent beacon. It was in use until 1916, when storms filled in the Cut, and Long Point became a peninsula once again. The Old Cut Lighthouse, as it came to be called, fell into disrepair, but was purchased and rebuilt as a private residence.

While the lighthouses dramatically reduced the natural hazards of Long Point, they inadvertently invited peril in a more sinister form: wreckers, or as they were called then, "Blackbirds"! A shipwreck certainly meant misfortune for the vessel's crew and owners, but for the residents along the Erie shore it was often a windfall. The ships that plied the Great Lakes did not carry treasures of gold, silver and precious stones. Their cargoes were the fruits of the labour of farmers, miners and loggers; and the manufactured goods needed in the booming frontier communities that were mushrooming around the lakes. When a ship went aground off Long Point, she would often be battered to pieces by the surf, and the cargo would wash ashore where jubilant scavengers awaited the bounty. Kegs of liquor, barrels of foodstuffs and crates of household goods all vanished from the beaches, sometimes even before attempts were made to rescue shipwrecked sailors. Even the timbers from the stricken vessels would be carried off for use in the construction of houses and barns. This was done in spite of a superstition that said that a house built with wood from a wrecked ship would be haunted by the cries of drowning sailors.

Blackbirds were land-based pirates who did not wait for chance to send them a wreck. Knowing that the night watch on a passing ship would be looking for the Long Point light or the lightship at the Cut, they would set up false lights to lure the victim into deadly waters. When the ship ran aground, the Blackbirds would row out to loot her, or just wait for the surf to bring the plunder ashore. No assistance was given to helpless victims in the water. When the bodies washed up on the beach, the Blackbirds simply rifled through their pockets. No one could say just how many Blackbirds skulked around Long Point. Most of them were probably vagabonds, with possibly a few locals joining their ranks.

One ship that fell into the hands of these blackguards was the schooner *Greenbush*. On a stormy December night in 1860 she was lured by a false light onto a shoal up the beach from the Cut. Her entire crew of 13 perished trying to make it to shore. When the weather calmed, the Blackbirds stole the ship's cargo of flour, which they could easily sell on the black market. There does not seem to be any record of Blackbirds ever being caught and tried. It seems that local residents and merchants began to suspect how they came by their wares, and refused to do business with them, so these unscrupulous men shook the sand of Long Point from their heels and drifted away, rather than risk being apprehended. It would almost certainly have meant a date with the hangman. They were evidently gone by the time the Cut lighthouse was built.

THE WRECK OF THE *JERSEY CITY*

Though many a vessel safely passed Long Point in the night thanks to the lighthouses, there were still times when ships were blown onto those dangerous shoals. On the night of November 24–25, 1860, the propeller *Jersey City*, bound for Buffalo from Cleveland, was seized by a November gale and driven toward the Long Point graveyard. When Captain W.T. Monroe saw the Long Point light winking through a blinding snowstorm, he immediately realized the peril his ship was in. Taking the wheel, he ordered the men in the engine room to shovel lard from his cargo into the boilers. The fires roared and the steam pressure rose to the danger point, but the desperate action was in vain. The *Jersey City* ran onto one of Long Point's murderous offshore sandbars. Almost immediately one of the passengers was swept away by the waves that crashed over the stranded vessel. Then a crewman was lost as he tried to launch the ship's yawl.

Knowing that his ship could not hold up long against the pounding of the surf, Captain Monroe ordered all hands and passengers to the hurricane deck. As he had expected, the deck was torn free from the hull and was carried, like a raft, toward the beach. But the people of the *Jersey City* were not out of danger yet. They were all soaked through, and the night was freezing cold. Those who made it to shore were numb and exhausted. Unfortunately, they were too far away from the lighthouse for the keeper to see them through the storm.

Captain Monroe's efforts to save lives were nothing short of heroic. He risked his own life to haul two people out of the water, one of them a young boy. Sadly, both died from the extreme cold. The skipper knew that the only hope for those still living lay in reaching the lighthouse. He tried valiantly to keep his shattered company moving toward it. But some wandered off in the wrong direction. Others surrendered to their exhaustion and sat down to rest. They froze to death on the spot. When lightkeeper Harry Clark took in the survivors, there were only five of them: the captain, three crewmen, and one passenger. Eleven frozen bodies littered the beach, and six more had been swallowed up by Lake Erie.

In the decade and a half that followed, it was a rare year that did not see at least one ship go down off Long Point. The schooners *Kate Norton*, *Junius*, *William G. Keith* and *Jessie Anderson* were among those that went to watery graves. In 1874 the schooner *Mockingbird* foundered while rounding Long Point. Fortunately, lightkeeper Harry Woodward saw the sinking vessel in time, and was able to row out and rescue the crew.

THE LEGEND OF ABIGAIL BECKER

While lighthouse men certainly did their part in keeping ships out of the clutches of Long Point, and in rescuing those who fell prey to the treacherous waters, the person most renowned for saving the lives of shipwrecked sailors was a woman. Abigail Becker lived with her husband and children in a cabin at a remote spot on Long Point. Jeremiah Becker made his living as a trapper and fisherman, and so was often away from home for days at a time. On the night of November 23, 1854, the schooner *Conductor* ran onto a sandbar half a mile (.8km) out from the Long Point beach. Crashing waves carried off the ship's yawl and were sweeping the deck, so Captain Henry Hackett and his seven crewmen lashed themselves to the rigging. They knew it would be only a matter of time before the pounding surf smashed the *Conductor* to pieces, but there was half a mile of frigid water between them and safety.

At dawn, Abigail Becker went down to the beach to see if there was any sign of her husband, who had gone to Port Rowan the day before to buy provisions. What she saw instead were the masts of the *Conductor* rising up from the water, with eight men clinging desperately to the rigging. Abigail hurried back to the house to fetch her oldest children and some blankets, tea and a kettle. She lit a bonfire on the beach and called to the men to come ashore.

The captain went first, telling his men that if he made it, they should follow one at a time. He was a good swimmer, but the cold water quickly sapped his strength. It looked as though he would not make it to the beach alive. Abigail could not swim, but she stood six-foot-two, and was a strong woman. She waded out into the lake as far as she could, and managed to grab Captain Hackett by the hand. Soon he was sitting by the fire, gulping down hot tea.

One by one, Abigail helped more crewmembers ashore. She even had to go to the rescue of her son Edward, who got in trouble trying to help one of the men in the water. Finally only the ship's cook was left. He couldn't swim, and none of his comrades had the strength to take him in tow. Abigail had to leave him there in the rigging while she took the other men to her cabin for food and warmth. The next morning the men built a raft and rescued

Abigail Becker earned international fame for her rescue work on Long Point.

Abigail Becker, in later years, displaying the medal she received from the Benevolent Life Saving Association of New York.

the unfortunate cook, who was nearly dead after spending another cold night dangling above the water. The man was in such a weakened condition that he could not accompany the others when they left. Abigail cared for him until he was well enough to travel. Upon hearing of the courageous rescue, the *City of Buffalo*, to which the *Conductor* had been bound, held a banquet in Abigail's honour and presented her with a purse of $550. Because two of the men on the *Conductor* were Americans, she was also awarded a medal by the Benevolent Life Saving Association of New York.

On another occasion, four half-frozen sailors stumbled into the Becker cabin. Their ship had struck a sandbar and broken up. Six men had drowned, and six had made it to shore. Two of them had collapsed on the beach, unable to make it to the cabin. Abigail and two of her sons went out into the sleet-driven night, found the barely conscious men, and carried them back home.

Abigail Becker became known as the Heroine of Long Point. She received a letter of commendation from Queen Victoria, a letter of congratulations from the Governor General of Canada and, in 1860, she was visited by the Prince of Wales. A highly romanticized ballad by Amanda T. Jones entitled "A Heroine

The Conductor *was like this typical two-masted schooner. Before the coming of steam, these vessels were the workhorses of the Great Lakes, and easy prey for shoals and reefs not marked by lighthouses.*

of '54" appeared in a textbook, *The Ontario High School Reader*. It went, in part:

O Mother Becker, seas are dread
Their treacherous paths are deep and blind
But widows soon may mourn their dead
If thou art slow to find

Abigail Becker certainly deserved credit for her actions, but the acclaim she received also had something to do with the Victorian psyche. The prevailing attitude held women to be helpless. Men were supposed to be the rescuers. So, when a woman did respond to an emergency with strength and resourcefulness, it was seen as exceptional.

Long Point is said to be a haunted place, a place of hidden graves and lost souls. The lighthouses there have witnessed shipwrecks and the despicable crimes of the Blackbirds. They have also seen the kindness of lightkeeper Harry Clark and the bravery of Abigail Becker. The sands may change the shape of Lake Erie's graveyard, but the legends endure.

PELEE ISLAND LIGHT: CASUALTY OF WAR

Pelee Island, 18 miles (29km) out in Lake Erie, is Canada's most southerly territory. It is a quiet place, known principally for its winery. It even has a romantic legend about a beautiful French-Indian woman named Huldah who fell in love with a dashing young Englishman, and then threw herself from the rock that now bears her name when he deserted her. But for all Pelee's peaceful atmosphere, it became the target of a "Patriot" attack in the Mackenzie Rebellion of 1837–38, and the scene of one of the more serious skirmishes of that hopeless attempt at a Canadian Revolution. In an uprising that was full of oddities, one of the victims of that attack was the island's lighthouse.

The Pelee Island Light, a stone tower built on the northeast shore, was the second Canadian lighthouse (after Long Point) to be erected on Lake Erie. It went into operation in 1834 as a guide for ships navigating the dangerous passage between the island and Point Pelee. Three years later, William Lyon Mackenzie initiated his ill-starred rebellion against the government of Upper Canada. Not many Canadians flocked to his banner. His "army" was routed, and he and a few followers fled to American territory, from which they tried

The Patriots (above) started to dismantle the Pelee Island Lighthouse (left). The arrival of British troops stopped the destruction.

to continue their insurrection. There they found a considerable number of Americans—mostly vagabonds and ne'er-do-wells—who were eager to join them in driving the British "tyrant" out of North America. Mackenzie's American supporters called themselves Patriots. Never did they have the support of their own government, although American authorities tended to be rather lax in dealing with them.

There had been farcical attempts at "invasions" at Bois Blanc Island and Fighting Island in the Detroit River, which British troops thwarted merely by showing up. Undiscouraged, the Patriots turned their sights on Pelee Island. The invasion came on February 26, 1838.

After a period of mild weather, the temperature dropped, and Lake Erie was covered by a layer of ice that was at some places 15 inches (38cm) thick. This was topped by deep, drifted snow. A party of 400 to 450 Patriots, with a few Canadian rebels among them, left Sandusky, Ohio, in sleighs and on foot, and took the island by surprise. Leading the Patriot force were "Colonels" H.C. Seward and E.D. Bradley, "Major" Lester

British Redcoats rout the Patriot army at Pelee Island with a bayonet charge. Some fleeing invaders went through the ice. (Inset) William Lyon Mackenzie. The Hunters and Patriots invaded Canada in the wake of his 1837–38 rebellion.

Hoadley, and "Captain" George Van Rensselaer. The invaders quickly took the few inhabitants prisoner, though the biggest landowner on the island, William McCormick, escaped to Amherstburg. The Patriots used his fine stone house as a headquarters.

With this bit of sovereign British territory in their possession, the liberators then degenerated into banditry. People coming from the Canadian mainland, unaware of the occupation, were taken prisoner or driven away with gunfire. The Patriots looted homes and farms. What they could not use themselves, they sent back to the American shore. Then they turned their attention to the lighthouse.

One historical account states that: "...in addition to these depredations the invaders dismantled the lighthouse and carried off whatever they considered of use". No explanation was ever given for the assault on the lighthouse. Was it an act of revenge for the destruction of the American ship *Caroline* in the Niagara River a few months earlier? Or was it simply wanton vandalism?

The "dismantling" of the lighthouse must have meant that it was pillaged of stores, equipment and interior fittings. The Patriots would not likely have had the equipment to actually tear the stone tower down; nor, considering the labour such a task would have required and the character of the men involved, would they have had the inclination. They also would

The Caroline *made a spectacular sight, going over Niagara Falls in flames.*

not have had the time. The British and Canadians were not about to sit back and allow a gang of ruffians to sack their island and destroy their lighthouse.

When William McCormick reached Amherstburg, he reported the attack to Colonel John Maitland. That officer led a force of about three hundred men to re-take the island. With this company of British Regulars and Canadian militia was Prideaux Girty, son of Simon Girty, the notorious "White Indian" of the American Revolution. Prideaux was a militia officer, and like his Loyalist father he had no love for the Americans. Most of the men rode in sleighs, with perhaps two dozen cavalrymen urging their struggling horses through the snow. Behind them dragged two six-pounder cannon.

Maitland didn't know what the enemy forces would be. There had been considerable traffic between Pelee Island and the American shore, and it seems that at one point there were as many as a thousand Patriots on the island. If that number is accurate, it would be the greatest concentration of foreign invaders on Canadian soil since the War of 1812, not to be matched until the Fenian invasion a generation later.

But even if the Patriot force standing in the shadow of the "dismantled" lighthouse was that large at some point, it quickly diminished. They were an undisciplined rabble, and once the looting was done, many of them drifted back to the American shore. Between 300 and 400 remained on Pelee Island, trying to decide whether or not to attack the Canadian mainland.

On March 3, Indian scouts who had been spying on the invaders, reported the Patriots' positions to the advancing British. Maitland deployed his troops on the frozen lake. He would lead the main body in an assault on the Patriot camp on the north end of the island. A smaller force would swing around to the south end of the island to cut off any retreat.

When they saw the British marching toward them, the Patriots released their prisoners and then formed ranks, their bayonets glittering in the sunlight.

Then, quite likely at the sight of the cannon, they turned and retreated to the heavily wooded south end of the island. The thick forest and deep snow prevented British pursuit.

Now the Patriots quarrelled over what to do next. Some were in favour of a hasty retreat across the lake. Others said they had come for a fight and wanted "to have the fun of it". Several sleighloads of American citizens from Sandusky, anticipating a show, had come across the ice to watch the battle. They saw a fight, but not the outcome they probably hoped for.

The Patriots evidently decided that discretion was the better part of valour. They emerged from the woods at the south end of the island, intent upon following their own trail through the snow back to the United States. They found the way blocked by ninety British Regulars and a handful of cavalry led by Captain John Browne. The Patriots formed a ragged line opposite the smaller, but ordered, British line. Then they opened fire.

Maitland and the main British force were still at the north end of the island, picking through the Patriot camp, where pots of potatoes still boiled on campfires. The lighthouse must have looked like an abused, innocent victim of marauders. Maitland did not know that the enemy had abandoned the woods at the south end, and were about to engage Browne's outnumbered command. He may have heard the sound of gunfire when the fighting started, but was too far away to be of immediate assistance.

For twenty minutes Browne's troops and the Patriots exchanged volleys. The British were taking casualties, and Captain Browne decided that if he stood there fighting on terms that were favourable to the enemy, he would suffer unacceptable losses. He was a veteran of Waterloo, where he had fought Napoleon, the French general whose military philosophy was, "When in doubt, attack!" Browne gave the order: "Fix bayonets! Charge!"

The British soldiers raced across the ice "at double-quick, with the half cheer, half roar of British troops..." according to an officer's description of the advance. With them were about twenty cavalrymen. One Patriot cried, "There come the cavalry! Fire on them!" They fired a volley and brought down one horseman. The British charge was not even slowed down.

Now the Patriots fled before the bayonet charge "like wild turkeys", in the words of one British officer. They ran back into the woods in complete disorder, dragging their dead and wounded with them, "staining the snow for a quarter of a mile in width with blood", as one witness stated. Then the desperate Patriots broke out of the trees farther along the shore in a frantic attempt to flee to safety. Captain Browne sent the cavalry after them, but thin ice prevented effective pursuit. For some of the fleeing Patriots, it also prevented escape. A large number of them eventually straggled into

Sandusky, where they were arrested and then released, but no one knew how many had broken through the ice and drowned.

The British losses were 5 men killed and 30 wounded. The Patriots left behind 11 dead (in addition to the ones who drowned). Another 11, some severely wounded, were taken prisoner. The following day, Prideaux Girty and a British officer spotted two Patriot fugitives in the vicinity of Colchester, and the pair was captured. Except for one who died of his injuries, they were all eventually released and sent back to the United States. Two of the Patriot leaders, Hoadley and Van Rensselaer, were among the dead.

American journalists tried to make much of the fiasco. There were accounts in which the Patriot freedom fighters poured "a death dealing volley" into the British lines, and claims that it was "one of the few times that British troops recoiled from a charge of bayonets". The Patriots, according to those chroniclers, battled their way through the British ranks to reach the safety of the American mainland.

A Patriot leader named David McLeod wrote to the mother of the slain Van Rensselaer and told her that when Canada became free, a monument to her son would be erected in that country. As it was, the only "monument" Van Rensselaer and the Patriots left behind was a vandalized lighthouse — one that was soon back in operation.

JACK SUTHERLAND AND THE *CISCOE*: ABOVE AND BEYOND

Jack Sutherland, 25, of Port Burwell, Ontario, was no stranger to lightkeeping. The Sutherland family had been tending the lighthouse in that community on the north shore of Lake Erie since it went into operation in 1840. Jack had inherited the lightkeeper's job from his late father. Jack was no stranger to peril, either, having served with the Canadian armed forces in the Korean War. On the night of March 22, 1955, Jack Sutherland the lightkeeper, rather than Jack Sutherland the soldier, showed his country the stuff that heroes are made of.

That spring night a storm of near-hurricane strength swept across Michigan and the Lakes and into Southern Ontario. Every vessel afloat dashed for safe harbour, and the landlubbing public was warned to stay away from the lakeshore areas. A cottage swept off its foundations by a raging Lake Erie was dumped on the pier of the Port Stanley Lighthouse. Even little Lake St. Clair showed muscle, and the U.S. Coast Guard had to

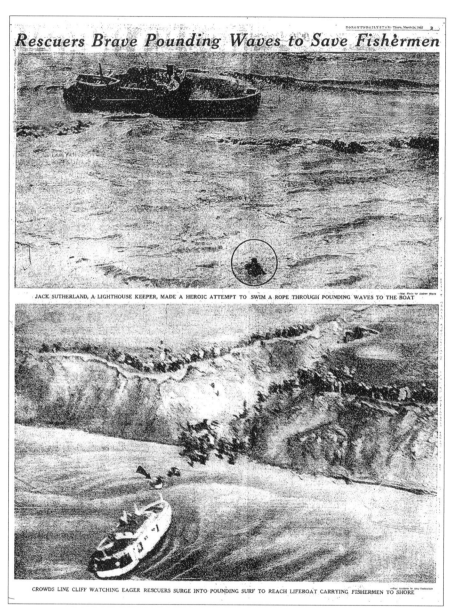

Rescuers Brave Pounding Waves to Save Fishermen

JACK SUTHERLAND, A LIGHTHOUSE KEEPER, MADE A HEROIC ATTEMPT TO SWIM A ROPE THROUGH POUNDING WAVES TO THE BOAT

CROWDS LINE CLIFF WATCHING EAGER RESCUERS SURGE INTO POUNDING SURF TO REACH LIFEBOAT CARRYING FISHERMEN TO SHORE

Lightkeeper Jack Sutherland, Korean War hero, braved Lake Erie's worst to try to take a line to the stricken Ciscoe.

send a cutter to Peche Island to rescue the lightkeepers who were stranded there by stormy waters and in danger of being swept away.

On Lake Erie's north shore, the 52-foot (15.8-m) fishing boat *Ciscoe* was disabled by engine failure while trying to outrun the storm, and the five men on board were at the mercy of the elements. One man was lost over the side before the boat was blown onto one of the notorious north shore shoals near Port Burwell. People on shore had been watching helplessly for hours as the lake toyed with the *Ciscoe*, and they knew it would not take long for the pounding waves to hammer the little craft to splinters. Then the four men still on board would be added to Erie's grim harvest.

Not one to stand and watch while the lake tore the *Ciscoe* to pieces, and knowing that time was crucial, young Sutherland was one of the first to try to go to the fishermen's aid. Before the eyes of astounded newspaper reporters and photographers who had rushed out to witness the drama, he grabbed a lifeline and plunged into a storm-tossed lake that was still frigid from the winter's ice. In the worst gale to hit Lake Erie in 25 years, he was going to *swim* out to where the *Ciscoe* was stranded, a few hundred feet from shore. One of the photographers took a picture of his gallant effort. Within two days it was seen in communities across the country.

Sutherland was a strong swimmer, and no one would doubt his courage. But in that cauldron he was just one more speck of flotsam to be tossed around or sucked under at Erie's whim. He soon found that he was no match for the raw power of the lake. Yet he still tried. The people on shore became alarmed when they saw him fighting a losing battle with the relentless waves. Fearful that Sutherland would drown rather than give up, they pulled him back to land with the lifeline he was trying to take to the fishermen. Sutherland was, indeed, exhausted and half-drowned when he was hauled onto the beach. He had failed, but somewhere his father's soul must have glowed with pride.

Jack Sutherland's heroic attempt to save the men on the *Ciscoe* had been for naught, and for the rest of that long night the watchers on shore stood helplessly as the lake pounded the little boat. The survivors on board could only pray.

Miraculously, the *Ciscoe* was still in one piece at dawn, and the surf had pushed her to within 100 feet (30m) of shore. Twice, boats tried to get out to the fishermen, but waves swamped them, and the would-be rescuers had to be rescued themselves. Men from the Royal Canadian Navy arrived and attempted to fire lifelines to the fishing boat with rockets, but in the howling wind this proved futile. Finally, a naval lifeboat from HMCS *Prescott* was able to battle through the surf and take the men off the *Ciscoe*. The stretch

he storm that disabled the Ciscoe was the worst to hit Lake Erie in twenty-five years.

of water between the ruined boat and the shore was still a no-man's-land of crashing waves and surging backwash, but the Navy men got a lifeline ashore, and gradually worked their lifeboat back to land. The fishermen, almost frozen to death and in shock, were rushed to hospital.

"No more dramatic a scene is imaginable", a Toronto *Globe and Mail* reporter wrote about the Navy's rescue of the fishermen. And for the Navy men it was deserved credit for a job well done. There was recognition for Jack Sutherland, too. His picture and his name made the papers, though he was difficult to recognize in the photograph, awash in a Lake Erie swell. But it was probably of little concern to him. Like the Navy men, he had been doing what he thought had to be done in an emergency. True mariners, including those who kept the beacons alight, were always ready to act above and beyond the call of duty.

MOHAWK ISLAND AND COLCHESTER REEF: LIFE AND DEATH ON LAKE ERIE

MOHAWK ISLAND

On December 13, 1932, James Foster of Dunnville, a community along Ontario's Grand River, set out in an 18-foot (5.4-m) rowboat for the lighthouse on Mohawk Island (also called Gull Island). This small island is about a mile and a half (2.5km) from the mainland, three miles (4.8km) east of Port Maitland, which is at the mouth of the Grand River. The stone lighthouse had been in operation since 1848, to warn of a dangerous reef at the approach to Port Maitland's harbour. The 60-foot (18.2-m) tower was built by John Brown, the architect of the Imperial Towers.

James's father, Richard, 61, had been the lightkeeper on Mohawk Island since 1921. He was an Englishman who had emigrated to Canada a few years before the First World War. In 1915 he'd gone back to Europe with the Canadian Army and had fought at Vimy Ridge. After the war he'd taken advantage of the Canadian government's policy of offering light-keeping positions to war veterans.

On that December day, James was following his father's annual routine for closing down the lighthouse at the end of the navigation season. Every year James rowed out to help with the job. He and his father would pack up and clean up. They would shut down the revolving light and turn on a battery-operated stationary light that would last for three months. In the morning they would take whatever food was left in the pantry and scatter it around for the flocks of seagulls that inhabited the island. Then James would row his father home.

James spent that night at the island. On the morning of Wednesday the 14th, Richard wrote in the lighthouse log, "Summer light out and winter light left burning". He noted the time as 7:45 a.m. Then he and James set off for home in the rowboat. They never made it.

That night, people on shore could see the beacon atop the lighthouse, but they could see no lights in the windows of the lightkeeper's cottage. Father and son had not arrived home in Dunnville. Over the next few days, police and volunteers tried to go out to the lighthouse to investigate, but ice made the crossing almost impossible. There were ice floes in the water, and slush ice along the shore was piled 15 feet (4.5m) high and extended 200 feet (over 60m) out into the lake.

While they waited to see if conditions on the lake would improve, police conducted a search along the shore in the Port Maitland vicinity. There was no sign of the Fosters. On Sunday, December 18, Richard Foster's younger son, Richard, Jr., could stand the waiting no longer. He and two other men set out in a rowboat and made a perilous crossing to Mohawk Island. The lighthouse was deserted. Young Foster could see that his father and brother had packed up and left. He and his friends made another hazardous crossing to return to the mainland and deliver the news that Richard and James were definitely not on the island.

People on shore knew something was wrong when they could not see light in the windows of the keeper's house on Mohawk Island.

LIGHTHOUSE KEEPER AND SON MISSING

The Mohawk Island Lighthouse is only a mile and a half (2.5km) from the mainland, but crossing that short distance in winter had terrible consequences for light-keeper Richard Foster (left) and his son James (right).

Now a major search was set in motion. Tug boats and fishing boats cruised up and down the lakeshore whenever weather conditions allowed. The American Coast Guard was notified so they could search their side of the lake. The federal government dispatched air force planes to assist the searchers on land and water. A plane from Buffalo swept the American shore. No one found a thing.

About a week after the men went missing, searchers found a pair of broken oars and a blanket that was believed to have come from the lighthouse, washed up on the beach between Port Maitland and Port Colborne (21 miles [34km] to the east). A few days later, on Christmas Eve, a woman walking her dog along the lakeshore, a few miles (over 3km) east of Port Colborne, found James Foster's body. Two days later, a family friend found Richard Foster's body in the rowboat, very close to where James had been found. Both had died of exposure. Foster's lighthouse log had a final entry in it, saying that they had run aground near Port Colborne on Friday, December 16. It was simply incredible that the searchers had missed them.

With the evidence at hand, investigators tried to reconstruct what had happened, and they came to the following conclusion: after closing down

(Top) Richard Foster. His lighthouse log had a final entry, telling when and where they had run aground. (Below) A year after the Foster tragedy, the Mohawk Island Light was automated.

the lighthouse, James and Richard began to row to the mainland through slush ice. Plummeting temperatures turned the slush into what was called "anchor ice". This coated the bottom of the rowboat, making it unmanageable. No matter how frantically the men pulled on the oars, the ice-laden boat drifted wherever wind and current would take it. Ice would have coated the oars, too, and the men evidently broke them trying to push their way to shore. If the date in Richard Foster's log was accurate, they were out on the lake for more than two days and nights.

When at last the boat did run up onto shelf ice, James was the only one with strength left to try to go for help. He stumbled or crawled across the ice to the shore. At that spot there was a high sand embankment. There was no snow, and marks in the sand showed that James had made a valiant effort to drag himself up the bank, trying to reach a house that was a mere

two-minute walk away. But those long, freezing hours out on Lake Erie had taken their toll. He died face down in the sand. Hidden from the view of the people in the house, he'd been there over a week before being discovered. The build-up of ice along the shore had kept his father's body hidden for another two days. Richard and James were buried together. One year later the Mohawk Island Light was automated.

Mohawk Island Lighthouse, built by John Brown of Imperial Tower fame. It has also been known as the Gull Island Lighthouse.

TWO ARE FEARED VICTIMS OF ICY WATERS OF LAKE

Richard Foster and His Son Reported Missing

Lighthouse Keeper Started Out For Home

Boat May Have Been Overwhelmed

From Our Own Correspondent

Dunnville, Dec. 18.—Richard Foster, Dunnville, the lighthouse keeper at Gull Island, east of Port Maitland, and his son, James Foster, are missing and believed to have drowned in Lake Erie.

Thursday being the last day of the navigation season, Mr. Foster was expected home from the lighthouse, along with his son, who had gone out to visit him. The island is 1½ miles from shore. When the two did not come home, Richard Foster, another son, notified Provincial Constable Hayes, of Dunnville, who called the coast guard station at Buffalo and the provincial police at Welland. The latter were requested to send a detachment of men to search the shore line from Port Colborne to Port Maitland.

DEATH GAINS A VICTORY

by A. H. Wells

Three days amid the ice and winds,
They fought their lives to save,
The sky o'erhead was dark with clouds,

And dark beneath their grave.
The slush ice closed about its prey,
Breaking with thudding crash,
And when the anchor ice gave way,
It fell with dull, low splash.

Father nor son, ne'er thought to
swerve,
As the boat drifted to and fro,
With weary heart and tranquil nerve,
Each felt his life's strength go:
Each felt his life's strength go and
knew,
As time drew slowly on,
That less and less their chances grew—
Night fell and hope was gone.

Their bodies numbed by the bitter cold;
No, not a crust of bread:
No shelter from the angry blast,
A sand bank was their bed;
Oh, Motherland, while thy native sons
Can live and die like these,
Keeping from shame that honored name,
As mistress of the seas.

Dunnville *Chronicle*, December 1932

COLCHESTER REEF

While searchers were combing land and water in the Port Maitland area looking for Richard and James Foster, another drama was being played out farther up the Erie shore at Colchester, near Windsor. John Knapp was the keeper of the Colchester Reef Light, a 60-foot (18.2-m) white wooden tower perched on a stone pier, five miles (8km) out in the lake. With Knapp was his assistant, Simeon Bock. Since Knapp had no telephone or radio, he had worked out a communications system with his wife. She would signal him with the headlights of their car to let him know when the shipping season was closed and he could come home. He would respond with a signal to confirm that he had received the message. For several years this arrangement had worked well. In 1932, however, things did not go quite so smoothly.

Ice conditions on Lake Erie were so bad that no boat had been able to reach the Colchester Light for a month. There was concern that Knapp and Bock would be out of food. When Mrs. Knapp was informed that the navigation season was officially closed, she drove out to the pre-arranged spot on the lakeshore and gave the signal with her headlights. No response came from the lighthouse out on the reef. The next night, and the night after that, Mrs. Knapp was at the water's edge, frantically flashing the car lights and looking over the dark water for a reply. Nothing! Had something happened to her husband and Bock in that long month since a boat had last visited the lighthouse? The beacon had been shining, but why didn't anyone answer her signals?

Very worried now, Mrs. Knapp took her concerns to three family friends: Clark Cornwall, Thomas Armstrong and Mahlan Halstead. Those three men used an ice boat in what newspapers called a "hazardous dash" across ice and water. They rowed across open water, and pushed the boat across ice for a gruelling two-and-a-half hours. When they reached the Colchester Light, they found Knapp and Bock preparing their small boat for what would have been an extremely dangerous crossing. They had a few days' supply of food left, but felt that if they waited any longer the weather would only deteriorate further.

The rescuers and the lightkeepers made the return trip guided by, according to the Toronto *Globe*, "a battery of automobile headlights". Mrs. Knapp had called upon friends to help light the way home for the men. John Knapp later said that he had been watching for his wife's signal every night, but must have confused it with other lights along the shore.

Colchester Reef Lighthouse keeper John Knapp and his assistant Simeon Bock were stranded because of ice. They were rescued through the efforts of Knapp's wife, who used her car headlights to flash signals to her husband.

A year later, Knapp and Bock were in trouble out on the Colchester Reef Light again. On December 11, 1933, Knapp saw the headlight signal flashed by his wife, telling him that he could close down the lighthouse and return home. But ice had again made a trip to the mainland impossible. It was too thick for his boat to break through, but not strong enough to risk walking on. Not until December 21, when the men had been ice-bound for ten days, was a motor launch finally able to reach them. Throughout the long wait, Mrs. Knapp went to the shore every night and flashed the car lights, asking her husband if he was okay. Each time he would reply that he was well. Just getting to and from an offshore lighthouse was a matter of life and death. After the tragedy that had occurred at Mohawk Island, John Knapp's reply signal must certainly have been a reassuring sight.

VERMILION OHIO: THE DISAPPEARING LIGHTHOUSE

The citizens of Vermilion, Ohio, a small Lake Erie port just west of Cleveland, were no doubt proud when, in 1877, a brand new lighthouse graced their harbour. The 30-foot (9-m), cast-iron tower stood at the end of the town's west pier, and replaced the old wooden tower that had lit the harbour entrance since 1859. For 52 years the Vermilion beacon was a familiar landmark to vessels sailing along the Ohio shore.

Then, in 1929, the lighthouse was badly damaged when it was crushed by lake ice. Concerned that it would be a hazard to navigation in its poor condition, the Coast Guard had it taken away by barge, supposedly for repairs. An 18-foot (5.4-m) steel tower took its place on the pier, but it just didn't have the appeal of the old lighthouse.

Their town's lighthouse was a familiar sight to the people of Vermilion, Ohio. It was removed for repairs in 1929, then it seemingly disappeared for 65 years. (Inset) A Vermilion resident finally solved the mystery when he saw a picture in a magazine.

Time passed, and the people of Vermilion began to wonder what had become of their lighthouse. But nobody, not even the Coast Guard, seemed to know. Was some sort of lighthouse-napping skullduggery going on? The case of the "Disappearing Lighthouse" would remain a mystery in that town for 65 years.

Meanwhile, the old Vermilion Lighthouse sat in storage in Buffalo for six years. Then, in 1935, it was disassembled, and reconstructed with up-to-date equipment. It was as good as new, and ready for service. But it was not returned to its old home in Vermilion. Instead, the lighthouse was taken to the East Charity Shoal in eastern Lake Ontario, about seven miles (11km) from Tibbetts Point, New York, and installed atop a concrete and iron bunker. There, at the busy entrance to the St. Lawrence River, far from little Vermilion, it warned shipping away from deadly rocks.

But nobody told the folks back in Vermilion. Not until 1994 would there be a clue to the mystery of the vanished lighthouse. That year a Vermilion resident saw an article about the East Charity Light in a magazine, accompanied by a photograph. The man compared the photo with pictures of the old Vermilion Light, and the mystery was solved.

In 1991, the town of Vermilion erected a 16-foot (4.8-m) tower that is a replica of the old Vermilion Light. It stands on the shore at the foot of the main street, and is an operational light. It is managed by the Inland Seas Maritime Museum. The old Vermilion Light, which first blinked into service in 1877, still stands lonely vigil (automated) on the East Charity Shoal.

SOUTHEAST SHOAL LIGHT: FLAMES ON LAKE ERIE

A cross-section illustration of the Great Lakes shows that Lakes Superior, Michigan, Huron and Ontario occupy very deep chasms, whilst Lake Erie is more like a saucer full of water. It is Erie's very lack of depth that poses a hazard to navigation. The lake abounds with shoals that have exacted a heavy toll in vessels and lives over the last two centuries.

The Southeast Shoal at the eastern end of Lake Erie's Pelee Passage is the shallowest part of the lake. But it is through these waters that the heavy traffic coming out of the Detroit River must pass, as ships fan out to go to major ports on the American shore, or to the Welland Canal. Upbound traffic, too, must pass through here en route to Detroit, Windsor, Sarnia and the Upper Lakes. The relatively deep water of the Pelee Passage is therefore the most important channel of the lake, and the close proximity of the Southeast Shoal makes a guiding beacon a vital necessity.

The shoal is in Canadian waters, but for several years in the early twentieth century it was marked by the United States Lightship *Kewaunee*. Then, in 1927, the Canadian government erected a 70-foot (21.3-m) concrete and steel lighthouse, with quarters for a keeper and two assistants. The first lightkeeper was William Moore, 41, an Englishman who had emigrated to Canada in 1910 and settled in the Lake Erie port town of Leamington, Ontario. Bill Moore would tend the Southeast Shoal Light for 23 years—the rest of his life.

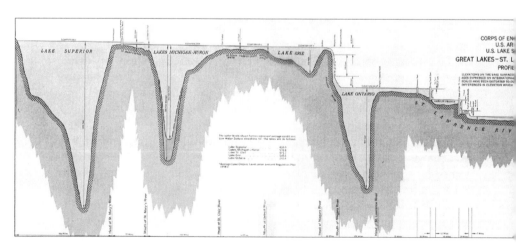

As this diagram shows, Lake Erie is by far the shallowest of the Great Lakes. Because of this, some areas of the lake are riddled with shoals.

For many years a lightship warned vessels away from the Southeast Shoal, the shallowest part of Lake Erie.

A lighthouse in the middle of a Great Lake, without even a small island on which to stretch one's legs, and with nothing to break the monotonous view, was nobody's notion of an idyllic posting. It was a tedious duty that meant long periods of separation from one's family, sometimes made longer by bad weather. The design of the Southeast Shoal Light was such that just getting on and off it could be perilous. The lower platform was too high for many small boats, which meant that a person had to time a jump with the rise of the water.

Nevertheless, for all the hardships of the job, Bill Moore stuck with it. After all, he had a wife, four sons, and three daughters in Leamington to support. By July 1950, he was 64 years old and looking forward to retirement in only nine months. It would be welcome, after so many years on the lonely shoal.

On Friday, July 7, 1950, Moore and his assistants, Lewis Shaw and George Henderson, were expecting a visit from the lighthouse tender *Grenville*. The ship was delivering six hundred gallons of gasoline to refill the storage tank at the lower level of the light station, as well as a supply of coal. The *Grenville* was also bringing Moore a new refrigerator (just the thing for storing his favourite food—bacon—which he liked to fry in thick slabs).

When Captain Oscar Morpheth brought the *Grenville* to the Southeast Shoal Light that morning, he had on board Dowsley Kingston, 42, of Prescott, Ontario. Kingston was a marine signals inspector for the Department of Transport. He was making what should have been a routine visit to the light station.

While the crew of the *Grenville* prepared to transfer the cargo to the station, Kingston went into the lower level to look at an electric motor that was located near the gasoline storage tank. Presumably, this was the motor

The tender Grenville *was delivering a supply of fuel to the lighthouse, and a new refrigerator for keeper Bill Moore.*

for the fog horn. Bill Moore was inside the lighthouse. Gerald McPherson, a crewmember of the *Grenville*, was shovelling coal into a bin near the storage tank.

Second Mate John Rice was in charge of refilling the gasoline tank. He stuck a broom handle into the opening to see how much fuel was already in it. Then he attached an anti-static hose to the tank. The gas was pumped into the tank by forcing compressed air into the fuel drums on the deck of the *Grenville*.

Things were going along smoothly, until Rice was called upon to supervise the hoisting of the refrigerator from the ship to the lighthouse. He ordered Gerald McPherson to keep an eye on the gasoline hose until he came back. But after Rice had left, McPherson put down his coal shovel and went to the *Grenville* for a glass of water because the fumes in the lower level were getting strong. He later claimed that he had not heard Rice's order.

Lewis Shaw was just outside the door to the lower level when he heard someone shout, "Shut it off!" A moment later an explosion shattered the air, and the flames from hundreds of gallons of gasoline shot up into the lighthouse. Dowsley Kingston was blown out through the door and landed in the water between the light station and the *Grenville*. Moore, the only man inside the lighthouse, suddenly found himself in the midst of an inferno. Walls of fire blocked the exits, so he crawled to another room and used a rope to lower himself to the ground.

The crew of the *Grenville* pulled Kingston out of the water and helped Moore onto the ship. Both men were horribly burned, though still conscious. Moore couldn't even remember how he'd escaped from the lighthouse. Captain Morpheth ordered the *Grenville* away from the lighthouse so that the flames wouldn't spread to the ship. Then the crew trained fire hoses on the pillar of flame towering above the Southeast Shoal.

The fire was completely out of control, and fighting it was useless. Captain Morpheth realized, moreover, that Kingston and Moore were seriously injured and in need of immediate medical attention. He ordered full speed ahead for Leamington, and radioed ahead for help. His message was picked up by the freighter *City of Kingston* and relayed to the mainland. By the time the *Grenville* pulled into Leamington harbour, a medical team was

Southeast Shoal Lighthouse in flames. Someone shouted, "Shut it off!" Then all hell broke loose.

waiting on the dock. Meanwhile, five U.S. Coast Guard cutters were racing from American ports to the burning lighthouse. There was little they could do, though, but watch as the gasoline-fed fire burned itself out.

At the Leamington dock, two doctors gave the victims immediate emergency care, then rushed them to Leamington Memorial Hospital to be treated for second and third degree burns to their faces and hands, and for shock. Sadly, the damage was too severe. Bill Moore died at 8:30 the following morning. Dowsley Kingston succumbed that same evening.

The Royal Canadian Mounted Police conducted an inquiry into the accident. They tried to determine who had shouted "Shut it off!" Everyone who had been at the scene of the tragedy denied having said it, so investigators decided that it could have been Kingston himself. But had he been calling for the engine or the gas to be shut off?

The investigators could not conclude just how the fire had started, only that the electric motor that Kingston had been inspecting was the probable cause. Either the untended hose had fallen out of the tank and the engine had ignited spilled gasoline, or sparks from the engine had ignited the fumes in the storage room. The one conclusion they did reach was that the electric engine should not have been in the same room as the gasoline tank. That, said the coroner's jury, was "inexcusable". The jury placed blame for the accident on "laxity in discipline and supervision of the crew" of the *Grenville*. They recommended tighter safety regulations for explosive materials, and stricter enforcement.

By the time the fire at Southeast Shoal was out, the lighthouse was a gutted ruin. The entire station had to be rebuilt and re-equipped, this time with diesel engines. A lightship stood duty until the construction was completed, guiding vessels safely past the shoal that for 23 years had been Bill Moore's post.

DETROIT RIVER LIGHT: FIRE ON THE *LUCILLE*

Lightkeepers in the more remote regions of the Upper Lakes were often the only human presence for many miles around. They were sometimes the only people mariners in trouble could look to for assistance. But in the more populated areas, too, like the western end of Lake Erie, the fact that a light-keeper was on duty could mean the difference between life and death.

The Detroit River Light, a 49-foot (14.9-m) tower built in 1885, was never a popular posting with lightkeepers. The lighthouse sat on a concrete pier in the mouth of the Detroit River, 28 miles (45km) from the city of Detroit and seven miles (11km) from Gibraltar, Michigan. It was considered an isolated light, and because of frequent fog was often damp and uncomfortable. Coastguardsmen who were stationed there in later years called it "The Rock" and "Alcatraz". It was, of course, an important navigational aid, situated in one of the most heavily travelled shipping channels in the world. (It is still in operation, automated.) One summer day in 1921, the light's keeper became a lifesaver when a freak accident almost claimed the lives of six people.

Toledo business tycoon William L. Urschel, his 18-year-old bride, along with three other men and another woman, were cruising Lake Erie near the mouth of the Detroit River on August 22, in Urschel's motor-driven yacht the *Lucille*. Someone in the party went below to make coffee on the gasoline stove in the galley. When that person lit the stove, it exploded! Liquid fire sprayed the galley, setting it ablaze. Urschel and the other men tried to fight the fire, while the two women huddled on a part of the deck farthest from the flames.

The Detroit River Light. Coastguardsmen would call it "Alcatraz", but it was a welcome sight to the people of the burning Lucille.

The Detroit River, actually a strait, is one of the busiest shipping lanes in the world.

However, fires seemed to be bursting out all over the vessel. The men had to retreat before the advancing flames.

The yacht's lifeboat must have been on fire, because there was nowhere for the Urschels and their friends to go but over the side. The men lowered the women into the water, then went overboard themselves. Some of them had already been badly burned. Now they clung to the side of the *Lucille* as the flames burned steadily down toward the waterline.

Fortunately, the Detroit River lightkeeper, whose name was not recorded, saw the flaming yacht and rowed to the scene as quickly as he could. He arrived at the *Lucille* just as the exhausted women were about to sink. He helped them into his boat, picked up the men, then took them back to the lighthouse. The uncomfortable "Rock" must have been a welcome sight indeed to the people from the charred remains of the *Lucille*. After the light became automated in 1979, the Urschel party would not have been as lucky.

MAEBELLE MASON: RESCUE ON THE RIVER

Maebelle Mason was not actually a lightkeeper, but her heroics on the Detroit River made her, for a while, the toast of the city of Detroit. Maebelle's father was Captain Orlo J. Mason, a Civil War veteran who in 1885 was appointed keeper of the light at Mamajuda Island, near Grosse Ile in the Detroit River. Mamajuda has been almost completely washed away, now, but at one time it was a serious navigational hazard in the busiest water corridor in the entire Great Lakes system, and had a substantial brick house and tower. Captain Mason's predecessor was, inciden-

Maebelle Mason, 14, proudly shows off the medals she was awarded for a daring rescue. Ships' captains blew their whistles to salute the lighthouse keeper's daughter.

tally, a woman, Caroline Litigot, who had kept the light for 11 years.

Maebelle would have been just nine years old when her father and her mother, Belle, took her to live on the island. Many children would have resented being so cut off from friends and the attractions of the big city, but Maebelle evidently loved her tiny island home. Her parents instilled in her such qualities as courage, modesty and a sense of responsibility. From her father, whom she adored, she learned how to operate the lighthouse machinery and how to handle a small boat expertly.

Maebelle's moment to shine came on May 11, 1890, when she was 14 years old. A man rowing on the river had thrown a line to the steamer *C.W. Elphicke*, looking for a tow. This was not an uncommon practice, as a free ride in the wake of a steamer was preferable to the labour of hauling on the oars. It was also dangerous, as was proven on this occasion when the rowboat capsized, dumping the lone occupant into the swift Detroit River current. The skipper of the *C.W. Elphicke* saw the man clinging desperately to the little boat, but would not have been able to stop and turn around in time to help him. As he passed the Mamajuda Lighthouse, he signaled that there was a man overboard and in danger of drowning.

Captain Mason was away from the island at the time, and had taken the light station's main boat. That left the rescue mission to Belle and Maebelle, and of the two, the daughter was the better rower. They hauled out the only boat left at the island, a small, flat-bottomed punt. With Maebelle handling the oars, they went after the helpless man. He was over a mile away, and the teenager rowed furiously in order to reach him before he slipped under. That she got to him in time was no mean feat. The Detroit River is actually a strait in a system connecting two Great Lakes. All of the water flowing from the huge Upper Lakes rushes through its channel on the way to Lake Erie, and the current is not gentle.

When at last they reached the man, who had just about given in to fatigue, Belle and Maebelle hauled him into the punt. Then Maebelle tied the overturned rowboat to the stern of her little craft and rowed back to Mamajuda Island.

Maebelle's heroic act caused a sensation. At a convention held in Detroit's Cadillac Hotel, she was awarded a silver lifesaving medal before an audience of cheering army veterans. The young lady humbly said that she had simply performed an act of humanity. An association of shipmasters felt that the silver medal, which was bestowed by the government, was not good enough. They had a gold medal struck, complete with a gold chain. Its inscription read, "Presented to Miss Maebelle L. Mason for heroism in saving life".

Again, Maebelle was modest in receiving the award. Perhaps for Maebelle and her parents, the greatest salutes to her brave deed were the blasts from their whistles that steamships gave in her honour as they passed Mamajuda Island.

The first Mamajuda Lighthouse. When keeper Barney Litigot died in 1873, his wife Caroline replaced him. The Masons were Caroline's successors.

Sault Ste. Marie

Thessalon

Clapperton Island

Little
Current

St. Marys River

NORTH CHANNEL

De Tour Reef

Badgeley Is.

Red Rock
Light

Sulphur Is.

Cockburn
Island

Gore Bay

Manitoulin
Island

Parry
Sound

Mackinac
Island

Great Duck Island

GEORGIAN BAY

Western Islands

Tobermory

Giants Tomb Is.

Alpena

Cove
Island

Mary Ward
Ledges

Thunder Bay

Bruce Peninsula

Christian
Island

LAKE HURON

Nottawasaga Light

Oscoda

Chantry Island

Owen Sound

Collingwood
Craigleith

Tawas Bay

Charity Islands Light
Point Lookout

Saginaw Bay

Southampton

Goderich

Port Huron Sarnia

PART FOUR

LAKE HURON

Charitable organizations gathered books and distributed them to light-keepers to help them pass the long hours of isolation. A package of books might include poetry, tales of adventure and romance, and action-packed "dime novels", but the emphasis was often on religious works.

CHARITY ISLANDS: GIFTS FROM GOD

Some might say that Big Charity Island and Little Charity Island, on the west side of Lake Huron, have been misnamed. Haven they may have been for Native people and early European traders travelling in surface-skimming canoes, but for ships drawing more than a few feet of water, the hidden shoals around the islands are anything but charitable.

The islands lie about a mile-and-a-half apart (2.4km) at the entrance to Saginaw Bay, about 6.5 miles (10km) off Point Lookout, Michigan. Because Saginaw Bay cuts a bite out of the mainland 60 miles (96.5km) long and 30 miles (48km) wide, travellers crossing in small craft risked being caught in the open by Lake Huron's sudden storms. The islands, which cover respectively 322 acres (130ha) and six acres (2.4ha), provided a safe refuge.

The Ojibwa called the larger island *Shawangunk* (Green Gull), and said it was a gift from the Great Spirit, Kitchi-Manitou. *Coureurs de bois* and voyageurs called the smaller islet *Ile aux Traverses* (the Crossing Island). The islands have been known since the mid-nineteenth century as the Charities, apparently because of a belief that they were gifts from God.

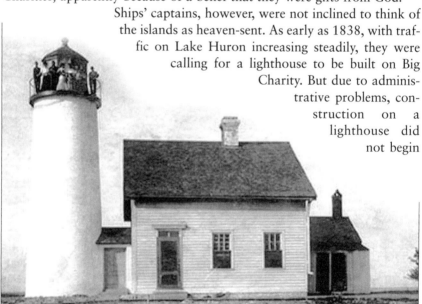

Ships' captains, however, were not inclined to think of the islands as heaven-sent. As early as 1838, with traffic on Lake Huron increasing steadily, they were calling for a lighthouse to be built on Big Charity. But due to administrative problems, construction on a lighthouse did not begin

Travellers in small boats considered the Charity Islands to be gifts from God, but to the sailors in larger vessels there was nothing charitable about the deadly shoals that lurked just off shore.

until 1856. The 39-foot (11.8-m) Charity Island Light, a conical, stone tower, was completed the following year. Its beacon was visible for 13 miles (21km) across the water.

The keepers of the light on Big Charity would have seen in microcosm the boom and waste that were to mark American expansion into the Great Lakes country. Many a westward bound adventurer took advantage of the island stopover, and camped near the lighthouse. The volume of shipping on this corner of Lake Huron grew rapidly, especially the transport of timber. Ships towed huge rafts of white pine past the Charities, as the hills of the mainland were denuded. The islands' own stands of indigenous oak were destroyed to make room for white pine, and then those trees, too, were cut down and shipped away.

Fishermen came in the 1850s and established a summer community that thrived for several years. Every evening, after they had hauled in their nets, the men in the fishing boats could look to the beacon of the Charity Island Light to guide them home. But uncontrolled exploitation of the fish stocks rendered the blue waters of the bay and the adjoining lake almost as barren as the now treeless islands, and the fishing industry eventually went belly-up. The fishermen departed, leaving the islands to the lightkeepers and the seabirds.

Then tourists came on sidewheel excursion boats and in small pleasure craft. Once again, the lighthouse was there to warn them away from the limestone reefs rising up from the lake bottom. But sometimes there were accidents when the light was obscured by fog. Occasionally, forest fires on the mainland caused navigational problems, too, because they shrouded the light with dense clouds of smoke. A vessel lost in the mist or smoke could be ripped open by jagged rocks, or have a propeller torn off. The captain would sound a distress signal, and the lightkeepers would render whatever assistance they could.

THE OCONTO: NIGHT OF TERROR

One of the most noteworthy wrecks to happen at the Charity Islands was that of the passenger steamer *Oconto* in December 1885. It was an accident in which the lightkeeper inadvertently played a part. The ship was making the final run of the season before being laid up for the winter. There were 47 passengers and crew on board. She left Oscoda, Michigan, just north of Saginaw Bay, outbound for Alpena, a little farther to the north, on Thunder Bay. The *Oconto* should not have had to go near the Charities at all.

But a sudden blizzard came howling across Lake Huron and tossed the *Oconto* around so violently that Captain G.W. McGregor ordered the wheelsman to turn about and head for the shelter of Tawas Bay. However, the wild wind and the crashing waves carried the *Oconto* past Tawas and down to Saginaw Bay. In the dark of night and the swirl of snow, the captain lost his bearings.

The gale battered the *Oconto*. The rolling of the ship caused objects that weren't fastened down to fly through the air. Walls of water smashed against doors and windows. There was pandemonium on the *Oconto* as the crew struggled to keep the ship afloat and the passengers cried in terror. Horses and cattle were on board, and these poor creatures, too, were thrown around like toys, many of them breaking their legs. Their shrieking neighs and terrified bellows added to the overall scene of bedlam. At any moment, Huron could pull the hapless vessel down.

First Mate Charles Reardon stumbled into the galley and found the ship's cook, William Brown, cringing on his bed and weeping from fear. Reardon was alarmed to see the stove glowing red hot. If the ship caught fire, the fate of all on board would most certainly be sealed. Reardon quickly doused the inferno in the stove's belly. Then he turned his attention to the panic-stricken cook. If he was about to blast the man verbally for his negligence and cowardice, he quickly swallowed the words. Brown was dead! He had seemingly died from sheer fright!

The *Oconto* was pitching so sharply as she rose and fell on the swells, that at times the propellers were right out of the water. The chief engineer had to turn the engine on and off in time with the waves. This was to keep the ship moving, but at the same time prevent the propellers from being damaged and perhaps made inoperable by spinning uselessly in the air.

All the cargo that had been loaded onto the main deck—sleighs and cages of poultry—was washed overboard, along with two lifeboats. The ship's loading cranes were smashed and the upper railings torn away. Mate Reardon found one of the gangways had been thrown open, and he managed to get it closed again.

Up on the bridge, Captain McGregor tried to find his bearings through the blinding snow. Visibility was almost zero, but the captain saw a light blinking off the starboard bow. Believing it to be the Tawas Point Light, he headed for it. He didn't realize it, but a twist of fate had caused him to misjudge his position.

The Charity Island beacon was a continuous light, while the light at Tawas Point, several miles to the south, blinked. Inside the Charity Light, unable to see the life-and-death struggle out on Lake Huron, lightkeeper Charles McDonald was trying to deal with the wet snow that was plastering the outside of the lamp room's glass. The snow was so thick, it threatened to block the light altogether. He went outside to clear it away, but more snow kept blowing onto the glass as fast as McDonald could wipe it off. From out on the lake, the beacon appeared to "blink"! Captain McGregor had mistaken the Charity Light for the Tawas Light, and now the *Oconto* was heading straight for the deadly Charity Islands reefs.

As he neared the islands, Captain McGregor realized his error and immediately ordered the ship to be brought about. But it was too late. With a sickening crunch the *Oconto* ran onto a reef about a mile out from the lighthouse.

In the long list of accounts of Great Lakes shipwrecks, the grounding of a ship is almost inevitably followed by the ship quickly being pounded to pieces by the raging surf. The crew of the *Oconto* was well aware of this, and at once they started passing out life preservers to the passengers. There were two women aboard, and one of them had a three-year-old child, whom the chief steward wrapped in heavy blankets over which he fastened a life preserver. The passengers were quiet and did not panic. But with only one of three lifeboats left aboard the *Oconto*, some of them surely doubted whether they would see another sunrise.

Amazingly, the *Oconto* held together. Lake Huron pounded her relentlessly, even stove in some bulwarks, but the stout timbers of the hull otherwise absorbed the punishment. Because the *Oconto* was firmly wedged, the surf could not pound her to pieces on the rocks.

By morning much of the raw power of the storm had been spent, though the weather was still foul. Captain McGregor hoisted the distress signals, and five of his men climbed into the ship's remaining lifeboat and rowed across the mile of choppy water to the lighthouse. Lightkeeper McDonald and his assistant sailed out to the wreck in their yawl, and soon had all of the *Oconto*'s relieved passengers and exhausted crew safely ashore.

Now, with over forty people all crowded into his little house, McDonald had the problem of feeding them. It was near the end of the navigation season, and the lighthouse would soon be closed for the winter. The lightkeeper's supplies would be very low. Fortunately, two days later the weather improved somewhat, and some of the crew returned to the *Oconto* for provisions. Then Captain McGregor and six others struck out in the yawl for Caseville, about 15 miles (24km) away.

It was no easy journey. The wind whipped up spray from the crests of the waves that stung the men's faces and froze to their clothing. Four miles (6.4km) from shore they encountered ice. Since it was not thick enough to walk across, they pulled out axes and hacked their way through, foot by foot. It took six hours to cover a distance they ordinarily would have covered in a fraction of the time. But they finally did reach shore and were able to enlist help for the castaways on Big Charity.

The following spring the *Oconto* was salvaged, repaired, and put back to work. Now she would haul freight instead of passengers. The change was fortuitous, because the *Oconto*'s new life was both short-lived and cursed. In that summer of 1886 she collided with a dock on the St. Clair River, then had another collision with a tug in the Toledo harbour. While out on Lake Erie she sprang a leak and had to put in at Cleveland for repairs. In the first week of July the *Oconto*, which had escaped a watery grave in Lake Huron, found one in the St. Lawrence River when she struck a rock and sank.

Lightkeepers continued to watch over the blue waters of Saginaw Bay from the Charity Island tower until 1916, when the lighthouse was automated. In 1939 a new light was constructed at nearby Gravelly Shoal, making the Charity Islands Light obsolete. The old stone tower was abandoned and deteriorated rapidly from the onslaught of weather and vandalism. The lightkeeper's house is no longer there, and the tower is but a dilapidated shell. There have been plans to restore and preserve the old lighthouse. In view of its long years of service to the mariners who sailed on stormy Lake Huron, such an undertaking would, at the very least, be charitable.

CHANTRY ISLAND LIGHT: A TRADITION OF SAVING LIVES

For lightkeepers, the light station was, first and foremost, an aid to navigation. The light had to be kept burning, and the keeper had to be ever vigilant for vessels in peril. Everything else was subordinate to that function.

Lake Huron's Chantry Island, just off the lumber and fishing centre of Southampton, Ontario, had long been in need of a light. The surrounding waters hid treacherous reefs, and even after the light became operational, there were frequent wrecks. In 1856, the steamer *Mazeppa* went down off Chantry while the lighthouse was being built on the island. The new light was an 80-foot (24.3-m) Imperial Tower. There was also a 540-foot (162-m) breakwater pier that became known as the Long Dock.

The first lightkeeper at Chantry Island was Duncan McGregor Lambert, a tough veteran of the Lakes who had also been a constable in Goderich. Lambert had been first mate on the steamer *Bruce Mines*, which sank in Lake Huron off Cape Hurd near Tobermory, Ontario, on November 28, 1854. It was one of the oddest shipwrecks in Great Lakes history. When the ship first began to founder, the carpenter wanted the crew to take to the lifeboats. The captain, a man named Frazer, pulled a pair of pistols and

threatened to shoot any man who stepped into a lifeboat without his orders.

Suddenly, the *Bruce Mines* was sucked down. However, the deck tore free of the hull and remained afloat, with the lifeboats still on it. Of the 24 people aboard the ship, only the carpenter, ironically, was lost. The passengers and crew piled into the lifeboats, with Frazer commanding one and Lambert the other.

The castaways rowed to Devil's Island, but after some time there they realized that owing to the lateness of the season, it was unlikely that they would be rescued. They returned to the lifeboats and, with only oars to propel them, embarked on a gruelling, four-day voyage around the Bruce Peninsula to Owen Sound. When they arrived there two weeks after the shipwreck, they learned that they had been given up as lost.

Lambert took charge of the Chantry Island Lighthouse in 1858. In his first year he rescued a boy adrift on a raft. The Lambert family would keep the light burning for almost fifty years. In addition to tending the lamp, Lambert also had to maintain the breakwater. With the constant battering of the lake, it was no easy task to keep up with repairs. In 1861, a 100-foot (30-m) section was washed away, and bad weather left the family stranded for six days. They were down to their last morsels of food by the time the weather eased up enough for Lambert to get to the mainland. That same year Lambert rescued four men from the wrecked scow *Grace Amelia*.

Duncan Campbell Lambert and his wife. A former mariner and constable, Lambert participated in many rescues. Any routine crossing on the Lakes could suddenly become a fight just to stay alive. In 1868 Lambert assisted survivors from the wreck of the Silver Spray.

Duncan Lambert, because he couldn't swim. Neither could his son Ross. But they were expert sailors, and many a person who might otherwise have drowned was taken to safety in the Lamberts' sailboat or rowboat. The list of vessels whose crews were rescued by the Lambert family, or who found shelter with them is an impressive one: the schooner *American Eagle* in 1864; the steamer *Silver Spray* in 1868; the barge *Bruno* in 1870; and the schooner *E. Fie* in 1877, to name but a few.

One rescue attempt, however, resulted in tragedy. On September 3, 1879, the schooner *Mary and Lucy* struck a reef south of Chantry Island during a storm. The crew climbed into the rigging to avoid being washed over-board, but one man was swept into the water. The steamer *Manitoba*, which was moored in the island's harbour, lowered a boat. In it were the skipper, a Captain Sims, and the ship's purser. At the same time, Duncan Lambert and some other men formed a human chain that stretched out into the foaming waters to try to grab the struggling sailor. Duncan, of course, took the most dangerous position at the very end. It was he who caught hold of the nearly drowned sailor.

William Lambert followed in his father's footsteps. He was awarded a gold watch for rescuing the crew of the Nettie Woodward *in 1892.*

Meanwhile, his son Ross, 23, had jumped into the rescue boat. He attached a lifeline to himself, but took it off when someone else chided him over it. The rescue attempt was gallant, but futile. The little boat might as well have been a toy. Driving seas flipped it over three times. The men managed to hang on the first two times it went over, but on the third, Ross Lambert lost his hold.

By now Duncan, having dragged the barely conscious sailor from the water, was standing on the dock, watching helplessly as Huron mauled the little boat. He saw Ross in the water, clinging to an oar. Then the waves swept over the young man, and he was gone. The body was recovered nine days later. The *Manitoba's* purser also drowned. Only Captain Sims made it back to shore alive.

Fortunately for the crew of the *Mary and Lucy*, their cargo was timber. The load of wood kept the ship afloat until the surf beached her, with the men still clinging to the rigging. The vessel was a complete wreck, but the crew got off safely.

Duncan Lambert was highly commended for his rescue efforts on that bleak day, but the death of his son weighed heavily upon him. In 1880, only a year later, he retired from the lighthouse service and passed the torch on to his son William. Duncan died just three years later, at the age of 70.

William McGregor Lambert was a man whose pride in his calling and in his light station knew no bounds. In his time as keeper, the Chantry Island Light became a showpiece. He wanted people to come out to the island and enjoy the spectacle of water and sky. He built a boardwalk from the lighthouse to the pier. He added benches and picnic tables for the benefit of tourists and local excursionists. He gathered relics from the many wrecks surrounding the island, and displayed them in his own marine museum.

But William Lambert was much more than just a friendly guide and raconteur. Like his father, he was very familiar with moody Huron and the dramas the big lake could produce. In 1884 he found a capsized sailboat from which four people had been swept to their deaths. A year later the

Unlike some lightkeepers who craved solitude, William Lambert liked to have visitors on the island, and tried to make it attractive to tourists.

schooner *Mary S. Gordon* was wrecked at Chantry. In 1889 Lambert was instrumental in the rescue of the crew of the schooner *Greyhound*, which ran aground on Chantry.

Two people drowned on September 1, 1892 when the schooner *Mary Woodward* was wrecked at Chantry Island. Five others were rescued by Lambert. On other occasions Lambert's wife and daughters, described in the press as "excellent seawomen", assisted him in rescuing nine people from a foundering American vessel, and the crew of an ice-bound tug from Kincardine.

Lambert also had a connection with a story that was initially considered to be a Great Lakes mystery. In mid-October 1905, the steamer *Kaliyuga* vanished from Lake Huron, seemingly without a trace. Search vessels found nothing. However, on October 29 William Lambert spotted some wreckage on the shore of Chantry Island. He picked up a piece of board that was broken at both ends. On it were the large letters *UG*. In all likelihood, the wreckage was from the missing *Kaliyuga*.

William Lambert was one of the most admired Canadian lightkeepers in the history of the Lakes. The "ruddy cheeked hero of wind and wave", as one Toronto journalist described him, was presented with a gold watch for rescue work in 1892, a Royal Canadian Humane Association medal for

Lightkeeper John Klippert kept the Chantry Light for twenty years. In one woman's recollection, "he worked all the time" and was "just a great old guy".

heroism in 1906, and in 1907 was awarded the Imperial Service Order medal for faithful service to the Dominion of Canada. Lambert retired from the lighthouse service that year, ending his family's dynasty on Chantry Island. He died January 7, 1921, a Great Lakes legend.

For the next decade, Malcolm MacIver kept the Chantry Island Light. Few details of his life are known, but he allegedly was presented with a silver watch for a successful rescue. This may have been in 1908, when the steamer *King Edward* ran aground on Chantry and all passengers and crew were safely taken ashore.

Chantry's next lightkeeper, John Klippert, stayed on the job from 1917 to 1937. Records indicate that aside from an occasional tug running aground, and a "deplorable accident" (for which there are no details) in which a man was killed, things were relatively quiet at Chantry during this period. However, the recollections of a woman who spent her childhood in Southampton and was friends with Klippert's daughter Ruth, give a warm impression of the man.

To Jean Scott, John Klippert was "a remarkable man in his day". He built boats, he was an expert fisherman, and he made his own weather forecaster by putting camphor and alcohol in a jar. When the concoction would "rile up", he'd know a storm was coming. Klippert would ride an old bicycle down to the end of the long pier to light the range light. Then he would take the girls up the tower. "Every night... we had to climb to the top to light the light. He had to pump it up and light the gas". Klippert also kept a garden. "He had the island so neat", Jean said. "It was wild, but it was organized. He worked all the time... Just a great old guy".

John Klippert retired (he died in 1950), and Clayton Knechtel, a former sawmill owner, took over the Chantry Light. He built a 30-foot (9-m), shallow draft boat that his friends dubbed "The Ruptured Duck", probably because of its flat bottom. It may have been the boat that Knechtel used in

Lightkeeper Clayton Knechtel (right) and friend Clive Morris. Clayton rescued two American boys whose boat had overturned, after a third boy swam across a mile (1.6km) of rough water to seek help.

a remarkable rescue in August 1937.

Three youths: Grant Peer of Guelph, Ontario, and two American friends were in a rowboat a mile (1.6km) from Chantry Island, when the boat capsized. They quickly realized that their plight could not be seen from shore. The American boys were struggling just to hold onto the overturned boat. Unlike Grant, they were not good swimmers. Water safety rules say that if a boat overturns, a person's best chance of survival lies in staying with the boat. But Grant could see that if help didn't arrive quickly, his friends would drown. He decided to swim to the island, a mile away through choppy water. All that is recorded of the brave deed is that Grant made it. He hauled himself ashore exhausted, staggered up to lightkeeper Knechtel, and told him what had happened.

Knechtel sped out to look for the two young Americans. Word of the drama quickly spread, and hundreds of cottagers stood along the shore watching. When Knechtel found the capsized boat, one of the youths was at the end of his strength and the other was "going down for the third time". Knechtel pulled them into his boat and took them to safety. Grant Peer's heroic swim made newspaper headlines, but for Clayton Knechtel, it was all in a day's work.

Knechtel left Chantry Island in 1941, and his immediate successor stayed only one season. Cameron Inkster Spencer manned the Chantry Light from 1942 until it was automated in 1954. Only five-foot, four inches tall,

Spencer was a decorated veteran of the First World War, and had, as a prized possession, a letter from King George V. Spencer's dedication to his duties on the island earned him the nickname "The Lamplighter". Whenever he had to go to Southampton he never failed to get back to the light, no matter how bad the weather.

Like his predecessors, Spencer took part in rescues. One year, however, the elements turned the tables and it was he who had to be saved. Ice had made it impossible for him to get to the mainland, and local residents had to chop their way through to take Spencer off the island.

Automation ended the era of the lightkeeper on Chantry Island, though sailors complained that the new battery-operated light was weak. In 1957, the island was designated as a Federal Migratory Bird Sanctuary, and was made off-limits to visitors. The condition of the lighthouse and the keeper's house deteriorated. Clayton Knechtel and Cameron Spencer died in the mid-1970s, taking with them the last living memories of the days when dedicated individuals were responsible for the beacon. In 1999, restoration work began on the buildings, and there are now tours to Chantry Island. The renovation of this lighthouse is significant, because many other old towers have been victims of neglect and vandalism. Though it is no longer necessary for someone to climb the stairs and light the lamp, the fact that the historic tower was saved from ruin indicates that the torch has, in a way, once more been passed.

THE NOTTAWASAGA LIGHT: GEORGE COLLINS AND THE *MARY WARD*

On November 22, 1872, the 139-foot (42.3-m) propeller *Mary Ward* left Sarnia, Ontario, bound for Collingwood, which was to be her new home port. The little steamer carried a cargo of salt, coal oil and general merchandise, as well as a few passengers. The skipper, a Captain Johnston, refuelled at Tobermory, and picked up a few more passengers there and at Owen Sound. This was apparently the *Mary Ward*'s first voyage on Georgian Bay, and one might wonder if the passengers would have been comfortable aboard the ship had they known her unlucky history.

Built at Montreal in 1864, the vessel had originally been called the *Simcoe*, and then the *North*. Some mariners considered it bad luck to rename a ship. In 1867 the *North* burned and sank in the St. Clair River just off Port Lambton, Ontario. A year later the ship was raised, repaired

Captain Johnston of the Mary Ward *testified that he mistook a light in a boarding house or tavern for the Nottawasaga Light. (Inset) Sophia Collins died in the Nottawasaga house after a bout of influenza.*

and refitted, and renamed yet again, the *Mary Ward.*

On the morning of Sunday, November 24th, the *Mary Ward* cleared Owen Sound harbour for Collingwood, ordinarily just a six-hour run. It was a clear, autumn day, with a mild southeast breeze rippling the blue waters of Georgian Bay. Pleasant enough for November, the passengers no doubt thought. But such days were what veteran sailors of the Lakes called "weather breeders", because they had a nasty habit of breeding foul weather; storms that could sweep down with astonishing suddenness.

Trouble began for the *Mary Ward* late in the afternoon. She was evidently already off-course, when the wind shifted to the northeast and grew in strength. Then the early darkness of autumn descended upon Georgian Bay. Captain Johnston scanned the shore for a light, saw one, and laid a course for it. He would later testify that he mistook a light shining from a tavern or boarding house in Craigleith (a small settlement near Collingwood) for the Nottawasaga Light. Johnston realized his error too late, and ran the *Mary Ward* onto a shoal of Miller's Reef about three miles (5km) from shore, and within sight of the Nottawasaga Light. It was about nine p.m.

The ship was stuck, but did not appear to have sustained serious damage. Captain Johnston did not think there was any immediate danger, so he allowed the passengers to retire for the night. He sent two men in a small boat to Collingwood to arrange for a tug to pull the *Mary Ward* off the shoal in the morning. One, apparently, was the ship's purser. The other was Frank Moberly, a local man whose family owned the Collingwood tug *Mary Ann.*

From his vantage point atop the Nottawasaga Lighthouse, an 80-foot (24.3-m) Imperial Tower, lightkeeper George Collins saw the grounded *Mary Ward.* Collins was an Englishman who had gone to sea at the age of 13, and had eventually wound up on the Great Lakes. He had been the Nottawasaga lightkeeper since the station went into operation in 1858, and had already participated in numerous rescues over the years.

When the Mary Ward *first struck the reef, the captain did not think there was any immediate danger. His passengers retired for the night.*

Collins knew that although the *Mary Ward* seemed to be in no immediate danger, things could change very quickly. He rowed out to the stranded steamer and offered to start ferrying passengers to shore right away. The first mate thanked him for his kind offer, but said that they had already sent for help. Collins felt that the passengers should be taken off, but as no one was inclined to go with him, he rowed his empty boat back to the lighthouse.

At about midnight the storm that Collins had been dreading struck with full fury. Accounts over just what was happening aboard the *Mary Ward* differ. At least two say that Captain Johnston and seven men had already left the ship in a lifeboat and gone to the Nottawasaga Lighthouse to get help, apparently concerned that Moberly and the purser had not made it to Collingwood. If that version is accurate, then Captain Johnston was certainly derelict in his duty for leaving passengers and crew in a dangerous situation.

In other accounts, however, the captain remained aboard the *Mary Ward*. An unidentified passenger recalled later:

> I was anxious and did not go to my cabin, although all the rest retired for the night. I sat up on deck. Shortly after midnight the wind suddenly shifted and heavy, black, swiftly moving clouds arose over the mountain and the moon and stars soon disappeared. There was an ominous moaning in the rigging, the import of which I knew too well. There was an uncanny stillness. I shall never, as long as I live, forget

the weird feeling of alarm and terror which came over me, nor shall I ever wholly forgive myself for not acting on the impulse I had to arouse everyone and tell them that a storm was about to break and that we better get to land while there was still time. But I had no authority and being young I was reluctant to exhibit signs of fear. After a little while I suggested to the watchman that he call the Captain. This he did and the Captain realized the danger at once and began blowing the *Mary Ward*'s whistle again frantically and calling all hands on deck. The storm increased in fury suddenly and by dawn huge breakers were sweeping over the stern. Had she not been well built she would have gone to pieces in a very short time but she held together despite the tremendous strain and pounding. In a few hours we were all hanging on for dear life and most of us had become reconciled to our fate.

Meanwhile, Moberly had in fact reached Collingwood early Monday morning. He alerted the crew of the *Mary Ann* of the *Mary Ward*'s predicament, and the little tug steamed out to the rescue. But by this time a full November gale was blowing, and high winds and raging seas drove the tug back.

Panic now gripped the people on the *Mary Ward*. It would be only a matter of time before the lake pounded the ship to pieces. Eight men (some accounts say six) tried to escape in the ship's only remaining lifeboat. One of them, a man named Charles Campbell, promised his pregnant wife, "I will make

According to legend, the ghosts of those who died when the Mary Ward *sank haunted the building that Captain Johnston allegedly mistook for the Nottawasaga Light.*

it". He didn't. Within a few yards of the steamer, the lifeboat capsized and the occupants were all drowned.

Back at the Nottawasaga Light, George Collins watched in helpless frustration. If those people had just listened! Now the water was far too rough for his little boat. But Collins was not a man to stand by and do nothing when people were in trouble. He and his 21-year-old son, Charles, began to row for Collingwood. It was a wild ride across heaving seas, and by the time they reached the harbour the two men were exhausted.

Maybe Collins' little rowboat couldn't take people off the *Mary Ward* in that storm, but a good, stout fishing boat could. Collins prevailed upon three fishermen to show some backbone and go to the helpless people's aid. With the help of George and Charles Collins, the fishermen made it to the stranded vessel and took the survivors off. Minutes later, the *Mary Ward* crumpled under the battering waves and slid beneath the surface. The shoal upon which the ship came to grief now bears her name.

People had serious doubts about Captain Johnston's claim that he had confused a light on the mainland with the Nottawasaga Light. There were

Captain George Collins, centre, was credited with saving 52 lives in his 31 years as a lightkeeper.

In 1879 the Masonic Lodge of Boston presented George Collins with this silver tea service for the dramatic rescue of four of their members. (Inset) George Collins.

those who said that he had been drinking, and that his compass was not working. The "mistaken light" story gave rise to a legend. It was said that the building whose light the captain insisted had confused him was haunted by the souls of those who had died in the *Mary Ward* wreck. The haunting ended only when the building was torn down.

George Collins, his son and the fishermen were each awarded 15 dollars for their daring rescue. Like other courageous Great Lakes lightkeepers, George was decorated for his lifesaving feats. In his 31 years on duty at the Nottawasaga Light, he rescued 52 people.

One sad day in 1880, however, George Collins was unable to go to the aid of his son, Charles, who drowned in a fishing accident. The Nottawasaga lightkeeper who had snatched so many lives from the maw of Lake Huron would spend his last years grieving over the one dear life he had not been able to save. The fates can be very unkind indeed.

ADAM BROWN: BIRD MAN OF RED ROCK

Red Rock Lighthouse takes up most of a tiny, steep-sided rock sticking up from the shoal-infested waters of Georgian Bay's eastern shore. It is about six miles (9.6km) from the mainland off Parry Sound. It was marked by two successive wooden towers before a 60-foot (18.2-m) concrete and steel lighthouse was built in 1911. A Canadian Parliamentary Paper of 1895 described Red Rock as "exposed to the full force of all westerly storms, and to the full sweep of the Georgian Bay. In bad weather the sea breaks completely over the whole building". Even when the new tower went up in 1911, it had to be equipped with steel shutters that could be closed during the most violent storms to prevent the monstrous waves from smashing the windows. For most people, Red Rock would not be an inviting place at all. But for fisherman-turned-lightkeeper Adam Brown, it was home from 1898 to 1937.

Brown was a jack-of-all-trades who filled his time—and supplemented his low lightkeeper's pay—with a variety of extra-curricular activities. He piloted ships into Parry Sound harbour, sold lumber and fish, and did carpentry work for cottagers. To tend the light while he was off moonlighting, Brown had an assistant named Alex Parker. Parker, who worked with Brown for 21 years, was a reclusive individual who earned the nickname "the Hermit of Red Rock". He preferred the solitude of the lighthouse to society ashore, and would spend long periods of time out there without setting foot on the mainland. He once even requested permission to stay at the lighthouse all winter. On one occasion, when stormy

Red Rock Lighthouse, lonely home to Adam Brown for forty years. (Inset) Assistant Alex Parker.

Brown's assistant, Alex Parker, asked permission to stay at the lighthouse all winter.

weather had kept Adam Brown ashore for a week, he apologized to Parker when he finally did make it back to the lighthouse. Parker replied, "I don't care if you never come back".

1903 was an eventful year for Adam Brown. On November 12 the steamer *Seattle* was wrecked on Green Island, about 20 miles (32km) from Red Rock, and Brown picked up the crew of 11 and took them to the mainland. Then he became involved in a scheme to "mislay" some of the ship's cargo of lumber. With the help of two confederates he salvaged the lumber and then hid it from investigating police and insurance agents. Once the coast was clear, he sold the lumber to locals and cottagers.

Toward the end of 1903, Adam Brown found himself in a serious situation. It was Christmas Day, and he was alone at the lighthouse. A government tender was to have picked him up on December 4, but ice and bad weather had made that impossible. He was almost out of food, and for the two weeks leading up to Christmas he'd been living on a ration of one biscuit a day. Now his last biscuit was gone, and he had no more fuel. He could no longer afford to wait for the ship. He would have to get himself out of the predicament.

Brown rigged up a crude derrick to lift his small boat over the build-up of ice that encrusted the Rock. When he had the boat in the water, he rowed for about a mile (1.6km) until he encountered drift ice. For two hours he probed along the edge of the icefield, looking for a place his boat could pass through, but without success. He had no choice but to get out and walk across the ice, stepping from one floe to another. He dragged his boat behind him because it was his duty to bring it in.

Adam Brown, (far right) was a jack-of-all-trades who, in addition to keeping the light, sold fish and lumber, did carpentry work and piloted boats into Parry Sound.

Brown finally reached solid shelf ice at a spot four miles (6.4km) from land. By that time he was exhausted. One biscuit a day for two weeks does not give a man the strength required for such an arduous trek. Brown lay down on the ice. He wanted to sleep, but he knew that to do so would be fatal. It was Christmas Day, a day when most people were home with their families. But Brown knew that men often went out to fish through the ice. He put two fingers in his mouth and blasted several sharp, shrill whistles.

Half a mile away, two men in a fishing camp on a small island heard the noise. One of them climbed up to a high point and scanned the horizon. He saw Brown stretched out beside his boat. The men hurried over to where Brown lay on the ice, cold, hungry and fighting sleep. Adam Brown completed his trip home in a dogsled. The ordeal did not turn him away from lightkeeping. He was back at Red Rock the following season, and for many seasons after that.

In his last years as a lightkeeper, Brown found a new vocation: the care of birds. He loved birds, and it saddened him that so many were injured or killed when they crashed into the lighthouse windows. The light attracted swarms of insects, which in turn attracted the birds, which were themselves hypnotized and confused by the light. The toll was especially high during migratory seasons. On one October day, Brown

Lightkeepers had to be prepared for visits from an inspector (centre, with notebook). Adam Brown is to the right, holding the mast.

Lonely Lightkeeper's Friends in Thousands: Georgian Bay Birds

Red Rock Dweller Saddened by Death of Hundreds Yearly, Lured by 15,000-Candlepower Beam

(By F. D. VAN LUVEN.)
(Staff Writer, The Globe and Mail.)

Parry Sound, Feb. 19. — Twenty miles due west up the Sound, six miles from mainland, a grim, red boulder of granite protrudes above the deep water of Georgian Bay.

Even in calm weather, the bald pate of Red Rock is washed by unending swells. During the stormiest days and nights when a southwest gale tears across the ninety-mile sweep from Owen Sound way, the boulder, and the structure of steel and concrete and glass roosting upon it that is Red Rock Lighthouse, are lost to all view except during brief intervals of huge waves and spray.

Few men could stand the monotony and rigor of life for months on end on this lonely rock, yet for many summers past it has been the only home known by Lighthouse-keeper Adam Brown. All lighthouse-keepers must be of a tough breed. Adam Brown is of the toughest.

Mistaken Conception.

If any one imagines that this man's isolated life has made of him a coarse, callous fellow, immune to all feeling except that required in his duty, that one is mistaken. Just the opposite is true. Outwardly, Adam Brown is hard enough and his blue eyes, one thinks, could be cold on special occasion, but when this reporter talked with him today they were soft and kindly and sparkling with anticipation.

Because, oddly enough, Adam Brown is counting the days and hours to the time when, with most of the ice gone, he will be taken out to Red Rock for another (and what is to be his last) summer's vigil. He longs for his friends out there—he has scores of thousands of them. Birds.

Birds, yes, of every kind and description, and because he loves them, and is a bit of a naturalist, too, one of his few real sorrows is that so many thousands must die a violent death under his eyes each year.

Hypnotized by the 15,000 candle-power of Red Rock light, millions of flying insects buzz around and it is this rich feeding-ground that attracts the birds. Hundreds of them, in turn, are blinded by the glare and fly with full force against the glass or framework of the beacon, to fall dead or maimed at the feet of their helpless human friend. The death toll is piteously large during the migratory seasons, spring and autumn.

300 Victims in Day.

On one day last autumn, Oct. 6, he picked up the bodies of nearly pery icicle. His rowboat couldn't be launched except by a crude derrick he painfully rigged that morning. Passing over the menace and anguish of that start, he finally got away and rowed a mile or so until he hit drift ice. His boat would have been smashed like an eggshell to have attempted its passage. After two hours of tiresome search, he found larger floes. He had to "bring in" his boat as well as himself, for the next quarter-mile it was a struggle of pulling his boat on to a floe, pulling or pushing it across, launching it on the other side, and repeating this terrific labor time until time until he staggered on to solid ice stretching four miles out from mainland. But he could go no further in his exhausted condition, and he made up his mind to spend the night there.

Rescued by Chance.

But for a freakish chance, it undoubtedly would have been his last night on earth. He had lain down in his overcoat beside the boat. Perhaps the piercing, subzero wind recalled to him the fact that occasionally fishermen plied their trade through the ice off an almost barren island half a mile away. He was pretty good at whistling, so, using two fingers in his mouth, he sent out a couple of blasts. It happened at this moment that one of two men, who fortunately were on the island, was cutting an ice-hole to draw a pail of water. He thought he heard something. Returning to the shack, he told his partner. One of them climbed to a bit of high ground and scanned the lake. Half a mile away he thought he saw a darker smudge against the late afternoon's growing twilight.

And so the courageous lighthouse-keeper, who should have been brought off by a Marine Department ship, in the end was rescued

BIRDS' FRIEND

ADAM BROWN.

(Left) In his last years as a lightkeeper, Adam Brown turned his lighthouse into a "bird hospital". (Above) Mesmerized by the light or attracted by the swarms of insects, birds frequently crashed into the glass and were killed or injured.

picked up over three hundred dead birds, "most of them rare songsters", he told the Toronto *Globe and Mail* in an interview.

Brown turned his lighthouse into a bird hospital. He picked up injured birds and tried to nurse them back to health. The lighthouse must have resounded with squawks, chirps and birdsong as Brown splinted broken wings and fed his patients. From the dead birds he selected the best specimens and sent them to an ornithologist in London, Ontario. There, the birds were preserved and donated to schools and museums.

When Brown spoke to the *Globe and Mail* reporter in 1937, his last year as a lightkeeper, he said that while he would never want another Christmas like the one he'd had in 1903, he would nonetheless miss his lighthouse. But most of all, he would miss the birds.

THE BECKONING OF THE BEACON
by Merrill H. Cook

Southward - Southward
In their long, long flight
Through the uncharted sky-roads
In the night,
By some eternal urge,
Within their feathered breasts,
The small birds have been passing,
Passing in the autumnal night.
Age-long a surge
Of Beauty passing by.
O'er forest, plain and sea they fly;
Undaunted.
'Till now, in this sad year, between two days,
Out of the miasmal maze
Of Erie's misty marsh
Fog-haunted—
Flashing
One hundred thousand candle strong,
The mighty beam of Long Point Light
Allured, alas! the winging host.
Bewildered, betrayed,
And victims of a strong momentum—
In quick decision made,
They gambled 'gainst the giant pane
—and lost.
In massed confusion
Crashing
At dawn's first kiss
The light-house keeper finds

Five hundred dead
Ah! Many a Southern glen shall miss
Their morning song
Hushed be their haunts
By northern trail and tree:
And Canada shall mourn the vanquished throng
And poorer be—forever.

Toronto *Globe & Mail*, December 1, 1936

(Top) Retiring in 1937 at age 75, Adam Brown takes a last look back at the Red Rock Lighthouse. Brown died in 1968 at the age of 106. (Middle and bottom) Different views of the tiny island that housed the light.

CLAPPERTON ISLAND LIGHT: THE LUCK OF THE BAKERS

BENJAMIN BAKER: UNSOLVED MYSTERY

The 35-foot (10.6-m) wooden lighthouse on the northern tip of Clapperton Island in Lake Huron's North Channel, was built in 1866 to warn ships away from a deadly shoal called Robertson Rock. Benjamin Baker, the light's second keeper, arrived on Clapperton Island with his family in 1875. Because Canadian lightkeepers were poorly paid, life on the rugged island was hard. Benjamin and his sons, George, William and Earl, supplemented their family income by growing hay on a farm in the island's interior, and raising sheep and cattle. They maintained channel buoys, fished and trapped furs. All this, in addition to the constant cleaning and polishing of brass and prisms in the lighthouse, made for a demanding schedule. But the Bakers weren't afraid of hard work, and the family got along well enough in their first 19 years on Clapperton. Then, in 1894, came the first of a series of disastrous events.

Occasionally Benjamin liked to sail to the town of Gore Bay, to the southwest on Manitoulin Island, to have a drink and play cards. One September day, Benjamin did not return from his card game. His son, Henry, 30, found

Benjamin's sailboat drifting on the water off Clapperton like a little *Mary Celeste* (the mystery ship that was found abandoned in the mid-Atlantic in 1872). Benjamin's dog was in the boat, but the only trace of Benjamin was his empty wallet lying on the seat. There was also a bottle of whiskey in the bottom of the boat. Benjamin Baker was never seen again.

It was quite possible that Benjamin had been drinking and that he stumbled, fell out of the boat, and drowned. But that empty wallet aroused suspicions in his family. Benjamin always carried money.

Clapperton Island lightkeeper Benjamin Baker mysteriously vanished. His family suspected murder.

And why would the wallet be on the seat of the boat? If he had indeed fallen overboard, the wallet would still be in his pocket. Had Benjamin won big at the card table, and then been robbed and murdered, and his body disposed of? Nobody in Gore Bay seemed to know anything about it. The mystery was never solved.

The Baker family didn't know that they had a clue in their possession until years later. Henry's wife, Jenny, was suffering from a terrible toothache. Henry still had that bottle of whiskey that had been in his father's boat. He suggested that a shot of whiskey might ease Jenny's pain. She poured a little of the liquor in a glass, and swished it around the aching tooth. She immediately became seriously ill. Probably because she had taken only a small amount of the whiskey, Jenny recovered. The Baker family strongly suspected that somebody had spiked Benjamin's whiskey with some kind of drug so they could rob him.

The only trace of Benjamin Baker was his empty wallet found lying on the seat of his boat.

HENRY BAKER: FAMILY TRIALS

Following his father's disappearance, Henry Baker became the lightkeeper at Clapperton. The family's history of tragedies had only just begun. In 1895, Earl Baker was accidentally shot and killed in a hunting accident on Clapperton. After Earl's funeral, things were quiet for almost twenty years.

In 1914 the Clapperton Lighthouse was struck by lightning. Fortunately, no one was hurt, and a new wooden tower was built. A decade later, the Baker family was touched by a grisly murder.

An Ojibwa named Angus Corbiere, from the West Bay Reserve on Manitoulin Island, had been working for Henry Baker. In November 1923, Corbiere disappeared. In July 1924, his headless body was found on the shore of Bedford Island, about nine miles (14.4km) east of Clapperton. The legs were tied together with wire. Henry Baker was called upon to identify the remains. Corbiere was evidently killed in a domestic quarrel. His wife and adult stepson were arrested, but were eventually released on the grounds that the killing had been an act of self-defence.

After that gruesome episode, bad luck seemed to leave the Bakers alone for a while. Henry tended the light and raised a family of his own. One of his duties was to look after the range lights along the shore of the island.

(Left) Lightkeeper Henry Baker wanted the government to move the range lights away from the shoreline, out of the reach of freezing spray. Ship captains argued him down. (Below) The Baker family took this picture to prove their point about dangerous ice conditions at the range lights. Henry Baker was fatally injured when an icy cable snapped and a lantern fell on him.

These lights were heavy, brass lanterns mounted on 30-foot (9m) poles. To refuel them, Henry had to lower them with a block and tackle, then replace them the same way. Because they were so close to the water, spray would coat the cables of Henry's block and tackle, making them brittle and putting an extra strain on them. He warned that one day a cable would break, and the heavy lantern would come crashing down. He wanted the lights moved back from the water's edge.

Ship captains argued against this. They wanted the lights to stay where they were. Otherwise, the captains said, they would be forced to bring their vessels too close to Clapperton Island and Robertson Rock. The

Department of Transport sided with the ship captains, and the range lights stayed put. It was an invitation to disaster, especially considering that Henry was getting on in years.

One evening in September of 1946, Henry was refuelling one of the range lights. The cable snapped, and the heavy lantern fell on him. It crushed his shoulder and smashed some ribs. Even so, Henry managed to climb onto his horse and ride over a mile (1.6km) back to the lighthouse. He was taken to the hospital in Little Current on Manitoulin Island, and died there on September 17, at the age of 82. A year later the Department of Transport moved the range lights back from the water.

BILL BAKER: THE MAN WHO CHEATED DEATH

Henry's brother Bill became Clapperton's next lightkeeper. During his tenure the old wooden tower was torn down, and a third one built. In his 16 years on the job, Bill had several close calls. On one occasion he ran his tug onto a deadhead and punched a hole in the hull. Bill couldn't swim, so he hung onto a life preserver and managed to kick his way to shore. Another time, a horse kicked him, breaking some ribs and puncturing a lung.

Bill's closest brush with death came one Friday night in 1950, when his appendix ruptured. He was alone in the lightkeeper's house, and in terrible pain. He was unable to handle the boat, and did not know what to do. As the hours of agony passed, the poison spread through his system. Bill

began to have blackout spells. He lay helpless all Friday night and throughout Saturday.

By Sunday, Bill's condition was critical. But when he saw that the light in the tower had gone out due to lack of fuel, Bill tried to crawl the 30 or 40 yards (27–36m) to the lighthouse. The effort was too much for him, and he collapsed.

For once, luck was with a member of the Baker family. A pair of Bill's friends, Harold Hutchings and Bert Bailey, paid a visit to the island to return some items they had borrowed. Bill had been lying on the ground for several

(Top) Lightkeeper Bill Baker, shown here with two of his pure-bred horses, very nearly became the next victim of his family's long run of misfortune. (Bottom) Crippled by an attack of appendicitis, Bill tried to crawl from the house to the lighthouse to light the lantern.

hours when they found him. Bill opened his eyes and whispered, "I'm done, boys. Get Norm Lloyd out of Kagawong to look after the light. It's out of oil." Norman Lloyd was Bill's great-nephew, his brother Henry's grandson, who had been living in the town of Kagawong just across the Clapperton Channel on Manitoulin Island. In what Bill Baker was sure were his dying moments, his last concern had been for the light.

Hutchings and Bailey put Bill in their boat and took him to Kagawong just as fast as they could row. From there they took him by car to the Red Cross Hospital at Mindemoya, about 20 miles (32km) to the south on Manitoulin. There, a doctor operated and saved Bill's life. Bill Baker recovered and returned to serve at Clapperton Island Light until he retired in 1962. The Baker family had served at the Clapperton Island Light for 88 years, and Bill was the only one to live to see another keeper (Beverly McFarlene) take his place.

SULPHUR ISLAND: CLOSED FOR THE WINTER

When winter's cold descended upon the shores of the Upper Lakes and navigation shut down, lighthouses were abandoned for the season, except for a few where the keepers had chosen to wait out the cold months. Vast stretches of water became locked in ice, ice that lay in craggy, wind-swept sheets across sub-bodies of water like Georgian Bay and Whitefish Bay. The ice gave the seascape the look of a mythological hell: Norse land of the Frost Giants. There was (and is) an aesthetic beauty to it, to be sure. But a beauty to be observed from a safe place. To go out on the ice was risky, sometimes fatal. Still, people who lived in shoreline communities or on islands had to maintain contact with the outside world, so they took the chance.

On Saturday, January 29, 1898, two men set out from Thessalon, Ontario, to cross the ice of Lake Huron's North Channel to Cockburn Island, 24 miles (38.6km) away. They were George Avis, local manager of the Island Cedar Company of Chicago, and a teamster named Pat Barry. They were taking a load of wood by sleigh to the island, where Avis resided with his wife and son. It should have been a routine crossing.

The two men were perhaps halfway to their destination when a blizzard came shrieking down on them. They might still have made it to safety, but Avis had lost his compass. Out on a vast expanse of ice, with white chaos swirling all around and no feature by which to fix a bearing, one has no sense of direction. Indeed, were it not for gravity, one would not even be

With their hands and feet frozen, George Avis and Pat Barry used their teeth to drag a lamp to the top of the tower.

able to tell the difference between up and down.

Avis and Barry wandered blindly for hours, quite possibly going in circles. They could have come within yards of the shore of an island and not known it. Finally conceding that they were lost and getting nowhere by their own reckoning, they placed their trust in their team, and let the horses go where they would, hoping the animals would lead them to safety. The horses turned their tails to the wind and trudged on in the direction in which it blew, changing direction when it did. When the struggling beasts could go no farther, they just stopped in their tracks. There was nothing for the exhausted men to do but wrap themselves up in blankets and robes, and curl up in the sleigh to await daybreak.

Morning, when it dawned, was no savior. The weather was as foul as it had been the night before. The temperature had, in fact, dropped to -26 F (-32C). Rather than spend another grim day in a futile attempt to find their way out of their labyrinth with no walls, Avis and Barry decided to stay put. Other men might have resorted to the old survival tactic of killing and gutting the horses, and then crawling inside the warm bodies. But this idea did not seem to have even occurred to Avis and Barry. Instead, they turned the horses loose, then spent another bleak night in the sleigh.

Monday morning broke clear but still cold. The men saw, not quite a mile (1.6km) away, Sulphur Island, an island with a lighthouse! It would be the hardest mile they had ever walked. The blizzard had dumped a knee-deep layer of snow on the frozen surface of the North Channel, and now under the bright sun that snow was turning to slush. Both men's hands and feet were already severely frostbitten, and now wading and stumbling through the slop made that condition even worse.

They reached the lighthouse at last, and found it locked up for the winter. They broke into the lightkeeper's house, and to their great relief found some fuel for a fire, and a little flour, oatmeal and tea. But sudden warmth is no friend to frostbitten limbs, and the pain Avis and Barry experienced as the numbness came out of their flesh was excruciating. The men knew that they were in no condition to make the eight-mile (13-km) walk back to

The people of Thessalon knew something was wrong when they saw the beacon from the Sulphur Island light, which was closed for the season.

Thessalon. They did not know, of course, that search parties had been out looking for them, but had lost their trail in the drifting snow. Their one hope lay in signalling the town. Since the lighthouse was closed for the winter, a light shining from the tower would certainly draw attention. The lamps, however, had been removed from the tower and placed in storage.

Avis and Barry could neither walk nor use their hands. They managed to get one of the lamps into a sack. Then, dragging the sack with his teeth, one of the men crawled up the stairs on his knees and elbows. Reports from the time do not specify which of the crippled men performed this arduous task, but in all likelihood they shared the job, because it seems to have taken considerable time to accomplish.

On Saturday night, February 5, they were at last able to light the lamp. But it was a clear, moonlit night, and the dim glow of the single lamp was not discernible in Thessalon. On Sunday night they tried again, and this time the light was seen and immediately recognized as a signal.

Rescuers hurried to the Sulphur Island lighthouse and found the two men barely alive. They were taken back to Thessalon and placed under the care of a doctor. The sleigh was found, but the horses were never seen again.

For a few days it looked as though the stricken men would recover. They were able to speak, and they told their harrowing tale, which reached the newspapers in far off Toronto. But on February 19, the *Manitoulin Expositor* reported that George Avis had died. Three days later the Toronto *Globe* announced that both men were dead.

Clearly, when Avis and Barry ventured out onto the ice, they should have been better prepared in case of an emergency. Weather on the Lakes is unpredictable at the best of times, and in winter it can be diabolical. Ships on the Lakes in the navigation season at least had the lighthouses to guide them. Ice travellers in the winter had not even that; the lightkeepers had gone home.

ALONE ON THE ICE: ALMOST A SEQUEL

But sometimes the lightkeepers were there in the winter, even though the shipping season was over. Almost thirty years after George Avis and Pat Barry found the Sulphur Island Lighthouse empty, two American fishermen were caught in a similar predicament. On December 28, 1926, Aleck McLean and C.R. Draper climbed into a horse-drawn sleigh and drove from the Dollar Settlement, two miles (3.2km) west of the American Soo, to Round Island out on Whitefish Bay. The ice was about eight inches (20cm) thick.

While they were tending their nets, the ice shelf upon which they were working broke loose and floated the men and their horse and sleigh out onto the open lake. The two men realized to their horror that they were adrift on an ice raft about half a mile in size. It was a terrifying situation. The ice could break up at any moment. Even if it didn't, they could die of exposure or starvation before they set foot on land again. Their only shelter was the sleigh, which they turned over and huddled under in an effort to stay warm.

For three days and nights, McLean and Draper drifted on cold Superior, praying for a miracle. Their prayers were answered when the ice raft ran ashore on Ile Parisienne, catching a tip of the island by a mere 50 feet (15m). The two men scrambled ashore, taking along their poor, starved horse. By this time of year most of the lighthouses on Lake Superior were closed, but a lightkeeper named Douglas and his wife were still at Ile Parisienne. They took the cold, hungry fishermen in and no doubt saved their lives. Had the lightkeepers not been there, the two Americans might well have suffered the same fate as Avis and Barry.

Two American fishermen adrift on an ice floe lived to tell the tale because the Ile Parisienne lightkeepers were at the lighthouse.

Squaw Island Light
High Island
Escanaba
Garden Island
Hog Island
Waugoshance
Point
Washington Island
Plum Island
Gull Island
Beaver Island
Death's Door Passage
North Fox Island
Little Traverse Bay
Chambers Island
Pilot Island
Charlevoix
South Fox Island
Green Bay
Door
Peninsula
South Manitou
Island
North Manitou Island
Manitou Passage
Traverse City

Manitowoc

White River Light

LAKE
MICHIGAN

Milwaukee

St. Joseph

Chicago

Michigan City

The lighthouse image is used yet again in an eye-catching advertisement, this time for an insurance company. What better symbol of security than the beacon shining from a tower that stands against the might of the sea!

SOUTH MANITOU ISLAND:

GRAVES IN THE WATER, GRAVES IN THE SAND

Considering the isolated locations of many Great Lakes lighthouses, and the dramatic, sometimes tragic, events that occurred within sight of their beacons—and even within the towers themselves—it is hardly surprising that some lighthouses are said to be haunted. Some of the tales of hauntings are but fanciful yarns spun by local guides for the entertainment of tourists, or perhaps in the hope that the notion of an unfriendly ghost or two will help to keep vandals away from abandoned but historically significant towers. Other stories, however, have their roots in factual events. One example of a lighthouse "haunting" that may well belong to the latter group concerns South Manitou Island in the northern part of Lake Michigan.

North Manitou and South Manitou are tiny islands lying just to the west of Traverse City, Michigan. North Manitou is seven and three-quarters miles (12.5km) long, and four and a quarter miles (6.8km) wide. South Manitou, a little under four miles (6.4km) to the southwest, is about half the size of North Manitou. Both islands are largely hilly and wooded. According to Ojibwa legend, they were formed by Kitchi-Manitou in memory of two bear cubs that had drowned there. There is another legend that the Manitous were the site of a bloody battle between warriors from rival nations.

With the westward expansion of America in the 1830s and 1840s, the islands were astride the busy shipping lane travelled by thousands of immigrants pouring into newly opened territories. The Manitou Passage, between the islands and the mainland, provided the shortest route for ships travelling up and down the lake. The islands themselves were a welcome source of firewood for the steamships' boilers. South Manitou had a good harbour in which vessels could take shelter from storms.

But the waters around the islands were treacherous, strewn with reefs and deadly shallows. There are more than fifty known wrecks on the lake bottom around the Manitous, and Great Lakes historians estimate there may be a hundred more that have not been located by divers.

Small lighthouses were built on South Manitou in 1840 and 1858. They were replaced with a 104-foot (31.6-m) white, conical tower in 1872. A lifesaving station was established in 1877. This was a building separate from the lighthouse, used to house boats and equipment for men specially trained in rescue work. A permanent light was not established on the North Manitou Shoal until 1935.

Crowded ships plied the Great Lakes carrying hopeful immigrants—and contagion.

But even a glowing beacon could not guarantee a ship's safe passage through the foggy, often turbulent Manitou Passage. Many an immigrant ship heading west, or eastward-bound freighter loaded with timber or grain, foundered in the shadow of the Manitous. Nor were shipwrecks the only tragedies to which the islands bore witness.

The cramped, dirty immigrant ships did not carry just human cargo. They also carried contagion! Irish and German poor travelling up the Lakes in search of new homes were decimated by sickness, just as they had been in the appalling Atlantic crossings. Sickness also struck down impoverished second- and third-generation Americans trying to escape the growing slums of the big cities in the East. Many diseases festered in the damp, foul holds of the ships, but typhoid and cholera were the worst. Captains would stop at South Manitou for fuel, and while half the crew was loading the cordwood on board, the other half would carry the dead ashore to be buried in shallow, mass graves. There was an evil rumour that some captains did not stop at burying those who were already dead, but also cast into the pit people who were still alive but had little chance of recovering. To a cold-hearted skipper looking at a short navigation season, there was no time to be wasted nursing a bunch of sick "foreigners". If they weren't already dead, they soon would be. Besides, a ship that had plague on board was required by law to fly a yellow flag as a signal to others, and ships flying the "plague" flag were not generally welcome in ports. How many suffering souls were buried alive will never be known.

War, shipwrecks and epidemics had caused more than enough death and pathos to provide South Manitou with lamenting spirits. Still, another series

South Manitou Lighthouse. It was rumoured that the beach was a graveyard for plague victims, some of whom were supposedly buried alive.

of incidents might have contributed yet another lost soul to the unquiet dead of South Manitou. The story involves a pair of shipwrecks that occurred many years apart and with no loss of life. But there was one subsequent tragedy.

On November 4, 1903, the wooden propeller *Walter L. Frost*, downbound from Chicago, was wrecked on the rocks off South Manitou during a storm. With the help of the men from the lifesaving station, all of the crew made it safely to shore. Fifty-seven years later, history repeated itself.

On November 24, 1960, the steel-hulled freighter *Francisco Morazan*, also downbound from Chicago, became lost in a blizzard and struck the same reef that had been the doom of the *Walter L. Frost*. When the *Morazan* eventually settled on the bottom, she was directly athwart the rotted wooden remains of the *Frost*. It was as though fate had guided the ship there.

The Francisco Morazan, *aground on the same reef that sank the* Walter L. Frost *in 1903.*

There were no casualties, but this time a little drama was played out on the beached ship.

Captain Eduardo Trizizas had his pregnant wife, Anastasis, aboard, along with his crew of 14 Cuban, Greek and Spanish sailors. When the U.S. Coast Guard cutter *Mackinaw* approached, Trizizas radioed that he was taking on some water, but did not think his ship was in imminent danger of sinking. He refused an order to back the *Morazan* off the reef, because then, he said, she would sink, and he could not allow that to happen before insurance agents had a chance to inspect the damage.

The captain insisted that he and his crew remain aboard, but he did want to see Anastasis safely ashore. The seas were too rough to launch the lifeboat from the *Morazan,* or for the *Mackinaw* to go alongside. There was an attempt to pick up the expectant mother by helicopter, but high winds thwarted that operation.

Not until December 1 was the Coast Guard able to send a party of men aboard the *Morazan* to rescue Mrs. Trizizas. She wanted to stay on the ship, but her husband insisted that she go with the Guardsmen. When she reached shore, a helicopter was waiting to take her to Traverse City. The captain and crew remained aboard while a trio of insurance men assessed the damage. The mariners hoped to unload some of the cargo, repair the hull, and then refloat the ship. But on December 4, with a powerful storm approaching, they had no choice but to abandon the ship.

Storms battered the *Francisco Morazan* over the winter. By spring only the upper portions were visible above the water. The wreck became a popular attraction for tourists and divers. Then tragedy struck. One day a local farm boy drowned while swimming around the hulk. The demise of the *Francisco Morazan* had, indirectly, cost one life.

The ghost of that drowned boy, it is said, is now one of an undetermined number of phantoms that haunt South Manitou. He has reportedly been seen numerous times on the beach near the rusted remains of the wreck. He shares his island haunts with the spirits of those who perished when their ships went down in the waters around the Manitous. People claim to have heard the screams of drowning sailors when there has been no one else around.

The lighthouse and the old lifesaving station, both now tourist attractions, have been scenes of alleged paranormal activity. Employees of Sleeping Bear Dunes National Park, which maintains the Manitous, have heard voices coming from the tower's lamp room, but upon investigation have found the lighthouse to be empty. The lifesaving station, too, has echoed to strange, unearthly voices, footsteps and other noises. When park personnel check the rooms from which the sounds have come, they find them to be just as empty as the lighthouse. Sometimes there is a knock on a door, and when someone opens it, nobody is there.

As always, the skeptics will say that people are imagining things, that they are seeing shadows or the tricks that light can play on water. What they are hearing is nothing but the wind, the water and the cries of seabirds. Superstition does not belong in this automated twenty-first century.

But witnesses keep seeing that sad, drowned boy. Wind, water and birds don't make heavy footsteps in a room directly above one's head. Nor can

(Left) South Manitou Light has seen much tragedy over the decades, and the light station is now said to be haunted. (Right) The ghost of a boy who drowned while swimming on the wreck of the Morazan *allegedly haunts the beach of South Manitou.*

they project human voices from an empty lighthouse with a securely locked door. Among the many attempts to explain the paranormal is a theory that ghostly "activity" that can be perceived by human senses— phantom apparitions, strange sounds—is the residue of powerful human emotions such as fear or sorrow. It remains, it is said, in places where traumatic events have occurred. South Manitou has certainly had a history of traumatic events, as is attested to by the bones that lie in its waters and in its sands.

WHITE RIVER LIGHT: 'TILL DEATH DO US PART

Captain William Robinson was a dedicated lightkeeper, so much so, that he was lighting a beacon to guide ships even before there was a lighthouse in which to house it. In the mid-1800s, White River, Michigan, on Lake Michigan's eastern shore, was a busy centre for the timber industry. Timber came down the White River from nearby White Lake, and was loaded onto ships to be taken to boomtowns like Chicago.

William Robinson, originally from England, arrived at White River in the 1860s. When he learned that wrecks were frequent out on the lake and that ships approaching White River had a difficult time finding the port at night, he took it upon himself to keep a light burning at the end of the settlement's pier.

The government finally built a 27-foot (8.2-m), wooden pierhead light in 1871, and appointed William Robinson its keeper. Then the White Lake Channel connecting White Lake to Lake Michigan was completed, and a more substantial light was required to guide ships

In the boom years of the timber industry, white pine was "king" on Lake Michigan, and communities like White River sprang up.

(Left) William Robinson, the oldest keeper in the American Lighthouse Service, died here on the very day that he was to vacate the premises. (Right) White River lighthouse.

to the new waterway. The government built a 38-foot (11.5-m) tower attached to a house, both made of brick and stone. William Robinson proudly lit the new light for the first time on May 31, 1876.

Captain Robinson faithfully served at the White River Light for a full 47 years. He and his wife, Sarah, raised nine children there (two others died in childhood). When Sarah herself passed away prematurely, Robinson's balm for his grief was to devote himself totally to his lighthouse.

In 1919, when Captain Robinson was 87 years old, the government forced him to retire. He was at that time the most elderly American light-keeper in active service. The old man was not about to give up his beloved lighthouse. He arranged to have his grandson, William Bush, who had been his assistant since 1911, appointed lightkeeper. Bush would keep the light for another 24 years.

With the younger William officially the White River lightkeeper, the elder William continued to live in the house and to do most of his old duties. This was against government regulations. Only the lightkeeper and his wife and children were allowed to live in the lightkeeper's house. Captain Robinson was served notice. He had to move out.

The old lightkeeper became depressed. After all his years of service, he was being forced out of the lighthouse that had been his home for forty

The White River Lighthouse, interior (left) and exterior (right).

years. He told his grandson that he was not leaving. On April 2, 1919, the very day that he was to vacate, William Robinson died. He had stayed with his lighthouse to the very end.

Captain Robinson was buried in a small cemetery within sight of the lighthouse, as was his wish. But the faithful old lightkeeper may still be on duty. The White River Lighthouse is now a museum, and visitors and guests have reported ghostly activity. In particular, they have heard the sounds of footsteps in the tower. Perhaps Captain Robinson is still up there, watching over the lighthouse that was his for so many years, and defying the government or anyone else to make him leave.

WOMEN AT THE LIGHTS: EQUAL TO THE TASK

There were relatively few female lightkeepers on the Great Lakes, perhaps no more than a few dozen. Twice that estimate probably worked as paid assistant lightkeepers. The number is miniscule compared to that of the thousands of males employed as lightkeepers and assistants. However, it would rise considerably if one were to include all of the wives and daughters who worked *unofficially* as assistants to their husbands and fathers, often taking full responsibility for the beacon if the chief keeper became incapacitated or died. One reason for this disparity in numbers, of course, was the belief that lightkeeping was "men's work". Women were thought to be physically and emotionally unequal to the rigours of the job.

But there was another reason. In both Canada and the United States lightkeeping positions were, in the early days, political appointments. What savvy congressman or member of parliament was going to squander a much-sought-after appointment on someone who couldn't even vote? Moreover, the press, the opposing political party, and the boys in the saloons would seriously question the intelligence and moral character of a politician who put a woman in charge of a lighthouse, when everybody knew damn well where her proper place was.

Yet, women did serve at the beacons, both officially and unofficially, and they did the job well. They endured the isolation, bent their backs to the never-ending work, tended vegetable gardens, caught fish, nursed the sick, and raised and educated their children. Some, like Esther Harvey of the Thessalon Light on Lake Huron's North Channel, even achieved fame in the hearts and minds of the tough, freshwater mariners. Esther took over the lighthouse after the death of her husband, James, in 1915. He had been

The Thessalon Lighthouse on Lake Huron's North Channel in September 1915, when Esther Harvey became lightkeeper.

the lightkeeper there since 1898. Esther not only did the job as efficiently as any man, but also risked her life to rescue a survivor from a wrecked gas boat. When she heard cries for help, she ran out and threw the man a line. It was a courageous act, because the boat could have exploded at any time. Ship captains admiringly called Esther "the brave little lady of the light". That may have a chauvinistic ring to it today, but at that time it was a considerable compliment.

ELIZABETH WILLIAMS: FORTY YEARS ON

Elizabeth Whitney, better known to Great Lakes historians as Elizabeth Williams, was island born and bred, and spent most of her adult life as a lightkeeper. Born on Mackinac Island in northern Lake Michigan in 1842, she was a child when the bizarre "Beaver Island War" took place in the early 1850s. Mormon leader James Jesse Strang had taken his small group of followers to Beaver Island, at the other end of the Straits of Mackinac from Mackinac Island, in 1848. Elizabeth's family was living on Beaver Island at the time. They were among the people forced to leave when Strang declared himself "king" and banished the "Gentiles" (non-Mormons) from the island. Because of that incident, Elizabeth detested Strang.

Strang was instrumental in having a lighthouse built at St. James, the largest community on the island. His enemies claimed (without substantial proof) that the Mormons would leave the beacon unlit, and set up false lights to lure vessels into dangerous waters where they could be plundered. Because of this and other accusations, violence flared up between the Mormons and neighbouring settlements. This very odd conflict ended when Strang was assassinated in 1856, and his followers were driven off Beaver Island.

Elizabeth Williams, born and raised on islands in Lake Michigan, was a lightkeeper for most of her adult life, serving at Beaver Island and Little Traverse Point.

(Left) Mormon leader James Jesse Strang was accused of leaving the Beaver Island Light unlit and setting false lights so that his followers could plunder wrecked ships. (Right) The Beaver Island Lighthouse at St. James. Elizabeth's husband, Clement Van Riper, was lightkeeper here when he was drowned trying to rescue the crew of a sinking schooner.

Over a decade later, Elizabeth was an unofficial assistant in the light-house built by the hated Strang. She had married Clement Van Riper, and in 1869 he became the Beaver Island lightkeeper. Then, in 1872, Clement was drowned while trying to rescue the crew of the sinking schooner *Thomas Hood.* "I was weak from sorrow", Elizabeth wrote in her 1905 autobiography *A Child of the Sea and Life Among the Mormons*, "but real-ized that though the life that was dearest to me was gone, yet there were others out in the dark and treacherous waters who need the rays from the shining light of my tower".

Elizabeth became the lightkeeper at the Beaver Island lighthouse at fifty dollars a month. In 1875 she remarried to a Daniel Williams. In 1884, she went to the mainland to be the lightkeeper at the new 40-foot (12-m) light-house at Little Traverse Point on the western shore of the Michigan mitt. She served there until her retirement in 1913 at the age of 71. Elizabeth Williams had spent over forty years as a lightkeeper.

MARY TERRY: WAS SHE MURDERED?

Lightkeeper Mary Terry came to an undeserved and cruel end. Late in 1867, Mary's husband, John, a Canadian from New Brunswick, was appointed keeper of the Sand Point Lighthouse still under construction at

U. S. Light House, Escanaba, Mich.

Lightkeeper Mary Terry died in a mysterious fire at Escanaba's Sand Point Lighthouse. Some people believed the fire was set to cover up a murder.

Escanaba, Michigan, on the north shore of Lake Michigan. But John died of consumption before the 41-foot (12.4-m) brick tower could be completed. The widowed Mary, past fifty, with no children to support her, must have somehow convinced the Lighthouse Service that she could do a good job because she was appointed the lightkeeper.

For 18 years Mary faithfully kept the light that guided the iron ore freighters and passenger steamers in and out of the busy little port. She was well respected in the community: "...a very methodical woman, very careful in the discharge of her duties and very particular in the care of the property under her charge", according to Escanaba's newspaper, the *Iron Port*.

Mary was known to be very careful with her money—there was no guarantee of job security in those days—and it was rumoured that over the years she had accumulated a respectable nest egg. Mary also lived alone. Her lighthouse was on a sand spit, somewhat removed from the residential part of town.

Like most northern lake ports, Escanaba was a rugged frontier community where sailors, loggers and miners converged to blow their pay on whiskey, gambling and women. These were for the most part tough characters, but men who nonetheless subscribed to a rough code of chivalry that forbade interfering with elderly widows. But there were also among them the drifters and the riff-raff, the sort who would rather steal than work, and who did not care whom they robbed. Escanaba would, in fact, one day be the home port of Roaring Dan Seavey, Lake Michigan's only known pirate.

At about one a.m. on March 4, 1886, an alarm was raised in the town. The lighthouse was on fire! Volunteer firefighters scrambled from their beds in answer to the call, but deep snow made it difficult for them to reach the blaze. By the time they got there, the roof was in flames and the interior was an inferno. Not until daylight were the stunned people able to start digging through the charred, smoking ruins. In a corner of what was once the oil room they found a few blackened bones, all that was left of 69-year-old Mary Terry.

Authorities were at once suspicious. Fires were certainly not uncommon, but it seemed inconceivable that a woman as careful in her ways as Mary had been would have an accident. And why, they wondered, had she been in the oil room at that hour, when on any other night she'd have been in bed? Moreover, there was evidence, even in the ruined state of the lighthouse, that the door had been forced open.

Had robbers broken in, awakened Mary, murdered her when she got up to investigate, and then set the fire to cover up their crime? Searchers found the old woman's hoard of hard-earned gold coins in the ashes, making the mystery all the more perplexing. *If* there had been thieves, why hadn't they grabbed the swag? Had they panicked after killing Mary and been in too much haste to get away? Or, in ransacking the place in search of the money had they accidentally started the fire? The questions would never be answered. A coroner's jury could only reach the verdict that Mary Terry had died due to "causes and means unknown". The sad legacy of the story is that Mary is remembered less for her work as a pioneer female lightkeeper than for her dramatic and mysterious death.

HARRIET COLFAX: FAMILY TIES

If Mary Terry had obtained her position of lightkeeper through already being on site, Harriet Colfax obtained her position as keeper of the light at Michigan City, Indiana, through political appointment. Her cousin was Congressman Schuyler Colfax, who would one day be President Ulysses S. Grant's vice-president. The congressman certainly took a risk with this bit of non-sexist nepotism, but his cousin did not let him down. She kept the light faithfully and efficiently from 1861 to 1904. In addition to the light in the 34-foot (10.3-m) tower, Harriet was also responsible for the light at the end of the harbour's long pier. On stormy, cold nights, walking down that pier could be as perilous as balancing on a greased tightrope. Strong winds and crashing waves were constant hazards. In winter, ice added to

Harriet Colfax became the Michigan City lightkeeper through a family connection in Washington. In spite of efforts to have her removed, she kept the post until she was eighty.

the danger. But Harriet took it all as part of the job. "Narrowly escaped being swept into the lake", was a frequent entry in Harriet's light-keeper's log.

During her tenure, Harriet endured not only Lake Michigan's storms, but also political attempts to have her removed and replaced with a man. No matter how well she did the job, there were people who simply could not accept the idea of a female light-keeper. It's quite likely, too, that Congressman Colfax's political foes would have seen Mary as a target through which to attack him.

Harriet's years as the Michigan City lightkeeper made her something of a legend on the Lakes. She stayed with the job long past the age at which most men would have retired. When Harriet finally lit the lamp for the last time, she was eighty years old!

Living in an era in which women were considered to be physically, emotionally and intellectually inferior to men, these women of the lighthouses were pioneers. They, and the many others whose names have been lost to history, showed that it did not matter if the hand that lit the lamp was a man's or a woman's, as long as the light was kept burning.

PILOT ISLAND: THE LIGHTHOUSE AT DEATH'S DOOR

Chroniclers of the Great Lakes have not had much good to say over the years about Lake Michigan's Pilot Island. Words like "bleak", "dreary" and "ugly" seem to be the most frequently used adjectives. The island sits in an eight-mile (12.8-km) -wide waterway that connects Green Bay on Lake Michigan's west shore with the main body of water. Early French explorers called this passage *Porte des Morts*—Death's Door. It was from a height of land overlooking Death's Door that the Jesuit priest Father Hennepin watched La Salle's *Griffin* sail off into mystery and legend in the late 1670s.

Pilot Island, the light-house at "Death's Door". Most lightkeep-ers dreaded this bleak location, but Martin Knudson stayed for eight years.

Death's Door, as the name implies, is one of the most deadly stretches of water on the Lakes. High winds, strong currents, fog and shoals have been the cause of many a wreck. Even before the coming of Europeans, Native people who travelled through here by canoe did so with caution. Those who didn't paid dearly.

Pilot Island, an isolated pile of rocks covering less than four acres (1.6ha), was never high on the list of lightkeepers' preferred assignments. Foul weather could make it difficult to approach and difficult to leave. One reluctant resident said that the only interesting thing to do there was to watch ships get wrecked on the reefs. An early assistant keeper, John Boyce, committed suicide there in 1880. It seems that his desperate last act was the result of a shattered love affair rather than despondency over his posting, but it nonetheless added to the grim atmosphere of the place. Another keeper, a Civil War veteran, compared it to a military prison. It was said that the fog whistle was so loud, it curdled milk and caused unhatched chicks to die in their shells.

But there is always someone who will find beauty in the most desolate of places. A Sturgeon Bay printer named Ben Fagg visited Pilot Island in 1890, and wrote of it:

> This is truly an isolated spot but I have spent five days on Pilot Island and they are among the happiest days of my eventuality... On moonlight nights it is like being in a dream of ideality to walk alone on the moss-covered rocks and listen to the swish of breakers that break over the breakwater at the boat landing, hear them roaring on all sides of the little island... it is a splendid place to raise an ample crop of good, pure thoughts.

Lightkeeper Martin Knudson must have shared Fagg's affinity for the unattractive little island, because, after serving as an assistant keeper there

(Left) Victims of "Death's Door": the J.P Gilmore (left) and the A.P. Nichols (right). Lightkeeper Martin Knudson used the hulk of an earlier wreck, the Forest, in a rescue of the crew of the Nichols. (Below) A breeches-buoy was used to transport survivors from a wrecked ship to safety.

in 1881–82, he returned as lightkeeper in 1889 and stayed for eight years. He often took his wife Theresa and their children along for company. In that time he saw many a ship come to grief in fearsome Death's Door. One such was the schooner *Forest*, which ran aground on Pilot Island in October, 1891. The partially submerged wreck was still there one year later, when Knudson performed the deed that made him a hero of the Lakes.

The autumn of 1892 was a bad season for shipping on Lake Michigan. Storms and high winds kept the lake in a nasty mood and ships ventured out of port at their peril. Nowhere on the vast body of water were sailing conditions worse than at treacherous Death's Door. Foaming water seethed through the passage and boiled around the deadly rocks. Night after night, Knudson looked down from his tower into a maelstrom.

On the night of October 17, as Knudson and his two assistants watched, a schooner hove into view from out of the darkness. The vessel was the 138-foot (42-m) schooner *J.P. Gilmore*. The *Gilmore* was battling against heavy seas and making no headway at all. As the lightkeepers looked on, contrary winds drove the wooden ship onto a reef not 30 feet (9m) from the wreck of the *Forest*. There the schooner was held fast.

Knudson and his men rigged up a breeches-buoy (a rescue device made of cables and a harness) to shuttle the crew ashore. But as the *Gilmore* did not appear to be in immediate danger of breaking up, the crew decided to wait for calmer seas before abandoning their ship. Once they were on the island, they were stuck there because the weather was too ornery for them to risk trying for the mainland in Knudson's small sailboat. They were in for a

The lighthouse on Pilot Island was bursting at the seams with the keeper, his wife and assistants, and the crews of two wrecked ships— 16 people in all.

long visit indeed. The *Gilmore* apparently had a crew of four, but that would have been enough to crowd things in the lightkeepers' quarters. The situation was going to get worse.

Eleven days later, on October 28, the seemingly unending bad weather turned even uglier. A northwest gale sliced through, bringing snow and sleet. Ships passing through Death's Door were having an extremely difficult time steering clear of the reefs. Some captains elected to ride out the tempest at anchor. One was Captain David Clow, Jr. of the schooner *A.P. Nichols*.

The 145-foot (44-m) *Nichols* was a fast, beautiful vessel, but one with a checkered past. In 1871, at the time of the Great Chicago Fire, she was tied to a dock there and suffered major damage. A year later she was almost wrecked in a storm and even temporarily reported as lost. In May 1888 she ran aground near Detour, Michigan. The wicked side of Fate, it seemed, had cast a covetous eye upon the *A.P. Nichols*.

Now Captain Clow was trying to cheat the lake and take the *Nichols* into the lee of Plum Island, not far from Pilot Island. Night was falling when he reached the island's shelter and dropped anchor. But this time the *Nichols* wasn't going to escape.

There was nothing on the lake bottom for the flukes of the anchor to hook onto to secure the schooner's position. As wind and waves carried the *Nichols* back into harm's way, the great iron dragged uselessly across the lake bed. Hard in the grip of the nor'wester, the ship was heading straight for the murderous rocks of Pilot Island, and there was nothing Captain Clow could do to avert disaster.

Martin Knudson, his wife Theresa, and the two assistants were in the lighthouse kitchen having coffee, and so did not see the *Nichols* being driven toward the rocks. Wherever the men of the *Gilmore* were, they did not see it either. A few minutes after eight p.m., there was a great crash, audible even above the sound of the storm. The four of them rushed outside and, through the snow and sleet, in the beam of the lighthouse lamp, they saw a shattered vessel on the shore only a few feet from the stranded *J.P. Gilmore*. The partly submerged hulk of the *Forest* was between them. Three schooners wrecked at the same spot, and within the space of a year! It was as though the lighthouse was drawing ships to destruction the way a candle attracts moths.

Unlike the *Gilmore*, which was fast upon the rocks, the *Nichols* was rolling in the surf, the timbers of her hull crunching on the rocks with each succeeding breaker. It wouldn't be long before the unlucky ship was hammered into driftwood. But if anyone thought that the crew of the *Nichols* was doomed, they hadn't reckoned on Martin Knudson.

The lightkeeper quickly saw that the remains of the *Forest* could be instrumental in the saving of the *Nichols'* crew. The hull of the wreck was on the bottom and the masts and cabin were long gone, but the deck was still above water, barely. Treading carefully on slippery timbers, and taking care to avoid open hatches and places where the boards had weakened, Knudson and an assistant crept out to the prow of the wreck, which jutted out into the lake. Through the raging storm Knudson shouted his instructions to the men on the *Nichols*.

Each time the surf roared in, it swept the stricken *Nichols* to within a few feet of the *Forest*, before the backwash sucked it back again. Knudson wanted the men to jump for it, one by one, each time the *Nichols* rolled inwards. He and his assistant would help them onto the deck of the *Forest*, and guide them back to land.

Ordinarily the captain is the last person to leave a crippled ship. But on this occasion, with the rescue operation being itself extremely dangerous, Captain Clow quite properly chose to go first. The rescue would be no piece of cake for Knudson, either. One wrong move on the slippery old timbers, and he would be in the savage waters, where in all likelihood he would be crushed between the wrecked *Forest* and the hull of the *Nichols*.

Captain Clow slipped as he made his leap from the rail of the lurching ship. He missed the prow of the *Forest* and plunged into the water. Knudson grabbed for him and caught him by the hair. He was able to wrap an arm around Clow and pull him onto the *Forest*. The assistant was waiting to escort him to shore, but Clow wasn't going just yet. There were still seven people aboard the *Nichols*, including a female cook and Captain Clow's own father.

Captain David Clow, Sr. was a retired ship's master. He was old, infirm and weighed 320 pounds. There was no way that he could manage that life-or-death leap from the battered ship. Knudson and the elder Clow had met before, under similar circumstances. Eleven years earlier the captain's own schooner, the *Lewis Day*, had been wrecked on Plum Island. Knudson had been there to rescue the captain and crew. Plum Island had, in fact, been

The Plum Island Lifesaving Station went into operation in 1896. (Inset) Lifesaving crew, men specially trained in rescue operations.

something of a demon in Captain Clow, Sr.'s career. He'd been wrecked there three times! But now it was Pilot Island, Plum Island's devilish twin, which threatened to be the old skipper's last port of call.

Sailors in trouble are a resourceful breed, and the people on the *Nichols*, in spite of the danger they themselves were in, were not about to abandon the old man to the fury of Lake Michigan. They slung a rope harness around Captain Clow, then hung a ladder over the side of the ship. The aged and bulky ex-skipper climbed down. He expected that when the *Nichols* was swept close to the *Forest*, his son and the two lightkeepers would grab him. But it wasn't going to be that easy.

A thundering wave caught the *Nichols* at a bad angle. It snatched away the ladder and left Captain Clow swinging in his harness. The old man was slammed against the hull of the *Nichols*. The crew hauled him back aboard, and made a second attempt. This time, when Captain Clow tried to step onto the *Forest*, he slipped and almost fell into the water. Clow Jr., Knudson and the assistant caught the heavy man and helped him to shore.

With Captain Clow, Sr. safely on land, the rescuers had relatively little trouble taking the remaining people off the doomed *Nichols* by means of the wrecked *Forest*. If ships have souls, as many mariners claim they do, the spirit of the old *Forest* might have felt somewhat vindicated.

Following the dramatic rescue of the *Nichols*' crew, dawn found the Pilot Island station bursting at the seams. What with Knudson, his wife and assistants, and the survivors of two shipwrecks, there were now 16 people on the little scrap of land. When the weather calmed at last, the men salvaged some food, clothing and bedding from the ruined *Nichols*. Those provisions would be vital, because two weeks passed before Knudson could put

Captain Clow, Jr. on a passing steamer. The young captain would send help and supplies to refill the island's depleted stores.

Americans soon learned of the courageous role Martin Knudson had played that stormy October. Two ships had been wrecked, and thanks to him not a life had been lost. The Lifesaving Benevolent Association of New York awarded him a gold medal on which was inscribed, "Presented to Martin Knudson Light House Keeper on Pilot Island in Lake Michigan in recognition of his courage and humanity in rescuing at great personal peril the crews of the schooners *J.P. Gilmore* and *A.P. Nichols* October 1892".

Knudson also received a silver medal and a letter of citation from the American government. He remained in the lighthouse service until 1924, at Pilot Island, Plum Island and other beacons. Lighthouses at critical danger points needed keepers who were above the ordinary. They required the courage and resourcefulness of keepers like Martin Knudson, the man who had watched over infamous Death's Door.

SQUAW ISLAND: ADRIFT ON LAKE MICHIGAN

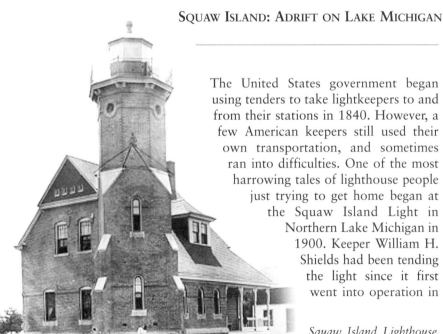

The United States government began using tenders to take lightkeepers to and from their stations in 1840. However, a few American keepers still used their own transportation, and sometimes ran into difficulties. One of the most harrowing tales of lighthouse people just trying to get home began at the Squaw Island Light in Northern Lake Michigan in 1900. Keeper William H. Shields had been tending the light since it first went into operation in

Squaw Island Lighthouse. Keeper William H. Shields and his party met with disaster on their voyage home from here in 1892.

1892, and knew too well that choosing the best time to leave in December was a gamble. One simply could not tell what weather conditions would be like from one hour to the next. December 14 dawned bitter cold, but the lake appeared calm, so Shields decided that the time was right.

Into a 25-foot (7.6-m) Mackinaw boat went Shields, his wife, their niece Mrs. Lucy Davis, and keeper's assistants Owen J. McCauley and Lucien Morden. They were bound for Beaver Island, a mere eight miles (13km) away. There, in the little community of St. James, McCauley's wife Mary was awaiting the birth of their child.

A Mackinaw boat was considered the ideal craft for lightkeepers. Two-masted, pointed at both prow and stern, and with enough room for a family and their belongings, the Mackinaw was nonetheless small enough for easy handling. But on this day, only ten minutes after the Shields party's departure, the gusting winds of northern Lake Michigan would prove to be too much for the usually trustworthy little vessel.

A sudden northwest squall, what one survivor would later call "a puff of wind", struck the Mackinaw like a broadside. The boat tipped completely over, so that the sails were in the water. The nimble McCauley scrambled over the gunwhale and avoided being pitched in, but everyone else was dumped into the December waters of Lake Michigan.

Instantly the air was filled with cries of panic and confusion. Shields held onto his wife, and Morden kept Lucy Davis's head above water. It must be remembered that at that time, relatively few people could swim, and if the women were wearing female attire typical of the period, they would have been encumbered by considerably more sodden clothing than the men.

Owen J. McCauley spent another 24 years as a light-keeper after his near-fatal experience on Lake Michigan. (Opposite page) Designed by William Watt, an Irish immigrant, the Mackinaw boat was considered ideal for lightkeepers.

The boat was still afloat, but on her side, and with the cold already draining their strength, the people in the water could not set her aright. They dragged themselves onto the side of the hull and lashed themselves down with strips cut from the rigging. But their lower legs were still dangling in the water; every wave on the surface washed over them, and the winter air bit into their flesh. Not even the numbness that followed could prevent violent shivering.

They saw some fishing boats heading out from Beaver Island to the south, and tried to hail them. But the boats were too far away for the men aboard to hear the weak cries or to see the almost invisible profile of the overturned Mackinaw. Still, the shipwrecked souls prayed that one of the fishermen would spot them and come to their aid. It was their only hope.

The hours passed, and the two women began to suffer convulsions. For them, clearly, the end was near. A tragic irony was that Lucy Davis, originally from Indiana, had gone north to Squaw Island on her doctor's advice, for her health. Now she lay near death on the side of a drifting wreck, pitifully trying to sing the hymn "Nearer My God to Thee". "The weeping and wailing of those innocent creatures through their untold suffering would melt the hardest of hearts", McCauley said later. "It is beyond my ability to describe the terrible scene and I prayed in silence for their sufferings to cease".

The cold winter sun went down, and in the darkness Lucy Davis died. Sometime before eight p.m., Mrs. Shields became delirious and begged her husband to let her slip into the cold water and put a finish to it. Reluctantly, he did. Still attached to the boat by a length of rope, Mrs. Shields's body trailed along underwater as the wreck drifted.

Now it was Morden who was reaching the end of his endurance. A scholarly type who spent most of his free time indoors studying law, he did not have the physical vitality of Shields and McCauley, who were outdoorsmen. Morden had been sitting upright on the side of the hull, out of the water but exposed to the spray and the frosty air. Now he released the lifeline securing him to the boat, and slid over the side. McCauley grabbed him and called to Shields for help, but Shields was barely conscious. Morden slipped free, and was gone.

McCauley and Shields drifted all night. Shields, the older man, was in far worse shape than McCauley. He became delirious, perhaps as much driven to the brink of madness by the death of his wife as by the murderous cold. McCauley pounded Shields with his fists and kicked him to try to jar him back to consciousness. At one point the old man muttered that he'd rather die naturally than be kicked to death.

A grey dawn found the castaways roughly between Whiskey Island and High Island. Falling snow further diminished the chance of being seen by the lookout on a passing boat. After almost 24 hours of exposure to the appalling cold, and with a dead woman lashed to the wreck and another drifting along like a wraith in the water, the two men by now were barely clinging to life. They would almost certainly be dead before the sun set again.

Then, like something out of a dream, a ship was bearing down on them. It was the steamer *Manhattan*, bound for Manitowoc, Wisconsin. A crewman spotted the floating wreck with its pathetic cargo of dead and near-dead. The skipper sent out four men in a lifeboat, and soon McCauley and Shields, and the bodies of Mrs. Shields and Lucy Davis, were aboard the *Manhattan*. The half-frozen men were somewhat revived with food and hot whiskey, and by the next morning they were in the hospital in Manitowoc.

McCauley had been in very good physical condition before the accident, and he recovered quickly, although he lost some toes and fingers to frostbite. Shields's condition was far more serious. The ordeal had damaged his lungs and left him partly paralyzed. He lost a leg to frostbite, and was a long time recovering from the emotional trauma he had suffered.

Meanwhile, out on Beaver Island, Mary McCauley was going through her own emotional torment. Communications between the island and the mainland were poor, especially in winter. On December 16 she learned from a fisherman that the Squaw Island Light had been shut down. Then for days she heard nothing. Not until the end of December was she finally told that her husband was alive and well.

Despite the ordeal they'd been through, McCauley and Shields both remained in the lighthouse service. But then, the keepers of the more remote lights were often from a tough breed. Despite the loss of a leg, Shields became the keeper of the light at Charlevoix on Lake Michigan, and stayed there until he retired in 1924, twenty-four years after this incident. He died one year later. McCauley became the head keeper at Squaw Island, a position he kept until the light was closed in 1928. He then was assigned to one of the lights at St. Joseph, on southern Lake Michigan, where he stayed until his retirement. After 36 years as a lightkeeper, he died at the age of 89; a long life that had so very nearly been cut short.

A schooner battles a storm in the Manitou Passage of Lake Michigan. The bluffs of the Sleeping Bear Dunes are in the distance.

Nipigon

Battle Island

Slate Islands

Marathon

Thunder Bay
(Fort William,
Port Arthur)

Talbot Island

CANADA

Silver Islet

Grand Portage

Passage Is.

Grand Marais

Michipicoten
Island

Isle Royale

Rock of Ages

LAKE SUPERIOR

Manitou Is.

Whitefish Point

Outer Island Light

Houghton

Gull Rock Light

Caribou
Island

Batchawana Bay

Duluth

Ile Parisienne

Au Sable Light

Whitefish Bay

Apostle
Islands

Keweenaw
Peninsula

Grand Island

Pt aux Pins

Stannard Rock Light

Grand Marais

Big Bay
Point Light

Marquette
Miners' Castle

Point Iroquois
Lighthouse

Pictured Rocks

U.S.A.

Sault Ste. Marie

PART SIX
LAKE SUPERIOR

Aground on Ile Parisienne 12/10/27

Ice envelops the steamer Lambton *(not the same vessel described on (p. 246) in this photo taken December 10, 1927, two days after the ship ran aground on Ile Parisienne in Lake Superior. Two men died before the crew could be rescued.*

AU SABLE LIGHT: DESERTION ON THE *KIOWA*

According to the July 29, 1871 issue of the Marquette, Michigan, *Mining Journal*, "In all navigation of Lake Superior, there is none more dreaded by mariners than from Whitefish Point to Grand Island". This stretch of rocky, foggy Michigan shoreline was once called "The Shipwreck Coast". The American government had established a lighthouse at Whitefish Point in 1849 and at Grand Island in 1856. But ships were still foundering in the 80-mile (129-km) gap in between, especially at a spot roughly halfway called Au Sable Reef. In 1873 construction began on the Au Sable Lighthouse (also called the Big Sable Light), on the mainland near the reef, 12 miles (19km) west of Grand Marais.

This light station, with its 86-foot (28-m), white brick tower was not a popular assignment with lightkeepers. It was in one of the stormiest regions of the Great Lakes, and the only connection with the outside world, aside from the occasional visit from a tender, was a footpath to Grand Marais—and that was often washed out. Many keepers resigned after only a season or two of duty there. One who did not seem to mind the isolation of Au Sable was Klass Hamringa, who took over the light in 1923 and stayed until his retirement in 1930 at about the age of about 68. Hamringa was at the light, therefore, when one of the most deplorable incidents in the history of Great Lakes navigation occurred practically in the shadow of the Au Sable tower.

The same November 30, 1929 storm that had thrown the *Sarniadoc* onto the rocks of Main Duck Island in Lake Ontario (see p.78), was also making a cauldron of Lake Superior. The 251-foot (76.5-m) steel freighter *Kiowa*, bound from Duluth to Chicago with a load of flax, was hugging the

The Au Sable Lighthouse stood guard over a stretch of Lake Superior shore called "The Shipwreck Coast".

The freighter Kiowa. *Captain Young committed one of the most shameful acts in the history of American navigation on the Lakes.*

south shore of the lake. Earlier, Captain Alex Young, son-in-law of the ship's owner, had tried waiting out the storm in a sheltered place. Why he changed his mind and decided to risk the deadly Shipwreck Coast in a monstrous storm no one knows. Perhaps he thought such a daring run would impress his father-in-law. It was a gamble, and one that he would lose.

As the *Kiowa* pitched and rolled on the raging lake, the cargo shifted. The *Kiowa* listed, and ran onto a reef within sight of the Au Sable Lighthouse. Lightkeeper Klass Hamringa would have seen the distress flares that were fired from the ship. What he could not see was the shocking drama that was being played out on board the freighter as it settled in shallow, but storm-tossed water.

It is the law of the sea, both written and unwritten, that the captain on an endangered ship must not leave the vessel until he has seen to the safety of all passengers and crew. Captain Young did not abide by that ancient and time-honoured code. He became hysterical. Crying that all was lost, he grabbed a loaded pistol from his cabin and used it to hold the crew at bay. Then he selected five men, including First Mate Arthur Cronk (or Kronk), to escape with him in the lifeboat. The other 16 sailors would simply be abandoned. Whether the five who accompanied Young did so willingly or were compelled by the captain's gun was never made satisfactorily clear.

Deserting his men in so cowardly a manner was a crime for which Young would have faced severe penalties ashore, but Fate had other plans for the captain. As the lifeboat with the six would-be survivors was being launched, a cable broke and it capsized, spilling the men into the churning, frigid water. Only Cronk managed to climb back aboard the wrecked *Kiowa*. Superior takes the craven as well as the brave.

The storm had disabled land communications, so lightkeeper Hamringa kept blowing the distress signal. It was not heard at the Grand Marais Coast Guard station until 3:15 p.m. the day after the *Kiowa* ran aground. A patrol boat was dispatched to investigate.

Meanwhile, a pair of civilians, Charles Chilson and Earl Howay, had seen the plight of the *Kiowa*'s crew. Showing considerably more courage than the late Captain Young, they used their small motorboat to start ferrying men from the partly submerged freighter to the lighthouse dock, and were in the process of doing this when the Coast Guard showed up. The Coast Guard vessel picked up the *Kiowa*'s crew, all of whom were suffering from exposure, but did not acknowledge the heroic act of the two civilians. Perhaps out of embarrassment because the patrol boat had arrived on the scene so late, the official report stated only that the surviving crewmen of the *Kiowa* had been rescued by the Coast Guard. It seemed that everything about the *Kiowa* incident became tarnished.

The first newspaper reports on the tragedy stated that Captain Young had died a hero, trying to save his men. But the shameful truth came out at the inquest into the sinking. Since Young was dead and beyond human justice, the court singled out First Mate Cronk for punishment, and suspended his licence for ninety days.

The Au Sable Light is still operating (automated), and the tower is managed as a tourist attraction by the Pictured Rocks National Lakeshore. The wreck of the *Kiowa*, in about 30 feet (9m) of water, is a popular dive site. Much of the ship's equipment was salvaged after the sinking. During the Second World War, with the high demand for steel, large portions of the superstructure and hull were salvaged for scrap. The remaining hulk lies as a silent reminder of the day a captain lost his nerve and forgot the rule of the sea.

Miners' Castle: The Wreck of the *Elma*

Lighthouse keeping was, indeed, an extraordinary occupation. Besides all the mundane tasks of cleaning, painting and polishing, it was part of the lightkeeper's job to watch for the unusual. He (or she) had to be alert for any sign of a ship in trouble. That could be difficult, given the monotony of the daily routine. When a lightkeeper did spot trouble, if it were at all possible, he would try to help. Thus, many lightkeepers became unsung heroes. Because of just such a one, the chroniclers of the Great Lakes would learn the incredible story of the wreck of the *Elma*.

Steamer towing a schooner barge. A large freighter might have two or three of these bulk-carriers in tow.

By 1895 the *Elma* had long since seen better days. She was originally built in 1873 as a schooner, 165 feet (50m) long and 35 feet (10.6m) in the beam. For years she had skimmed across the freshwater seas as a graceful ship, powered by the wind that filled the sails rigged to her tall masts. But in time the *Elma* suffered the fate of many a beautiful sailing vessel. Her masts were shortened to hold but a small amount of canvas, and she was reduced to the undignified status of sailing barge. For most of her trips across the water now, she would be towed by a steamship.

On Saturday, September 28, 1895, the steamer *P.H. Birkhead* chugged through Whitefish Bay en route to a Lake Superior port to pick up a load of lumber for Tonawanda, New York. To carry the extra cargo she had three barges in tow: the *Commodore*, the *Chester B. Jones*, and the *Elma*. Each barge had a crew of six or seven men. The little fleet moved slowly because the *Birkhead* had not been built for speed, and with three barges to haul—even empty ones—she seemed to barely move.

Leaving Whitefish Point behind, the *Birkhead* had about one hundred miles

In stormy weather, vessels sought shelter in the lee of Grand Island.

(161km) ahead of her before she would reach the shelter of Grand Island. That was one hundred miles along Superior's south shore, with the wide open lake to the starboard—a long stretch for the plodding little fleet, and Superior had never been known for patience.

In the afternoon a strong wind swept down on them from the northwest and a heavy sea was running. By late afternoon the nor'wester had become a gale, and huge waves cresting in whitecaps rolled across the surface of angry Superior. The *Birkhead* had no hope of making the safety of Grand Island before the full force of the storm was unleashed, so the skipper decided to turn back for Whitefish Bay.

As he swung the *Birkhead* around in a big half-circle, the ship was carried from crest to trough as though on a roller coaster, and tossed around mercilessly. The three barges were given equal ill-treatment, but were holding their own well enough, as long as they were tied fast to the *Birkhead*. But the strain on those umbilicals to the mother ship was enormous, and suddenly the lines broke!

The captain of the *Birkhead* tried to round up his scattered barges, but the only one he could get a line to was the *Elma*. The *Commodore* eventually made it to Sault Ste. Marie (some barges were equipped with sails in case of such an emergency), while the *Chester P. Jones* rode out the storm at anchor.

With only one barge in tow now, the *Birkhead*'s skipper decided to try once more for Grand Island. All Saturday night and into Sunday morning the *Birkhead* plodded on, with the *Elma* struggling behind. They had Grand Island in sight at last, when ill fortune struck the *Elma* a double blow. First the tow line broke again. Then the vessel's steering mechanism was damaged. The *Elma* was now at the mercy of the elements. With the power of the storm rising, there was nothing the crew of the *Birkhead* could do for the lost barge. They fled for the safety of Grand Island.

The crashing seas tossed the *Elma* around like a toy. They swept over her, carrying away her masts and rigging. Water poured into the hold, and the crew worked desperately at the pumps. But it was clear that they were fighting a losing battle.

The *Elma* was foundering off a stretch of the south Superior shore known as Pictured Rocks. This is a series of brilliantly coloured sandstone bluffs rising straight up from the water to heights varying from 50 to 200 feet (15-61m). Standing out like a sentinel at one end of this unique formation, and not far from Grand Island, is a spectacular limestone promontory called Miners' Castle, because it closely resembles the ruined battlements of a medieval fortification, and the principal occupation in that region was mining. This magnificent example of nature's architecture would become a

Miners' Castle. George Johnson managed to climb the craggy landmark, but Rudolph Yack was battered to death against the rock face.

grand attraction for tourists, but the rocky shoreline was no place for a rudderless wooden ship. Superior shrugged, and the *Elma* was smashed against a rock about 100 feet (30m) from shore, directly in front of Miners' Castle.

The barge was impaled on the rock, held fast as though by teeth. The seven sailors aboard knew, though, that she could become dislodged at any moment and sink, or be hammered to pieces by the surf. They had to somehow make it to Miners' Castle. It was not just the lives of the crew that were in danger; one of the men had brought along his three-year-old son.

There was a yawl on the *Elma*, but getting it across that hundred feet of water was going to be dangerous. The gap was strewn with jagged rocks, and the water from which they protruded was boiling with the violence of the gale. A man named George M. Johnson volunteered to try it. With considerable difficulty the crew launched the yawl on the leeward side of the *Elma*. Johnson got in and tied lines to it, which the crew on the wreck played out as he fought his way across the churning water. If Johnson could secure lines to Miners' Castle, the others could use them to ferry themselves and the child off the doomed *Elma*.

Johnson managed to steer his way through the deadly reefs, but as he neared Miners' Castle the wind suddenly propelled the yawl forward and smashed it to splinters against the base of the great rock. The lines fell into the water in a useless tangle. Johnson was left clinging to the rock like a spider, with the surf threatening to sweep him off just as easily as it had wrecked his ship.

Searching desperately for handholds, Johnson slowly started to pull himself up the wall of the Castle. It took tremendous effort, but at last he was out of the reach of those killer waves. He kept climbing until he reached a large cavity he could crawl into. But now he was helpless to do anything for the people still on the *Elma*.

Another courageous mariner, Rudolph Yack, volunteered to swim to Miners' Castle with lines tied to his body. He could then climb the wall, as they had seen Johnson do, and the two of them could rig up lifelines. Yack dove into the foaming waters. He was a strong swimmer, and he made it to the base of the Castle. But he could not find a handhold in the rock. While Yack searched frantically for something to grasp, the powerful surf bashed him against the massive rock again and again, until he was dead. The crew of the *Elma* tried to retrieve the brave man's body by means of the lines Yack had tied around himself. However, as they were pulling the body up the side of the ship, it slipped free of the lines. Yack disappeared into the swirling water and was never seen again.

Prospects for those aboard the *Elma* now seemed truly bleak, but the men were not about to give up. They tied lines to some buoyant objects and tossed them into the water. From his perch on Miners' Castle, Johnson could see that his shipmates were attempting to float lines to him. Climbing down a rock face is even more difficult than climbing up one, but Johnson did it. He somehow managed, without losing his grip, to snatch up one of the floating lines. Then he climbed back up to his little hole in the wall. By now it was dark, so the rescue operation would have to be put off until morning. Johnson tied the line around his waist so it wouldn't be lost. It was the last, slender chance his shipmates had. The men on the *Elma* prayed that the timbers beneath their feet wouldn't be ripped apart during the night.

At dawn one of the stranded sailors tied the Castle-line around his body, and then another one that he would drag behind him from the wreck, his fellow crewmen making it secure. With Johnson working from one end, and the *Elma* men from the other, the man was drawn across the water and up the Castle wall. The procedure was repeated until all of the men were safely on the rock. For the little boy they drew the lines taut and rigged a "traveller" (a type of suspended chair) to carry him above the waves to safety.

Except for the unfortunate Rudolph Yack, the people of the *Elma* had survived the wreck, but they were not out of danger yet. Behind their refuge on Miners' Castle was a 140-foot (43-m) cliff. Even if they could scale it, which wasn't likely, they were in wild, cold country, with only two loaves of bread and a few blankets they had brought with them from the *Elma*. If they were going to get off Miners' Castle, it would have to be by water.

The men climbed higher up, and found a larger cavity that would accommodate all of them. There were some logs that had somehow been deposited in the hole, so they were able to build a fire. Even so, they were cold and exhausted, and the loaves of bread did not go far.

By Tuesday morning, October 1, the storm had died down. There wasn't much left of the *Elma*. The waves had pounded the once-proud schooner to flotsam. But the men thought there might be some food in the submerged hull, which was still impaled on the rock. They climbed down to the base of the Castle, where wreckage had washed in. They fished out as many planks as they could, with the intention of binding them together to make a raft so they could go out to the wreck. While they were doing this, however, one of the men spotted a small boat coming their way.

It was a lighthouse keeper! He had seen the smoke from their fire two days before, and had caught a glimpse of the stranded *Elma* before the lake reduced her to floating debris. Once the storm had abated, he set out in his boat to investigate.

Neither the lightkeeper's name nor the lighthouse from which he had come appears to have been recorded. Most likely he came from the Grand Island North Light, about eight miles (13km) away, the only one with a clear view of the Pictured Rock shoreline and Miners' Castle. Thus far, a list of the names of the nineteenth-century keepers of that lighthouse has not been found. What is important is that the vigilant lightkeeper, whomever he was, took the marooned crew of the *Elma* off Miners' Castle. He soon found the *P.H. Birkhead* where she had taken shelter behind some rocks, out of sight of Miners' Castle, and delivered the survivors to the ship.

The lightkeeper's role in the story of the wreck of the *Elma* was a small, but crucial one, because it was the link by which the whole tale came to be known. It's possible that the six men and the boy might have been rescued by some other means, but it is just as possible that if the lightkeeper had not gone out to make his investigation, they would have perished. Then no one would ever have known of the courage of George M. Johnson and Rudolph Yack, nor of the last hours of the *Elma*. Their fate would be one more secret of the deep waters of the Lakes.

STANNARD ROCK: THE LONELIEST PLACE IN AMERICA

No other American lighthouse is farther from land and, according to the United States Coast Guard, there is no lighthouse in the world in a more desolate location. Some people might challenge that opinion, but it provides a fair assessment of the Rock's isolation. From the lantern room of the Stannard Rock Light, 110 feet (33.5m) above Lake Superior, one can see nothing in any direction but water and sky. The nearest land, Manitou Island, is 24 miles (38.6km) to the northwest. The closest mainland community is Marquette, Michigan, 45 miles (72.4km) to the south. There is not even a speck of island, for the shoal the Stannard Rock Light stands in warning against is several feet below the surface, a mountain rising up from the bottom of the lake and lurking in ambush like a monster of the deep.

When Charles C. Stannard, captain of the schooner *John Jacob Astor*, discovered the Rock in 1835, it was immediately recognized as a hazard—"the most serious danger to navigation on Lake Superior" said the Lighthouse Board. Putting a lighthouse on it would be one of the greatest feats of maritime engineering of that period.

Construction did not begin until 1868. First a stone crib, 12 feet (3.6m) in diameter, was fastened to the shallowest part of the shoal. Then a wrought-iron shaft, 20 feet (6m) high and six feet (1.8m) in diameter was installed. On top of this went a temporary day beacon. Then the engineers waited to see

The Stannard Rock Lighthouse sits on the peak of a submerged mountain in the middle of Lake Superior. The isolation drove some men to the brink of insanity.

how this structure stood up to the assaults of Lake Superior. When the beacon had withstood ten years of ice, storms and pounding waves, the engineers
started work on the actual lighthouse at a site about 2,000 feet (609m) from
the experimental crib.

Building a lighthouse where there was no land was challenge enough.
Building one in the water wilderness of hostile Superior was testing human
skill and nerve. Any construction site can be a hazardous place; but that
site, literally in the middle of nowhere, called for men willing to risk the
vehemence of a Great Lake notorious for its storms and unruly disposition.
Cut and dressed granite blocks weighing up to 30 tons each had to be taken
out by barge and manoeuvred into position to form the base. This was the
bulwark that would stand up to Superior's battering. When the tower was
completed, a Second Order Fresnel lens that cost $25,000 (over $400,000
in today's terms) was taken out to the site. The component parts were carried up the tower's 141 steps to the lantern room and assembled there. The
light went into operation on July 4th, 1882. At a cost of $305,000, the
Stannard Rock Lighthouse was one of the most expensive edifices of its
type in the world.

Built to endure the elements, Stannard Rock Light also proved to be a
test for the ability of any lightkeeper to endure isolation. The fact that the
pay was better for this posting than for any others on the Great Lakes was
a strong incentive, and there were indeed men who were equal to the trial.
But others were not. One man had to be removed after he threatened to
jump in the water and swim for shore, an impossible feat considering the
distances to the nearest land. Another was taken away in a straitjacket.
When the United States Coast Guard took over the operation of the light,
guardsmen assigned to duty there grimly called it "Stranded Rock". It was
scuttlebutt among the rank and file of the Coast Guard that an assignment
to Stannard Rock was a punishment detail, though this was never the official policy of the Coast Guard. Women and children were not allowed on
the Rock, and aside from his duties, there was nothing for the lightkeeper
to do but fish and read. If he had an assistant they could play cards, but two
or three men confined to a small space for weeks at a time could grow more
than a little weary of each other's company.

Besides the mind-numbing loneliness, the keepers at the Rock had to be
stalwart when Lake Superior's temper was unleashed. Even with walls ten
feet (3m) thick at the base and three feet (.9m) thick at the top (making the
interior very cramped indeed) the tower would tremble in the teeth of a
northern gale, and spray from the waves would fly over the top—110 feet
(33.5m) up. The dishes would rattle and the furniture shake, and there
must have been moments when the men in the station doubted that the

Low-lying shoals like the ones at Stannard Rock can be all but invisible from the bridge of a ship.

foundation upon which it stood was the immovable object it was supposed to be.

Ice was one of the greatest dangers to lightkeepers stationed at Stannard Rock. When a lighthouse tender arrived at the end of the navigation season to take the keepers off, the crew often found the Rock surrounded by a barrier of ice hundreds of feet wide. The keepers would be obliged to walk across this treacherous shelf to a small boat that would transport them to the ship. Sometimes the entire structure would be encased in ice many feet thick. In November 1913, after a particularly horrific storm, it took the crew of the tender five days to hack through the ice to get the keepers out. This was not a coating of ice such as would be found on a tree after a night of freezing rain. Rather, it was an accumulation caused by the freezing spray from the constant pounding of mountainous breakers. The sheath of ice steadily thickened, until the lighthouse resembled a giant icicle turned upside-down. The men inside were actually trapped in a prison of ice, that could well have become an ice-tomb if the rescuers had not chopped their way through in time. In the spring, the lightkeepers frequently had to chop through more ice to get back in.

In 1944, the Stannard Rock Lighthouse was electrified, its power coming from gasoline-fuelled generators. It was scheduled to be automated in 1961. No more would lightkeepers have to endure the privations and the unnerving weather conditions of the Rock. Aside from those incidents of men cracking up under the strain of loneliness, the record of the Stannard Rock Light had been an impressive one. Human ingenuity and human hands had built a lighthouse at the most difficult location Nature could provide, and for almost eighty years the tower had defiantly withstood everything Superior could throw at it. But Fate was not going to allow mere mortals to get away with such impudence unscathed.

DEATH ON THE ROCK

In June 1961, Electrician's Mate Oscar R. Daniels, 23, was sent to Stannard Rock from Sault Ste. Marie, Michigan, to repair one of the generators. Already at the Rock on lightkeeper duty were Engineer First Class William A. Maxwell, 43; Seaman Walter Scobie, 22; and Seaman's Apprentice Richard Horne, 18. There would ordinarily have been an officer of higher rank present, but on this occasion he was on shore leave.

Shortly after 9:30 a.m. on June 18, Scobie was asleep in the seamen's quarters, and Horne and Daniels were in the galley. The fourth, Maxwell, was supposed to be on duty in the watch room, but instead was (apparently) in the engine room. Suddenly a tremendous explosion rocked the lighthouse as 1,800 gallons (6,813 L) of gasoline and propane went up in flames. The tiny world of Stannard Rock became a microcosm of hell as smoke and flame enveloped everything and a fireball shot into the sky. The sleeping Scobie was thrown from his bed, and Horne and Daniels were hurled across the galley. Daniels was badly burned and suffered severe lacerations to one leg. Scobie and Horne received only minor injuries.

"As soon as it happened the rooms of the lighthouse became filled with black smoke and objects began flying through the air. The windows blew out", Horne said later. The inferno had shot up through the lighthouse tower, destroying everything. Horne, Scobie and Daniels got out through one of the shattered windows, dropping 12 feet (3.6m) to the concrete apron below. Daniels was wearing pants but no shirt, and Scobie was dressed only in his underwear. It was cold and windy, and all they'd managed to grab before escaping was a tarpaulin. They rigged it into a tent at a spot by the north side of the tower, as far as they could get from the fire raging in the coal bunker and the engine room. They couldn't was no sign of Maxwell.

The Lighthouse after the explosion of June 18, 1961. One man was killed.

The men tried to launch even approach the blaze for warmth, because of fumes. There The men tried to launch the station's lifeboat, but somehow the rope slipped and it got away from them. "I climbed ten feet down a ladder and dived into the lake, thinking maybe I could catch the boat", Horne said. "But I am not a good swimmer and I couldn't reach it. I began to get quite tired and Scobie threw me a life ring. I caught it and they pulled me back to the rock". June can be cold out on Superior, and the half-naked men were in for a miserable time, wondering all the while if Maxwell was alive somewhere out in the water.

The next day they found two cans of beans in the locker room, and some rags that they tried to fashion into clothing. They were certain that help was already on the way, but it would be two days before rescue arrived. No passing freighter saw the smoke. Nor, inexplicably, did the Coast Guardsmen's radio contacts in Marquette or on Manitou Island initiate an investigation when they failed to make their regular reports. It seemed that the disaster had gone entirely unnoticed.

Finally, the Coast Guard did receive a report that the Stannard Rock Light was out. The cutter *Woodrush* was sent out from Duluth to investigate. The vessel reached the Rock at 11:30 p.m. on June 20. The skipper, Lieutenant Mike O'Brien, was stunned when he saw the devastation. But the men on "Stranded Rock" were more than relieved. "It was like seeing God when the *Woodrush* showed up", Horne said. "Scobie and I could have made it longer, but I don't know about Daniels".

Lieutenant O'Brien took the three survivors off the light station and rushed them to Houghton, Michigan. Then he returned to the Rock to put out the fire still smouldering in the coal bunker and to search for Maxwell. The only trace ever found of the man who had a wife and five children back in Houghton was a key chain. "I would not like to go back there again", Horne admitted. "But I will if I am ordered. I have too many memories. It would be living like a ghost".

No one could conclusively determine just what had caused the explosion, but the Coast Guard speculated that Maxwell might have been at fault. He had been on watch duty, and he was a pipe smoker. He had evidently left the watch room, which he should not have done, and gone to the engine room. If he had a lighted pipe in his mouth, that would have been enough to ignite gas fumes in the engine room as he opened the door, setting off the explosion and blowing himself into oblivion. Maxwell died only weeks before the Stannard Rock Light was scheduled to be automated.

Today the light station on Stannard Rock is fully automated, and is visited only by Coast Guard maintenance crews. Off limits to the public, it is as desolate a place as ever. But stories persist among those people who have to service the light that there is still "someone" there—the ghost of the missing

William Maxwell, or of some long-dead lightkeeper who feels bound to remain on duty at the loneliest place in America.

It has been said that a lighthouse's beacon is its "soul". After the explosion, the Fresnel lens in the Stannard tower was dismantled and placed in storage. For decades no one knew where the historical artifact was. Then, in 1999, Great Lakes historian Frederick Stonehouse learned that the Stannard Light lens was in a Coast Guard warehouse in Forestville, Maryland. He arranged to have the old light transported to the Marquette Maritime Museum. There it was cleaned and reassembled, and is now on display. Most people will never have an opportunity to visit the Stannard Rock Lighthouse, though it can be viewed from tour boats. In the museum, however, they can see the light that was the "soul" of "Stranded Rock".

BIG BAY POINT: A HARD MAN TO WORK FOR

The Big Bay Point Lighthouse, a tower rising to 60 feet (18.2m) from a two-storey brick house, is said to be haunted. The lighthouse was constructed in 1896, on the south shore of Lake Superior, 25 miles (40km) northwest of Marquette, Michigan. Accommodations were rather spacious, as lightkeeper dwellings went. The house was actually a duplex, with quarters for the keeper and his family on one side, and duplicate quarters on the other side for the assistant and his family. As it turned out, having a wall between the families was something of a blessing.

The first lightkeeper at Big Bay was William Prior, formerly the lightkeeper at Stannard Rock. Prior's record shows that he rose from being a third assistant to head lightkeeper, so he was obviously good at his job. Unfortunately, he was not an easy man to get along with. He was

William Prior, keeper of the Big Bay Lighthouse, could not find a satisfactory assistant until his son took the job. Then tragedy struck.

apparently demanding, and something of a perfectionist. He expected others to live up to his high standards, and he was very critical when they didn't. As a result, Prior had a difficult time keeping assistants. His first assistant, Thomas Gallagher, lasted a little over a month.

Of his second assistant, Ralph Heater, Prior wrote in his lightkeeper's log: "I can not see that the assistant has done any work around the station since I left. He has not the energy to carry him down the hill, and if I speak to him about it he makes no answer, but goes on just as if he did not hear me...." Prior also recorded his opinion of Heater's wife: "...she is altogether a person totally unfit to be in a place like this as she is discontented and jealous and has succeeded in making life miserable for everyone at the station".

Heater worked one season with Prior, then transferred to another station. Prior wrote in his log that he was "thankful". The next assistant was George Beamer. He stayed for a month in 1898, then went to fight in the Spanish-American War. In his absence, his wife Jennie was Prior's assistant. She was the only woman to be a keeper at Big Bay. Jennie worked with Prior, apparently without too much trouble, from May until September, when her husband returned. Then the caustic entries about Beamer began to appear in Prior's log: "Asst. Beamer does not take hold of his work as he should". "When will I get an assistant who will fit the place?" "He is too high strung for a lightkeeper's asst...."

After two months the Beamers transferred out. Prior wrote, "This Beamer... is without exception the most ungrateful and the meanest man I ever met".

On April 23, 1899, William Crisp became Prior's assistant. He fared no better than Gallagher, Heater or Beamer. On July 11, Prior wrote in his log, "...he [Crisp] has decided to resign and wishes to leave at once and will go to Marquette at first opportunity if he has to walk".

Considering Prior's difficult personality, one can only speculate what it must have been like to work with him in the confines of Stannard Rock. Finally, a solution to the problem at Big Bay was found. Prior's next assistant was his 19-year-old-son, George, who took the post on January 18, 1900. William Prior finally had an assistant he felt he could rely upon. Unfortunately, it was not to last.

In April 1901, George fell while working on the dock and badly injured his leg. It seems that he did not seek immediate medical attention. In those days before the discovery of antibiotics, any injury was potentially dangerous because of the threat of infection. George's leg became gangrenous, and his father finally took him to the hospital in Marquette. But it was too late. George died there in June.

William Prior was devastated over the loss of his son. After George's funeral, acquaintances said that Prior showed signs of being mentally deranged. On June 28, he left the lighthouse and was seen heading into the woods with a gun and a container of strychnine. It was feared that he planned to commit suicide, so a search was made. The lightkeeper, however, had disappeared. A reward was offered for information on Prior's disappearance, but nobody came forward. The man seemed to have vanished from the face of the earth. It would be 17 months before the mystery was solved.

On November 14, 1902, a man named Fred Babcock was hunting in the woods about a mile (1.6km) south of the lighthouse, when he came upon the skeleton of a man hanging from a tree. The remains were identified by the clothing as being those of William Prior. One part of the mystery that would never be solved was why Prior took poison and a gun into the woods, and then chose to hang himself.

It is said that suicides are damned, and it could be that William Prior is still at the lighthouse. The old Big Bay Light is now privately owned, and has been operating as a bed-and-breakfast inn since 1986. Guests at the inn have reported hearing strange noises like howling wind and slamming doors—when there has been no wind, and no doors being slammed. They have also claimed to have seen an apparition: a man dressed in the uniform worn by old-time lightkeepers. This "ghost" has been seen on the grounds around the building, and in the half of the house that was once the lightkeeper's residence. Perhaps William Prior is doomed to forever lament the untimely loss of his son. Or maybe he's still looking for an acceptable assistant.

ROCK OF AGES: THE DEVIL ROCK

Rock of ages cleft for me
Let me hide myself in thee

When English clergyman Augustus M. Toplady wrote the lyrics of his famous hymn in 1776, he would hardly have guessed that one day the title would be sardonically applied to a deadly hazard to shipping in a vast lake in far-off America. Rising only 16 feet (4.8m) above the surface of Lake Superior, Rock of Ages is 205 feet (62.4m) long and 50 feet (15.2m) wide.

It is but the tip of a ship-killing minefield of rocks and shoals about two and a half miles (4km) off the western tip of Isle Royale, on the American side of the international boundary. It lies right in the path of a major shipping lane for traffic going to and from the Canadian port of Thunder Bay (formerly Port Arthur and Fort William), and the American port of Duluth. The frequent occurrences of heavy fog compound the danger.

Mariners had known of the Rock for many years, and continually badgered Washington to appropriate funds for a lighthouse. But a tight-fisted Congress ignored their warnings until 1905. In the meantime, the Rock claimed two known victims: the 418-ton sidewheeler *Cumberland* in July 1877, and the 1,773-ton propeller *Henry Chisholm* in October 1898. Both vessels went to the bottom with no loss of life, but it was clear that with the volume of shipping on Superior steadily increasing, it would be but a matter of time before a catastrophe happened. Preventative measures needed to be taken, and so, in the spring of 1908, engineers were finally dispatched to the isolated location.

A base station was established at Washington Harbor on Isle Royale for the storage of supplies. This would also be barracks for the workmen until they had quarters out at the Rock. A crew of fifty men blasted the western end of the Rock flat. Then they built a concrete and steel pier upon which the tower would stand. This massive structure was 25 feet (7.6m) high and 50 feet (15.2m) in diameter, and solidly bolted to the native rock, a bulwark against Superior's strength. The upper portion flared out to deflect waves. With the pier completed, the men built a bunkhouse, which would be home until the tower was finished.

On September 15, 1910, a light visible for 19 miles (30.5km) shone from the eight-storey tower perched on the barren rock. Within the tower were relatively large and comfortable quarters for the keeper and three assistants. There was a steam heating plant, kitchen and office, as well as a fog-signal plant. A crane was used to hoist supplies from tenders and to raise and lower the station's boat, which was kept safely on the pier deck. Topping it all was a huge Second Order Fresnel lens.

But even with the Rock of Ages Light standing its lonely vigil, the waters at the western tip of Isle Royale remained treacherous, and in June 1928 the 183-foot (55.7-m) passenger steamer *America* struck a shoal near the Rock and sank. Fortunately, all on board made it to the island in lifeboats.

(Opposite page) Rock of Ages Lighthouse, shown here in various stages of construction, took two years to build. A crew of fifty workmen lived in the bunkhouse at right.

THE COX: CRUISE INTO DANGER

According to maritime lore, it is bad luck to change a ship's name. But George M. Cox, a New Orleans lumber and shipping tycoon, was not one to pay heed to sailors' superstitions. In 1933 he bought the 32-year-old steamer *Puritan*, a 259-foot (78.9-m) passenger ship that for most of her career had plied the waters of Lake Michigan. Cox refurbished the *Puritan*, transforming her into a luxury cruise ship for his new enterprise, the Isle Royale Transport Company. Though Canada and the United States were in the grip of the Great Depression, Cox believed there would be no shortage of vacationers and conventioneers who would happily climb aboard for excursions on the Lakes. Cox, a big, sandy-haired, good-natured fellow, indulged himself a little by re-christening the ship with his own name: the *George M. Cox*. Before the vessel embarked upon her maiden voyage as the *Cox*, the owner told the press that his ship would be "clean": no gambling or disorder on board. He said he'd rather sink the boat—a statement that turned out to be eerily prophetic.

That year Chicago was holding the Century of Progress Exposition to commemorate the city's centennial. The *Cox* was to sail to Port Arthur to pick up 250 Canadians and take them to Chicago for the big bash. On board for the outward journey were 120 people. Roughly three dozen were George Cox's business associates and personal friends enjoying a free pleasure trip. There were three children aboard, all boys under the age of eleven. The crew of over 80 included sailors and black gang (engine-room men), kitchen and wait staff, stewardesses and entertainers. Among them were ship's nurse Adeline Keeling, 23, and stewardess Beatrice Cote, 21. The two women had grown up together in Manistee, Michigan, but this was the first time they would sail together.

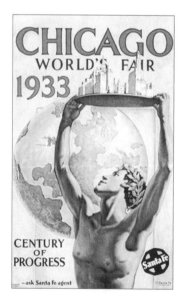

The Cox *was taking 250 Canadians from Port Arthur to an Exposition in Chicago when disaster struck.*

The trip from Chicago to Houghton on Michigan's Upper Peninsula went smoothly, with nothing more eventful than whatever was going on behind cabin doors. It seems that in spite of what jovial George had told the reporters, whiskey and women were aboard for those who wanted to partake of a little not-quite-clean fun. Should the lake rise up in sudden anger, the *Cox* had Captain George Johnson, a veteran Great Lakes skipper, on the bridge.

But not all on board the *George M. Cox* could boast of a record as impeccable as Johnson's. The first mate, a man named Cronk (Kronk), (see p. 205) had once been reprimanded for conduct unbecoming a ship's officer, and had his license suspended for ninety days. There would also be allegations that some of the crew on the *Cox* were drunk when the vessel passed through the locks at Sault Ste. Marie. But when the steamer docked at Houghton, George Cox had only praise for her seaworthiness and luxurious accommodations. "First class!" he told the press.

At about two p.m. on May 28, 1933, the *George M. Cox* left Houghton, cutting through the canal that bisects the Keweenaw Peninsula. It was a clear day with Lake Superior, as all would later recall, as calm as anyone had ever seen that body of water. The captain set a course for Rock of Ages, where the *Cox* would make a starboard turn for Port Arthur. Then he went below, leaving the bridge to First Mate Cronk.

As the *Cox* approached the Rock, fog rolled in, patchy at first, but then thick and enveloping. Cronk called the captain back to the bridge. Johnson said that the ship was off course and called for reduced speed (or so he later testified). The passengers were sitting down to dinner and the orchestra was playing what Nurse Keeling called "a dreamy waltz", when from somewhere out of the pea-soup came the blast of a foghorn.

From atop the Rock of Ages tower, lightkeeper John Soldenski tried to warn the Cox *with blasts of the foghorn.*

The wreck of the Cox *made front-page headlines, as shown in this Toronto newspaper.*

From his station in the lamp room atop the Rock of Ages tower, keeper John F. Soldenski saw the masts of an unknown ship that moved like a phantom through the grey cloud hanging over the gently rolling Superior waters. To his horror, he saw the masts turn as the ship changed direction and took a course aimed right at Rock of Ages.

Alarmed, Soldenski blew the warning signal on the foghorn. Still the ghostly ship came on. When the standard warning signal—a two-second blast every 28 seconds—failed to alert the vessel, Soldenski overrode it and sounded the danger signal—the foghorn version of "Red Alert!" But it seemed that whoever was in charge of the vessel ignored the signal. Sometime between 6:20 and 6:30 p.m. (no one could agree on the exact time), the gleaming white hull of the *George M. Cox* crashed into the immovable Rock of Ages.

Adeline Keeling later told the press that the passengers were having dinner and enjoying the music. "Everyone was happy. Then without warning there was a sickening crash and a deafening noise, followed by a second and louder one. I felt the boat turning over".

On impact, the bottom of the *Cox* was ripped open, and the prow shot high into the air, plunging the stern down into the water. Inside the ship,

(Above) The Cox *impaled on Rock of Ages. Ship's nurse Adeline Keeling said, "Everyone was happy. Then without warning there was a sickening crash...." (Right) Captain Johnson was cleared of any blame, but he never sailed again.*

furniture, dishes and people were thrown against walls and each other. In the galley, deckhand John Gancarz was severely burned by hot oil from the deep fryer. He would eventually die as a result of the scalding.

At first there was pandemonium within the *Cox*. The sounds of shattering glass and the screams of terrified people rent the air. Steam from broken pipes mixed with the swirling fog to create a hellish atmosphere.

In an interview with a Toronto reporter, Adeline Keeling said, "A buffet came charging across the hall and knocked me into a stateroom. Beatrice Cote, the stewardess, saw I was dazed, and pulled me out and helped me clamber up to the starboard deck. I looked back to see the stateroom I had just left filling with water". As Cote helped Keeling climb the steep incline to the deck, she herself was struck by flying furniture and received a painful back injury. Nonetheless, she was among the most helpful in getting people fitted with lifejackets and assisting them off the ship.

The *Cox* was listing at a 45-degree angle, but was impaled on the Rock. As it turned out, this was fortunate because if the ship had slid off the Rock she'd have sunk in minutes, taking dozens of people to a watery grave.

On the bridge, Captain Johnson sent out an SOS signal, then went out on deck to oversee an orderly evacuation of the ship. At the inquiry that was held later, he accused First Mate Cronk of abandoning his post in order to save his own skin, a charge that Cronk tearfully denied.

George Cox tried to calm the frightened passengers. "Naturally, the women started screaming", he said later. "I have a good, loud voice when I want to be heard, and I just told everybody to be quiet. 'We've hit something', I said, 'but we are going to get out all right'. The panic was soon over". When Captain Johnson came down from the bridge and began barking orders to passengers and crew, Cox repeated the skipper's instructions in his megaphone of a voice.

Crewmembers passed out life jackets and lowered the boats on the port side. (Those on the starboard side were rendered useless by the angle at which the ship was listing). Women, children and the most seriously injured were taken off first. Aside from the scalded Gancarz, the worst injury was a broken leg. One of the little boys was heard to tell his mother, "Don't cry, mamma. I'm having a swell time".

In the Rock of Ages lighthouse, John Soldenski and his three assistants leapt into action. They lowered their powerboat from its storage platform, then Soldenski pushed out into the thick fog. By the time he found the stricken *Cox*, all of the ship's company were huddled in five lifeboats and two rafts, George Cox and Captain Johnson being the last to leave the ship. Soldenski tossed them a line and towed them all back to the lighthouse.

The castaways spent a miserable night on Rock of Ages. They were cold and wet, and the small lighthouse could accommodate only a few at a time. They took turns going inside for warmth, but even in the tower it was cold. There had been no time to grab coats, so people shivered in their thin clothing. Off-duty crewmen had been in their bunks when the collision

Salvage operation at the wreck of the Cox. *The ship was stripped of all moveable property and equipment before it finally slid beneath the waves.*

happened, and escaped wearing only their underwear. For the sake of modesty, the maids gave the men their aprons to wrap around themselves.

Though she had her own aches and pains after being banged around in the wreck, Adeline Keeling became the heroine of the hour as she tended to the injured and tried to keep spirits up. The many cuts and bruises soon used up the lighthouse's first aid kit, so women tore up their slips to make bandages. There was little the nurse could do, though, for the badly burned Gancarz, who lay in agony. George Cox would have words of high praise for Keeling when he spoke to the press, saying that she had won the admiration of all with her tireless efforts to help the injured.

Soldenski and his assistants did what they could to help, passing out hot coffee and food from their small larder. But they were not provisioned to feed over a hundred people, and there was no liquor to provide a little inner warmth and relief from pain. To go back to the *Cox* for supplies was too dangerous, because the ship could have slipped off the rock at any moment.

The distress signal from the *Cox* had been picked up in Port Arthur and re-broadcast from there. At about 4:30 on the morning after the wreck, the lifeboat from Portage Station on the Keweenaw Peninsula arrived, and began ferrying some of the shipwrecked people to Washington Harbor on Isle Royale, where they could be temporarily lodged in the Singer Hotel. Two hours later the Coast Guard cutter *Crawford* arrived from the base at Two Harbors, Minnesota, 125 miles (201km) away. In spite of the fog, the *Crawford*'s skipper had powered his vessel at top speed to reach the site of the wreck. The freighter *Morris Tremaine* also responded to the distress call.

The *Crawford*'s commander wanted to take all of the refugees from the *Cox* aboard his vessel for the trip back to Houghton, but Nurse Keeling said that four of the injured, including her friend Beatrice Cote, needed immediate hospital care. They were transferred to the *Morris Tremaine* and taken to Fort William for treatment in St. Joseph's Hospital. Exhausted as she was, Keeling went with them. George Cox went, too, dutifully staying with the injured people until they were safe. His ship, valued at $150,000, was a total loss. But Cox took it all philosophically. "We can always get another boat".

While the *George M. Cox* lay in shattered splendour on Rock of Ages, all moveable property and equipment was salvaged. Within a year, the pounding of the surf did its work, and the wreck slid beneath the Superior waters. (The wreck is now a popular dive site. The bow is in 15 feet (4.5m) of water and the stern sits keel-up between depths of 50 and 90 feet (15 and 27m). At the inquest that was held in Houghton, Captain Johnson was absolved of any blame for the accident. He had heard the lighthouse's foghorn, but because fog can distort sound, he had made what was considered an understandable error in misjudging the direction from which the signal had come. Moreover, crewmen supported Johnson's claim that First Mate Cronk had put the *Cox* off course.

Captain Johnson was cleared, but the loss of a ship does not sit well with a skipper. The captain retired, and never sailed the Lakes again. If there was any responsibility for the sinking of the *Cox*, perhaps it lay with amiable George Cox himself, for courting bad luck by changing the ship's name.

PASSAGE ISLAND LIGHT: LIGHT ON THE FRONTIER

A DEAL BETWEEN NATIONS

The international line that divides Lake Superior between Canada and the United States lies where it does because Benjamin Franklin was a much sharper negotiator than his British counterparts. In the months following the Revolutionary War, when Great Britain and the newly independent United States were haggling over where the boundary should be drawn on the map of North America, Isle Royale did not appear to be of much value; at least as far as the British were concerned. It was a big, uninhabited rock, sitting off the North Shore of Lake Superior, far from anything that could be called civilization. The British, who would consistently show short-sightedness in their negotiations over the border between Canada and the United States, decided that if the damn-fool Yankees wanted that useless rock, they could have it.

Because Benjamin Franklin out-negotiated his British counterparts, mineral-rich Isle Royale went to the United States even though it is closer to Canada. A pinnacle on the island is named in Franklin's honour.

The Americans agreed to build a lighthouse on Passage Island (left) in Lake Superior, if the Canadians would build one on Colchester Reef (right) in Lake Erie. For ten years each country sat back and waited for the other to go first.

Franklin, on the other hand, believed there might be valuable iron and copper deposits there, and he was right. Thus Isle Royale, along with Passage Island and several other islets, became American territory in 1783, though it is only 18 miles (29km) from the Ontario shore. A high point on the island is called Mount Franklin in the great American's honour.

For many years, however, American ships rarely ventured anywhere near Isle Royale. Traffic going in and out of U.S. ports like Duluth tended to hug the south shore of the lake. But as the Canadian cities of Port Arthur and Fort William grew, and Canadian shipping on the northern part of Superior increased, the three-mile-wide (5-km) strait between Isle Royale and Passage Island became an important shortcut. It shaved 50 miles (80km) off the route between the Lakehead and Sault Ste. Marie. But it was a dangerous passage due to Canoe Rock and other reefs. The Canadians suggested that, as a gesture of goodwill, the Americans build a lighthouse on Passage Island.

Goodwill notwithstanding, lighthouses were expensive to build and operate. The Americans did not see why they should go to the trouble of constructing and maintaining a lighthouse that would benefit only Canadian ships. So, in the tradition of Ben Franklin, they decided to negotiate.

For a long time the Americans had wanted the Canadians to build a lighthouse at Colchester, on the Ontario side of Lake Erie, to help guide ships past a dangerous reef as they entered the Detroit River. The Canadians had considered a light at that location an unnecessary expense, and so had not acted on the American request. Now the United States said that if the Canadians would build the Colchester Light, as a gesture of goodwill, the Americans would put a lighthouse on Passage Island. The Canadians hemmed and hawed, discussed it among themselves in Ottawa, then hemmed and hawed some more. Finally, in 1870, they agreed to the American proposal. Then each side sat back and waited for the other to go first. After a decade, the exasperated Americans went to work, and on July 1 (Canada's Dominion Day), 1882, the lamp was lit on the 44-foot-high (13.4-m) Passage Island Light. It would be another three years before the Canadian government kept its end of the deal and built the Colchester Light, a 60-foot (18.2-m) wooden tower on a stone pier.

THE *ALGOMA* DISASTER

Like other light stations on vast, wild Superior, the one on Passage Island was a lonely place, especially so for American lightkeepers because even though the island was in American waters, the only ships they ever saw flew the Canadian flag. Still, the skippers of those vessels blew their whistles in friendly appreciation as they passed by. But even the light station with its beacon, fog bell and gas buoy did not always guarantee safe passage through the treacherous waterway. There were numerous wrecks, due to storms and to the fact that the high iron content in Isle Royale's rock played hell with ships' compasses. The most disastrous was that of the Canadian passenger steamer *Algoma*.

The Algoma, *considered a wonder in the 1880s, could reach a top speed of 16 knots.* Algoma *and sister ships* Alberta *and* Athabascan *were the first ships on the Great Lakes equipped with electric lights.*

The *Algoma* was one of three steel ships (the others were the *Athabascan* and the *Alberta*) built in Scotland in 1883 for the Canadian Pacific Railway. They crossed the Atlantic under their own steam. At Montreal they were cut in half amidships so they could be towed through the St. Lawrence Canal. They were reassembled at Buffalo, outfitted at Port Colborne, then sailed to their new home port of Owen Sound. In 1884 they went into passenger service between Owen Sound and Port Arthur (Thunder Bay).

These ships were considered marvels of the time. Each was 270 feet (82.2m) long and 38 feet (11.5m) in the beam. They were the first ships on the Great Lakes to be equipped with electric lights. They each had a capacity of 1,000 passengers. The *Algoma* was the first of the three to sail into Owen Sound's harbour, and people flocked to the waterfront to admire the big, new steamer (which was also equipped with sails). Tragically, the *Algoma*'s career was short-lived.

On November 5, 1885, the *Algoma* cleared port at Owen Sound for the regular run to Port Arthur. Due to the lateness of the season, there were only 11 passengers on board. But there were 530 tons of freight in the hold. The *Algoma* could reach a top speed of 16 knots, and by the night of November 6, Captain John I. Moore of Owen Sound had his ship slicing across Lake Superior.

After the Algoma *split in two, the forward section sank, but the aft section, with a handful of survivors clinging to it, remained on the rocks.*

That night a furious gale roared across the lake. It began as an icy rain, then turned into a blizzard that reduced visibility to zero. Captain Moore was a veteran skipper, but on this occasion he misjudged his ship's position.

(Left) Debris from the Algoma washed ashore (foreground). The aft section of the steamer can be seen in the background. (Below) The site of the wreck as it appears today, with no visible evidence of the disaster.

He thought he stood about 15 miles (24km) off Isle Royale, when in fact he was almost on top of it. He gave the order, "Put the wheel hard over to starboard". Just as the *Algoma* came about, a strong wind caught the ship and slammed the enormous hulk onto Greenstone Rock, one of the many outcroppings that lurk in the waters off the eastern tip of the big island. It was the morning of November 7. On that same day, the last spike was driven in the Canadian Pacific Railway. A day of national triumph was to be marred by tragedy.

The *Algoma*'s rudder and propeller were smashed, leaving the vessel helpless. Huge grey waves pounded the ship against the rocks and swept across the decks. Even the *Algoma*'s steel structure could not stand up to the monstrous weight of the crashing waves. The captain ordered the seacocks opened, hoping that by flooding the ship, he could settle her on a ledge. But the *Algoma* was doomed. The raging lake tore the steamer in two, and the forward half sank immediately, taking with it any souls unlucky enough to be in that part of the ship. The aft section was resting on some rocks, but waves continued to batter it and sweep over it. Screaming victims were carried off into the foaming seas.

Captain Moore did everything he could to save lives. He ordered lines of strong rope to be strung across the

Salvaging the aft section of the Algoma. The forward section has never been located.

deck, and urged everyone to hold on tight. He was everywhere on that piti-ful remnant of the once-proud *Algoma* as it shuddered and rolled with every violent blow Superior dealt it. He encouraged frightened people to hang on, not to give up hope. Help would come with daylight, he promised. Then a piece of cabin jarred loose and fell on him, leaving him badly hurt and pinned to the deck. Those who were near enough to him heard the captain pray for their safety.

When daylight came, the survivors could see that they were only sixty feet (18.2m) from land. But it was sixty feet of wild water seething around deadly rocks. Corpses rolled in the surf. The storm seemed to be subsiding a little, but the water still heaved and surged. Several of the crew tried to launch the one remaining lifeboat. It capsized almost at once. Most of the men crawled back onto the wreck, but a few hung onto the overturned lifeboat and were carried to the island.

There were now four or five men on the island, and eight or nine people still clinging to the stern of the *Algoma*. At any moment the waters could suck that piece of the ship down to join the forward section. But the storm still howled, and there was no way the remaining survivors could get off. There was nothing anybody could do but shiver in miserable cold and fear.

By Sunday morning the weather had improved enough for the men on the island to go in search of help. The people on the wreck, in the mean-time, began to make a raft out of pieces of shattered cabin. The crewmen on the island came back with some fishermen who were able to run a life-line out to the wreck. The crossing was not easy, but everyone still on the *Algoma*, including the injured captain, made it to safety. There were 14 sur-vivors. Forty-five passengers and crew had died.

DEATH OF THE *MONARCH*

Although the Passage Island Light had been in operation since 1882, the *Algoma* was wrecked too far from the lighthouse for the keeper to be aware of it and go to the survivors' assistance. Twenty-one years later a similar wreck would occur. This time there would be a lightkeeper nearby. And he would make a difference.

The *Monarch*, a 240-ft. (73-m) wooden propeller, left Port Arthur on December 6, 1906, bound for Sault Ste. Marie with ten passengers and a cargo of wheat, oats and flour. She had a crew of thirty, and her skipper, 38-year-old Captain Edward Robertson of Sarnia, was considered one of the best navigators on the Lakes. In many years of sailing, he had never had an accident. Indeed, the *Monarch* herself had a spotless record, with no mishaps. But Superior could be a vengeful lake, and on this voyage both ship and master would meet their match. As the *Monarch* embarked on the last scheduled run of the season, a blinding snowstorm shrouded Isle Royale and the Passage Island Light.

Captain Robertson had actually taken his ship safely through the passage, when severe weather on the open lake forced him to turn back and seek shelter. He saw two flashes of the Passage Island Light, and then lost it in the thick curtain of swirling snow. To make matters worse, his compass wouldn't work properly. He proceeded cautiously, but with no bearings to guide him, he was groping in the dark. At about 11:00 p.m. the people on the *Monarch* felt a terrific jolt as the ship struck a rock at the eastern end of Isle Royale, about five miles (8km) from the Passage Island Light. The hull was ripped open and water was pouring in. Almost immediately the ship began to list. Robertson knew that he had to get the passengers and crew off without delay.

The ship was about thirty feet (9m) from shore. Charles McLaughlin, brother of the first mate, offered to have a rope tied around his waist so that he could be swung from the *Monarch* to a projecting rock. The first attempt failed, and McLaughlin slammed hard against the side of the ship. On the second try the rope broke, and all on board thought that McLaughlin was lost. But he had managed to grab hold of the rock, and he laboriously pulled himself up. The crew tossed him another line, which he secured to a tree. Since the ship's yawl could take but a few people at a time, and no one could be sure how long the *Monarch* would remain afloat, some faced a harrowing, hand-over-hand crossing on the lifeline. One by one they stepped off the sinking ship and hung suspended in the black night. Stinging snow struck their faces while cold hands gripped the coarse rope. The wind tugged at their dangling bodies. Below, the dark, icy water swirled. One slip meant a plunge into oblivion. But each person to attempt this made it across and finally stepped onto solid ground.

Most of those who crossed in the yawl also reached safety, but there was one sailor who did not. Deckhand James Jacques was afflicted with a condition that caused him to suffer periodic spells of temporary near-blindness. At the time of the collision he was handicapped by such an attack, and could not see objects more than three feet away. After the passengers had been safely put ashore, Jacques was anxious to get off the ship quickly. In his panic, he thought that his shipmates were going to abandon him. Instead of waiting to be assisted into the yawl, he made a desperate jump for it—and missed. He plunged into the dark water, and did not come back up. His body was never found.

Captain Robertson stayed on the *Monarch* until the following morning so that he could take a thorough look around in the light. By that time only

The Monarch *and Captain Edward Robertson had spotless records that came to an end on the rocks of Isle Royale.*

fifty feet (15m) of the forward deck was above water. When he was certain that no one was left aboard, and once he had saved the ship's log, he went ashore. Soon the pilothouse was all that could be seen of the *Monarch*.

The passengers and crew were on solid ground, but they were far from being saved. Thirty-eight men and one woman—Mrs. Gregory, a stewardess—were stranded on Isle Royale in mid-December. The prospects of freezing or starving to death were very real. They could only huddle in the bush, and hope that help would come by soon. Their prospects looked poor at best. There might be no more ships this late in the season. If one did pass by, there was no guarantee that anyone would spot them. Without shelter or provisions, the survivors of the *Monarch* had little chance of surviving the winter. They might as well have been on an island in the Arctic.

They built a rough windbreak, but it provided scant protection from the icy blast of the gale. Friday dawned grey and bleak, with the storm still howling. After that first perishing night, one of the men found that he had some dry matches in his pocket. They lit a beacon fire, which they struggled to keep going in the snowstorm. But there was nobody else to see it. Even if Alexander Shaw or Klass Hamringa, the keepers at the Passage Island Lighthouse, had been looking in their direction, the snow would have hidden the light.

For yet another day and night the storm continued unabated, and several in the group began to feel the effects of frostbite. One of the passengers fell ill, apparently from pneumonia. The hours dragged by—cold, miserable hours that must have seemed endless. As fingers and toes, hands and feet became numb, hunger pangs began to bite from within. The castaways

The dreadful ordeal of the Monarch's *survivors was reported in newspapers across the country.*

managed to keep their fire burning, but dragging firewood drained what little strength they had. And still the wind knifed across the island. Not until Sunday morning did that relentless demon ease up a little on the forlorn camp at the rocky edge of Isle Royale.

That morning, with hunger gnawing as painfully as the cold, two or three of the crew risked going back to the *Monarch*. This was a dangerous undertaking, as the wreck was hanging on the rock and taking a pounding from the surf. She could have slipped off and sunk to the bottom at any moment. But this time fortune was kind. Though the ship was mostly submerged, the men were somehow able to salvage a bag of flour. How they extracted this treasure from the wreck was not recorded, but it was a lifesaver for the people on the island. Hardtack biscuits gave them some strength to battle yet another ordeal.

At last, on Sunday afternoon, three days after they'd been shipwrecked, they saw a small boat approaching! Lightkeepers Shaw and Hamringa had seen the smoke from their fire, and one of them rowed out to investigate. The seas were too rough for the lightkeeper to land on the island, and it seems that the castaways had lost their yawl, because one of them was compelled to perform a heroic act. Ship's Purser Reginald Beaumont, the only man who had any strength left, dived into the frigid

The tug Whalen, *shown here cutting through ice 32 inches (81 cm) thick, was sent to rescue the survivors stranded on Isle Royale.*

water and *swam* out to the lightkeeper. The water was cold enough to kill, but he reached the rowboat, climbed in, and explained what had happened.

With both men pulling on the oars, the rowboat made good time returning to the lighthouse. Not long after, the steamer *Edmonton* hove into sight of Passage Island. One of the keepers rowed out to her and told the skipper of the plight of the *Monarch*'s survivors. There was no way the *Edmonton* could approach that rocky shore of Isle Royale, so she carried the word to Port Arthur. This took time, and for the almost delirious people on Isle Royale, every minute counted. One man was already deathly ill, and the rest were reaching the end of their endurance.

Two tugs, the *Whalen* and the *Grace*, were dispatched from Port Arthur to pick up the Isle Royale castaways. The band of haggard survivors cheered when they saw rescue at hand, but their privations were not over yet. Rough seas and the rocky shoreline at that eastern end of Isle Royale made it impossible for the tugs to land. There was, in fact, only one place at that end of the island that a vessel could safely approach: Linis Harbor, on the north side of the island. The *Monarch* had been wrecked on the south side. The tugs signalled that information to Captain Robertson.

Now the wretched survivors had a brutal, three-hour trek north through deep snow ahead of them. Those who were able, carried the man who was too sick to walk. Some of them, by this point, were losing their minds. They wanted only to lie down in the snow and go to sleep. But to fall asleep in the bitter cold was to surrender to death, and Edward Robertson wouldn't permit it. He had already lost one man, and that was one man too many. He hauled stragglers to their feet and told them to get moving. All during that torturous hike across the eastern tip of Isle Royale he barked orders, pushed people forward, threatened them with physical violence if they did not keep walking. There could be no stopping, no resting. Some members of the group undoubtedly cursed Robertson, but he was saving their lives. He himself had a frozen foot and a frozen hand, but he kept the stumbling band moving, and he did not lose a single person as they tramped their way through unbroken drifts of snow.

At last the *Monarch* survivors reached Linis Harbor, a small, natural anchorage in the vicinity of what is now called The Pallisades. There, the *Whalen* and the *Grace* were waiting for them. There was food on board, and doctors. In addition to frostbite, the physicians had to treat burns caused when some of the survivors, in their terrible condition, had fallen into the fire. Mrs. Gregory fainted as soon as she was taken aboard ship. Several of the men just paced back and forth and wept. After such a horrible ordeal, it must have been hard to believe that within a few hours they would be safe in Fort William.

The *Monarch* was written off as a total loss, and no attempt was made to raise the wreck. The steamer eventually broke up and slid into deep water, and still lies there today. Captain Robertson was not found to be in any way at fault for the wreck. He was, in fact, highly praised for his leadership. A banquet was held in Port Arthur in his honour. Later, there was a big reception for Robertson and all of the *Monarch*'s crew in their home port of Sarnia.

Accounts of the wreck of the *Monarch* and the rescue of the survivors say only that the Passage Island lightkeeper found them, and alerted the *Edmonton*. His name is not recorded at all. We know however from the list of keepers who served at Passage Island that Alexander Shaw was the head keeper there from 1893 until 1907, and Klass Hamringa was an assistant at the light from 1905 to 1908. One of them had to have been the man in the small boat that Beaumont swam out to. We know little more about these men, except that had they not been there, the wreck of the *Monarch* might have been a tragedy equal in scope to the loss of the *Algoma*. One might say that the lightkeeper in question was only doing the job for which he was paid, but on that occasion an American on a remote island in Lake Superior was the difference between life and death for some very fortunate Canadians.

PERIL ON THE WATER: COMMUTING AS A LIFE AND DEATH STRUGGLE

For many lightkeepers posted at remote locations, the most hazardous time of year was the close of the navigation season in December. Though occasionally lightkeepers wintered at the lighthouse, most chose not to. They had to make their way through foul weather and ice-choked water to their winter residences. This was especially true for Canadian lightkeepers, whose government frequently left them to their own resources as far as transportation home was concerned. But American lightkeepers, too, could find themselves in trouble when bad weather prevented tenders from reaching them.

Superior had the worst reputation for turning a routine journey home into a nightmare. Lightkeepers there generally had the longest distances to travel, winter temperatures were colder there than elsewhere on the Lakes, and it had the longest stretches of sparsely populated shoreline. All these factors combined to make the journey home a race with disaster.

ST. IGNACE LIGHT

The St. Ignace Light on tiny Talbot Island in northern Lake Superior was the first Canadian lighthouse on the lake. Talbot Island lies east of the southern tip of the much larger St. Ignace Island. According to Ojibwa legend, Talbot Island was cursed ground. But that didn't stop the government from erecting a white, wooden lighthouse there to warn ships of some nearby shoals. In 1867 William Perry became the first keeper. At the time, it was so remote that there were no sizeable Canadian towns on Lake Superior at all—the nearest was Sault Ste. Marie on the St. Marys River, about 200 miles (322km) to the southeast.

Perry lived there alone, and put in that first season apparently without mishap. At the end of November he set out in a small boat for the Hudson's Bay Company post at Nipigon on Superior's North Shore, over 25 miles (40km) away.

Perry's first season at St. Ignace was also his last. He never reached the Hudson's Bay post. In the spring of 1868, Perry's body and his boat were found on the shore of Nipigon Bay. He had evidently frozen to death.

Misfortune of a different sort befell Thomas Lamphier and his wife, who succeeded Perry at St. Ignace (see p.256). In 1872, Andrew Hynes took over the St. Ignace Light. Like Perry, he lived there alone. Also like Perry, he evidently put in an uneventful season. Then the shipping season closed, and Hynes shut down the lighthouse for the winter. He set off in a

Every lightkeeper at the short-lived St. Ignace Lighthouse met with disaster. This lighthouse at Killarney on Georgian Bay was built in the same style as the one at St. Ignace.

(Left) These foundation stones are all that remain of the "Lighthouse of Doom".
(Right) Talbot Island. Ojibwa legend said it was cursed.

small boat for Silver Islet, a community along the North Shore, 60 miles (96.5km) southwest of Talbot.

The weather was clear when he started, but as often happens on Lake Superior, it suddenly turned stormy. Hynes' journey took 18 wind-blown, frigid days. When he finally reached Silver Islet, he was so wasted by hunger and ravaged by frostbite that he died within a few days. After Hynes' death, the government abandoned the St. Ignace Light, which by that time was being called "The Lighthouse of Doom".

PASSAGE ISLAND LIGHT: WINTER OF HUNGER

In 1883 W.F. Demant was the keeper of the Passage Island Light, on a small island three miles (4.8km) off the northeastern tip of Isle Royale. It was the northernmost American lighthouse on the Great Lakes, and much closer to the Canadian mainland than to the American shore. Unlike Perry and Hynes, Demant was not alone at his isolated station. He had with him his Chipewyan wife and three children. Demant intended to spend the winter at the lighthouse, but had to go to Port Arthur, Ontario, to purchase supplies. When the shipping season closed, Demant set out for the mainland, leaving his family on Passage Island. He probably expected to be absent for no more than a week.

While Demant was in Port Arthur, severe cold fell upon the North Superior country, and treacherous ice conditions made his return to Passage Island impossible. Demant could do nothing but wait out the winter in Port Arthur while he worried about the safety of his family. He was well aware that his wife knew how to look after herself and the children in what was really a wilderness camp, but how were they going to find food on frozen Passage Island?

Passage Island Lighthouse. W.F. Demant's wife and children spent a winter of near-starvation here while the lightkeeper was stranded in Port Arthur.

Out on that rocky island, Mrs. Demant and the children spent lonely months battling against cold and hunger. There was plenty of wood for fires, but chopping firewood expended a lot of energy, and it is difficult to keep up one's strength when food is in short supply. When Mrs. Demant and the children had used up the scanty supplies in the station, they turned to snaring and fishing. They evidently had no gun.

In order to catch fish, they would have had to chop through the ice, another chore that sapped a person's strength. They caught rabbits in their snares, but only enough, it seems, to keep barely alive. By the time Demant was able to return with provisions in the spring of 1884, his wife and children were close to starvation.

CARIBOU ISLAND: BLEAK CHRISTMAS

The close of the 1904 shipping season was the setting for a drama on Lake Superior that the Toronto *Globe* called "no unusual chapter in the history of lightkeepers on the lakes". Such a statement was typical of newspaper reporting of the time. The Great Lakes—especially Superior, so far from "civilization"—were a constant source for the tales of shipwrecks, privation and daring-do that the papers liked to feed to an adventure-hungry public. Lightkeepers were seen as romantic figures, along with cowboys, ship captains and other adventurers.

The story to which the *Globe* referred took place at Caribou Island in eastern Lake Superior. The lighthouse, actually on a rock just off the main island, is the most isolated light on the Great Lakes. In the week before Christmas, the tug *Reid* picked up the Canadian keepers of the lights at

The Reid (left), *the tug that rescued the keepers of the Caribou Island Lighthouse on Christmas Eve, 1904.*

Gargantua and Otter Island, and the American keepers of Victoria and Passage Island Lights, then went to pick up the keepers at Caribou Island. However, when the captain of the tug signalled the lighthouse, he received no response. Because of ice, the tug could not go right up to the island. From where his boat sat out on the lake, the lighthouse appeared deserted. The *Reid* went back to Sault Ste. Marie, where the skipper reported the situation.

There was concern now over the safety of lightkeeper W.O. Demers and his assistant Fred Pelletier. The *Reid* went back to the island, the captain hoping to land men on the rock. But a heavy fog rolled in and he was unsuccessful. Once again the tug returned to port. Another tug, the *Boynton*, signalled the Caribou Light while passing the island en route from the Lakehead to the Soo, but received no response. The skipper assumed that the keepers had already been picked up. Ice and fog still prevented any approach to the lighthouse.

Now it was assumed that Demers and Pelletier had left the lighthouse on their own. A search was made of Caribou Island and of the Superior shore as far as Michipicoten. There was no sign of the two men, and their families feared the worst.

Actually, Demers and Pelletier were *in* the lighthouse. When the *Reid* first signalled, instead of responding, the two keepers had gone inside to shut things down and pack up their gear for the trip home. Then, when the tug departed, they assumed that they were being left to winter at their lonely outpost on provisions of half a barrel of flour and a supply of frozen fish. Not expecting to see another ship until spring, they were unprepared to respond to signals when the *Reid* returned and when the *Boynton* passed by.

A barren rock in the middle of ice-strewn North Superior is a desolate place in the dead of winter. Demers and Pelletier would have had a desperate time of it if they'd been obliged to wait out the long, cold months. But the skipper of the *Reid* decided to try one more time. He took aboard "special equipment", as the *Globe* called it, for docking at an ice-encrusted rock, and set out on December 23. Newspapers were telling their readers that there was little hope of the men being found alive.

By noon on Christmas Eve, the *Reid* was as near the rock as the skipper dared go. The captain was preparing an assault on the ice with the men and equipment he had brought for the purpose, when he saw a small boat cutting through the icy water in a frantic dash for the *Reid*. The two men in it were soon aboard the tug. Demers was so overcome with emotion at being rescued, that he sat on the deck and cried. It was not for himself that he wept, he said, but for his wife and children. His family would endure a bleak Christmas before they learned the next day that he was alive.

ROCK OF AGES

Twenty-two years later, the skipper of another tender met with a surprise when he arrived at a lighthouse to pick up the keepers. On Friday, December 17, 1926, the captain of a tug sent to Rock of Ages Lighthouse found the station deserted and a note pinned to the door. Lightkeeper Emil Mueller, assistants Robert Marrow, Colin McKay, and a third unidentified assistant, were gone. Due to bad weather that had prevented supply ships from reaching the Rock, they had run out of fuel and food and had endured a week with no tobacco. After four days with nothing to eat, and fearful that they might starve before help could reach them, they had decided to take their chances in an open boat on wind-tossed Superior. It was uncertain how long it had been since the men abandoned the lighthouse.

In December, 1926, the lightkeepers on Rock of Ages had a choice: face starvation, or brave Lake Superior in an open boat.

When news of the men's departure reached the mainland, the Coast Guard tender *Marigold* was sent out to look for them, but found nothing. Newspaper reports on the men's chances for survival were not hopeful. Even if they reached land, the Superior shore was a hostile place in winter.

Then, on December 20, Robert Marrow limped into Duluth, exhausted and starving. He and his companions had crossed the open water and come ashore somewhere between Duluth and Grand Portage, 150 miles (241km) to the northeast. They made their way by boat down the ice-bound shore until they came to a place called Pigeon Point. There they went ashore, probably because the lake was becoming too rough for them to continue on to Duluth by boat. Of the four, only Marrow was able to continue on. Leaving the others at Pigeon Point—probably in an abandoned fishing camp—Marrow hiked for miles through waist-deep snow until he reached Duluth, and told authorities where the other men could be found. Despite the harrowing ordeal, records show that Mueller, McKay and Marrow were back at Rock of Ages the following year.

GEORGE JOHNSTON: LONELY CARIBOU ISLAND

With the coming of spring, winter does not easily relinquish its chill grip on Lake Superior. Weeks after the ice has gone out of the other Great Lakes, large pans of it still drift around Superior, presenting a hazard to shipping. And devastating storms can blow in at anytime. In the heyday of the light-keepers, this could make the journey *to* the lighthouse at the opening of the navigation season just as dangerous as the trip *from* the station after ship-ping had closed. Moreover, some of the Superior lighthouses were among the most inaccessible on the Lakes. One such was Caribou Island Light.

If Michigan's Stannard Rock Light could lay claim to the title "The Most Lonely Place in America", then the Caribou Island Light could make a sim-ilar claim for Canada. It was, in fact, 65 miles (104.6km) from the nearest port, even farther out than Stannard. The one advantage Caribou had over the Rock was a small island on which the lightkeeper could stretch his legs a little. (The Caribou Light is actually on an acre of rock a short distance from the main island.)

It took a tough, resourceful brand of keeper to manage the light in this remote, windswept corner of Lake Superior. George Johnston, the keeper there from 1912 to 1922, was just the right man for the job. The isolation did not bother him, he was no stranger to hard work, and he had the guts and the brains to handle any crisis that might arise. In his first season at the Caribou Light, Johnston discovered that he had forgotten to bring along his rifle, though he had plenty of ammunition. Without a gun to bring down

Though American Coastguardsmen called Stannard Rock, "the most lonely place in America", Canada's Caribou Island Light is even farther from the nearest port. (Inset) George Johnston, lightkeeper at Caribou Island for over a decade, warned the Canadian government that the Lambton *was not adequate as a tender. He refused to go aboard the boat.*

game, his family would have to get by on a steady diet of fish. Instead of moaning, Johnston used materials at hand to put together a homemade rifle that worked just fine. It may not have been a Winchester, but it put meat on the table. When Johnston broke his leg in an accident, he set the bone himself, and then splinted the leg. He made himself a pair of crutches and a peg leg to get around on so he could resume his duties. The word "can't" was not part of his vocabulary.

During his years at the Caribou Light, George Johnston helped ships in distress, endured the furies of Lake Superior, and faithfully kept the beacon lit. He did all that was asked of a lightkeeper, and then some. But he must have been stunned when, in 1915, he received a letter from the Canadian government informing him that, in an effort to cut costs, Ottawa would no longer provide a ship to take lightkeepers to and from their stations at the start and end of the navigation season. The decision was made by people who did not understand that telling the lightkeeper of a remote station like Caribou Island to cross 65 miles of turbulent, frigid Lake Superior at the most deadly times of the year, in the station's small, open boat, was like inviting him to play Russian roulette with a revolver that had five loaded chambers. Meanwhile, on the American side, a fleet of fine vessels known

The resourceful Johnston converted a sailing sloop (left) into an engine-driven boat (right). In this vessel, Johnston and his assistant endured an eight-day ordeal of storms and ice on Lake Superior.

as light tenders carried lightkeepers to and from their stations.

But Johnston was not a man to complain. He converted his sailing sloop to a boat that was driven by a kerosene engine, and added a cabin with a coal-fired heater. It was the best he could do, but Superior proved too tough an adversary. In 1919, because of bad weather, Johnston and his assistant were stranded on the island a full ten days past the close of the navigation season. They finally left on Christmas Day and headed for Quebec Harbour, a fishing station on Michipicoten Island, 30 miles (48km) north, where they intended to put in for the night. Another storm arose however, and dangerous ice conditions around the island forced Johnston to withdraw to open water. For eight nerve-wracking days the little boat was buffeted by wind and ice as it drifted with the sea anchor out, totally at the mercy of the elements. The men were finally able to make it to the mainland once the storm died down, but it was a hellish way to bring in the New Year.

THE LOSS OF THE *LAMBTON*

A few years later, in 1922, George Johnston gave up his lightkeeping position at Caribou to become a fog alarm inspector. His replacement, George Penefold, was outraged when he learned that the government expected him to travel between the mainland and the island in a small boat. He wrote letters of protest that finally convinced the stubborn government in Ottawa to deliver the lightkeepers to their stations by ship, as the Americans had been doing all along. The choice of a vessel, however, was questionable.

Four unidentified men (two in the pilothouse) pose on the Lambton. *One critic said that the* Lambton *had been "wished on the government" during the war.*

(Left) Sailors said the Lambton *was too small for the job, and didn't answer the helm well in bad weather. (Below) In sub-zero weather, spray coated everything with ice, making equipment difficult to operate and decks treacherous.*

The *Lambton,* 108 feet (32.9m) long and 25 (7.6) in the beam, was a propeller-driven ship built at Sorel, Quebec in 1909. One Great Lakes historian has described her as "a tough little tug", very seaworthy and manoeuvrable. But in an article published in 1922, the Toronto *Globe* said that the *Lambton* had been "wished on the government during the war" (probably meaning that during the war the government had been forced to put almost anything that floated into service) and that, in the opinion of experienced seamen, she was too small for the work assigned to her. One man who had sailed in the *Lambton* said that she didn't answer the helm very well in bad weather.

George Johnston wasn't impressed when he saw the ship. Because she rode low in the water, the steering quadrant was exposed to freezing spray. Johnston actually saw the crew chopping ice from the steering cable, not at all a comforting sight. He and his wife both wrote to the government, telling the men in charge about these problems. Johnston also pointed out that the *Lambton*'s lifeboats were kept on the uppermost deck, and that in an emergency the crew might not be able to reach them. But they didn't listen to Johnston, despite his experience. Johnston refused to go aboard the *Lambton* in the spring of 1922. But George Penefold, who had complained about being sent to the Caribou Light in a small boat, probably felt that he had no choice. He had demanded a ship, and

The crew of the Glenlivet *were among the last people to see the* Lambton *before the tender vanished.*

At about 10:30 a.m., April 18, 1922, the *Lambton*, in the charge of Captain Alex Brown, sailed from Sault Ste. Marie, Ontario, with Penefold on board, as well as lightkeepers going to Ile Parisienne and Michipicoten Island. There were, in all, 22 men on board. The decks were piled high with supplies for the lighthouses. In the company of the steamers *Glenfinnan* and *Glenlivet*, the *Lambton* sailed out into Whitefish Bay for an appointment with destiny.

The bay had been relatively free of ice, but strong winds now blew drifting packs of it in from the main body of the lake. Soon the winds were blowing gale force and carrying snow. The *Glenfinnan* became stuck in the ice, and the *Lambton* went to her assistance. In the course of breaking the *Glenfinnan* free, the *Lambton* collided with the larger ship. According to a report made later by the captain of the *Glenfinnan*, the *Lambton* was not damaged in the accident. But before the three vessels could put the icefield behind them, the *Lambton* broke her steering gear. The crew jury-rigged a substitute steering mechanism by attaching lines directly to the rudder quadrant. If, as that other sailor had claimed, the *Lambton* was already difficult to manoeuvre in bad weather, this makeshift repair would render her very vulnerable indeed.

With the sailing conditions on the lake steadily deteriorating, the *Glenfinnan* and the *Glenlivet* changed course and made for the shelter of Whitefish Point. But the *Lambton* pressed on. Why, is anybody's guess. Perhaps Captain Brown believed it to be of the utmost importance that he deliver Penefold and the other lightkeepers to their stations without delay. Maybe he wanted to prove that George Johnston and the others had been wrong about his ship. Whatever the reasons for the captain's decision, it was a bad one.

There were only brief glimpses of the *Lambton* between the time she part-ed company with the *Glenfinnan* and the *Glenlivet*, and the moment that she was officially declared "missing". The steamers *Osler* and *Westmount* reported sighting her on April 19th, about 40 miles (64km) from Whitefish Point, just before the worst of the gales roared in. The steamer *Midland Prince* saw the *Lambton* on the afternoon of the same day. Both ships were battling against a powerful southeast wind. Then the direction of the tempest suddenly shifted to the southwest. The resulting cross-seas, said the skipper of the *Midland Prince*, were among the worst he had ever seen. It had been all he could do to keep his own ship and crew from going to the bottom. When the gale had blown itself out, the *Lambton* was nowhere to be seen.

J.N. Arthurs, the Canadian Superintendent of Lights, received word on April 23 that the lights on Ile Parisienne and Caribou Island were not in operation. The *Lambton* had not been seen for days. Arthurs immediately ordered a search. He himself was aboard the steamer *G.R. Gray* that set out to look for the missing ship. Though he hoped to find survivors in a boat or camped somewhere on the shore, he took along replacement lightkeepers in case his worst fears were realized. The pack ice in Whitefish Bay was still so thick that the *G.R. Gray* had to follow in the wake of a large freighter to make it through.

Arthurs searched for five days, and found no trace of the *Lambton*. No bodies, no debris, nothing! Lighthouse keepers all along the Canadian shore were instructed to keep a lookout for any sign of the vessel. On the American side, the U.S. Coast Guard cutter *Cook* made a sweeping search. Then Arthurs received word that the freighter *Valcartier* had spotted what appeared to be the top of a pilothouse in the water, about 25 miles (40km) southeast of Michipicoten Island and 15 miles (24km) east of Caribou. That ship's wheelsman had sailed on the *Lambton* the previous year, and said he was certain it was her pilothouse.

On May 9 the tug *Reliance*, with George Johnston aboard, found one of the *Lambton*'s lifeboats about twenty miles (32km) southeast of Michipicoten Island. The lifeboat was empty, and its air tanks had been crushed. This indicated that the lifeboat had sunk with the ship and that in the great depths the tanks had collapsed under pressure before the little boat broke loose and rose to the surface.

The wreck of the *Lambton* has never been found, and what exactly hap-pened to her remains a mystery. From the slim amount of evidence, it seems that the ship lost her ability to steer, and in that crippled condition was no match for Superior. The men evidently could not get to the lifeboats, and so had gone down with their ship. Lightkeeper George Penefold had died in the line of duty before he could even reach his lighthouse.

(Top) George Johnston's wife, Louise, and their infant son, Pat, in 1912. Johnston, who was a wizard at fashioning useful items out of materials at hand, made the baby's swinging cradle from a meat basket. (Left) The Caribou Island light tower. George Penefold never made it to his post. (Right) Young Pat with the Johnston family's pet eagles. The bird on the left just had an accidental dunking in the lake. The eagles were eventually given to the Toronto Zoo.

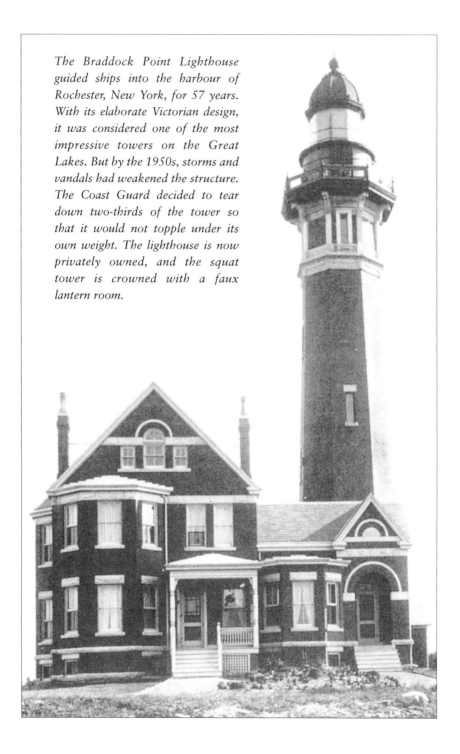

The Braddock Point Lighthouse guided ships into the harbour of Rochester, New York, for 57 years. With its elaborate Victorian design, it was considered one of the most impressive towers on the Great Lakes. But by the 1950s, storms and vandals had weakened the structure. The Coast Guard decided to tear down two-thirds of the tower so that it would not topple under its own weight. The lighthouse is now privately owned, and the squat tower is crowned with a faux lantern room.

PART SEVEN
AROUND THE LAKES

The Mississagi Strait lighthouse on Manitoulin Island in Lake Huron is connected to French explorer La Salle, and one of the earliest mysteries on the Great Lakes. His barque, the Griffon, *was built in 1678 and vanished the following year. In the 1930s, artifacts from a shipwreck near the Mississagi Strait lighthouse were sent to marine specialists in Paris, France. They confirmed that the wreck's iron bolts were of a manufacture consistent with those used at the time that La Salle had the* Griffon *constructed. The Mississagi Strait wreck could be the remains of the* Griffon, *but the claim has also been made for several other wrecks.*

ALONE WITH THEIR DEAD

In his famous ballad, "The Cremation of Sam McGee", Robert W. Service tells in poetic rhyme the tall tale of a man in a rather morbid situation. While the man and his partner, Sam McGee, are searching for gold in the Yukon, Sam dies, leaving the man with the unpleasant task of lugging a corpse all over the countryside until he can find a place to cremate it, in accordance with Sam's dying request. Service's yarn is, of course, an exercise in dark humour. The situation was much more serious for people at remote locations on the Great Lakes. A death at a lighthouse could pose a very unsettling problem for the colleagues or family of the deceased. At some locations, the grieving people had no place to give the body a decent burial. And sometimes, adverse weather conditions prevented them from taking the remains to a nearby community cemetery for interment.

Such was the case for the keeper at Giants Tomb Island, that mysterious monolith rising out of southern Georgian Bay. For 22 years in the early 1900s, Alfred H. Griffith and his wife kept the light at the southern end of the island. On the great rock that was often shrouded by fog, they lived with only each other's company in a small white frame house attached to a 40-foot (12.1-m) tower. In the summer there were frequent visits from tourists, because the big rock was one of the best known attractions in Georgian Bay. But for the rest of the year it was a lonely place.

Alfred Griffith and his wife on Giants Tomb Island in Georgian Bay. When Mrs. Griffith passed away, Alfred kept a solitary vigil over her body while a storm raged for three days.

LIGHTHOUSE KEEPER ALONE THREE DAYS WITH HIS DEAD

Alfred Griffith Stormbound on Giant's Tomb Rock Following Death of Wife—Tended the Lamps Together for 22 Years

(Special Despatch to The Globe.)

Midland, Nov. 16.—Mrs. Alfred H. Griffith, wife of the keeper of the lighthouse at the Giant's Tomb, died last Friday night. Owing to heavy weather, it was not until last night that her husband succeeded in The island, or rock known as the Giant's Tomb, upon which Mr. Griffith was left for three days and three nights with the body of his wife, is one of the most conspicuous in the waters of the Georgian Bay. Around it a great deal of Indian lore

Tales of lighthouses and their keepers, including melancholy accounts of lonely deaths, were always of interest to the public.

The nearest neighbours were 12 miles (19km) away, and only the occasional freighter passed by.

After more than two decades of working at her husband's side, Mrs. Griffith passed away in November 1920. A storm was blowing, and Alfred was unable to leave the island to seek assistance. For three long days he was alone with his grief and the remains of his beloved wife; the sole mourner at a lonesome wake.

Some twenty years later, at the Patterson Island Light in the Slate Islands off Superior's North Shore, lightkeeper Charlie Lockwood died suddenly. His wife was left all alone, and had no way of contacting the mainland from the remote station. The bereaved Mrs. Lockwood had to keep her late husband's remains in a shed until spring, when she could arrange a proper burial on the mainland.

Another situation occurred on the American side of eastern Lake Ontario. In late March 1932 at the Galloo Island Lighthouse, just off Sackets Harbor, New York, assistant lightkeeper William E. Framer died suddenly. Lightkeeper Robert Graves and another assistant, William Friedsberg, placed the body in a boat and set out for Framer's home in Cape Vincent, New York, the point at which Lake Ontario drains into the St. Lawrence River. It should have been an easy trip, but ice conditions were terrible. The men couldn't get through to Cape Vincent, or return to

Galloo Island. They were forced to land on Grenadier Island, about seven miles (11km) off Cape Vincent. There, according to a newspaper headline of the time, they were "Marooned With Corpse" for two days before the U.S. Coast Guard finally picked them up.

TALBOT ISLAND: CURSED GROUND

Perhaps the saddest incident of one person being left in the company of the dead took place at the St. Ignace Light on Talbot Island in northern Lake Superior. Thomas Lamphier was hired as the keeper of the St. Ignace Light in 1868, following the demise of the first keeper, William Perry (see p.239). Local Ojibwa said that Talbot Island, a narrow, rocky, spit of land, was haunted by evil spirits, and they generally stayed away from it. The misfortune that had befallen Mr. Perry had done nothing to alter official skepticism for Native "superstition", and so the government looked for a replacement.

Thomas Lamphier was well qualified for the job. For twenty years he had sailed Lake Superior on Hudson's Bay Company schooners. He knew the North Superior country and what it took to survive in it. The St. Ignace Lighthouse, a white, square wooden tower, was the first Canadian lighthouse on Lake Superior. The American shore of the lake was already relatively well lit, with eight lights in operation. But settlement and development had been slower on the more remote Canadian shore, and so traffic on that part of the lake had been lighter.

Lamphier moved into the lighthouse with his Native wife, who was also his unpaid assistant. Mrs. Lamphier's first name does not seem to have been recorded, although we know she was from the shores of Hudson Bay. She would be well acquainted with severe cold and with life in a wilderness location. According to legend, Mrs. Lamphier was a raven-haired beauty. More importantly, she was a strong woman who could handle the rigours of the job.

Thomas Lamphier's grave on Bowman Island, about a mile (1.6km) from Talbot Island, where he died. Mrs. Lamphier had been obliged to wrap the body in canvas and wedge it in a cleft in the rocks behind the lighthouse until spring.

After the navigation season ended, Lamphier and his wife planned to spend the winter on the island in order to avoid the dangerous journey back to civilization. The government had enlarged the lightkeeper's house, and had winterized both it and the tower. All boded well for the St. Ignace Light.

The navigation season passed without incident. Husband and wife kept the station in good order. The little contact they had with the outside world came from sailors who waved from the occasional passing ship. Freeze-up came, and they settled in for the long winter. Then Thomas suddenly fell ill. There was no nearby settlement to which Mrs. Lamphier could go in search of a doctor. And the remedies she administered proved not to help. Lamphier sank deeper into the clutches of whatever malady had seized him, and finally died.

Now Mrs. Lamphier was left with solitude. There was no one to talk to, no one with whom to share her grief. Moreover, there was no one to share the workload of all the daily chores. And if she herself should fall ill or be injured, no one else would know. It must have seemed as though she were the only person in the world.

Mrs. Lamphier also had a body that she could not bury. There was simply no place to dig a grave in the rocky, frozen ground. She wrapped Thomas in a canvas sail from their small boat, and wedged the body into a cleft in the rocks behind the lighthouse. For the rest of the long winter she did not see another living human being. Such absolute solitude has been known to drive some people mad.

When spring arrived, a party of Ojibwa passing by in their canoes saw a woman signalling to them from the shore of Talbot Island. In spite of their fear of the place, they landed. They were met by Lamphier's widow, now a thin, haggard woman. Her black hair had turned completely white. "The winter took it", she said of her lost beauty.

The Ojibwa took the body of Thomas Lamphier to Bowman Island, about a mile away, and buried it there, marking the grave with a small white cross. Within a few years, after yet another lightkeeper died under horrendous circumstances, the St. Ignace Lighthouse would be abandoned. The elements would destroy the wooden structures, and eventually even the stone foundation would be virtually erased, leaving little evidence that human beings had ever lived there. Talbot Island would be left with its legacy of a curse and untimely death. Some local fishermen claimed that at night the ghost of a long-haired woman wandered the island, as though in search of something. But whether Talbot Island was haunted or not, the St. Ignace Light entered the lore of the Great Lakes as "The Lighthouse of Doom".

(Top) Freighter covered with ice in the fall. Spray and waves breaking over a vessel formed what sailors called "little ice devils". The name sounds almost playful, but the ice was, in fact, deadly. Its sheer weight could cause a ship to sink like a rock.

(Middle) Lighthouses, too, became entombed in ice, as shown here with the Port Colborne Light, and the Cleveland West Pierhead Light (bottom), both on Lake Erie.

Ice gives an other-worldly appearance to the Oswego Lighthouse on Lake Ontario.

From 1938 to 1946, Arnold Wing and his family tended the light on Double Top Island at the Western Islands in Georgian Bay. They compiled a lightkeeping family's photo-journal. (Top) Steamers cutting through the ice as they head for open water in the spring. (Middle) The Wing family makes its way across the ice to the lighthouse on Double Top Island. (Bottom) Arnold Wing at the lighthouse in late fall. The ice turned the island into a steep mound, requiring the use of cleats. Water from the lake had to be hauled up the slope in a bucket attached to a rope. By the time the bucket reached the top, it was often empty.

(Top left) The Wings arrive at the island with their belongings. The tender St. Heliers *is in the background. (Top right) Arnold, Lillian, Beth and Lois Wing being lowered from the* St. Heliers. *(Left) A lighthouse family poses in front of their tower.*

THE STORM OF 1905: GUIDING LIGHTS

As previous chapters have illustrated, sailing the Great Lakes has always been a perilous business. Even with the installation of lights at the danger points, ships have foundered, capsized, collided with each other, or simply been overwhelmed by the sheer power of the freshwater seas. The thousands of wrecks that litter the bottoms of these giant lakes are chilling evidence of that. But for every vessel that lies in silent ruin in the murky depths, there have been thousands of others that have passed safely in darkness, fog and storm because of a lighthouse. Their voyages are little noted, outside of entries in captains' logs, because there is nothing remarkable to catch the public's attention. The account of one such voyage provides a dramatic picture of a vessel making it through a journey fraught with danger, thanks to the presence of lighthouses and the people who kept the beacons shining.

Most Great Lakes historians agree that the Big Blow of 1913 was the worst storm on record. But in terms of savage sailing conditions, the infamous gale of 1905 would be a close runner-up. That storm turned the Upper Lakes into witches' cauldrons that sucked down ships and men, or hurled vessels against rocks to be shattered like glass ornaments. It was a gale of which old timers still spoke in superlatives over half a century later, telling awe-struck younger sailors that they were on the

A funeral procession in Goderich, Ontario, on Lake Huron, after the "Big Blow" of November 1913.

Bodies from the steamer Wexford *washed ashore near Goderich after the Big Blow. Note ship's name on the life-jacket on the corpse in the foreground. Knowing what ship a man had been on could help investigators to identify the dead.*

The Charles S. Price, *shown in this composite photo afloat and as an over-turned wreck, was one of at least 17 ships sunk or stranded on November 11, 1913. The* Price *drifted as a "mystery ship" for six days before identification was finally made. The storm of November 1905 was a close runner-up to 1913's Big Blow in terms of ferocity and losses. But thanks to those beacons on the shore, the* Joseph Butler, Jr. *had a fighting chance.*

Monkshaven, or the *George Spencer*, or the *Argo*—or some other vessel that had come within an inch of disaster—in the 1905 Blow.

On November 25, 1905, the brand new freighter *Joseph G. Butler, Jr.* sailed out of Lorain, Ohio, bound for Duluth, Minnesota. In command of the 525-foot (160-m) *Butler* was Captain William P. Benham. The ship's owners were aboard as passengers for the first leg of the *Butler*'s maiden voyage. It was a chilly, damp evening as Benham put the lights of Lorain's harbour behind him and set a course for the Detroit River. He kept an eye on an unusually high barometer. By dawn of the 26th the ship had passed Detroit, crossed Lake St. Clair, and was off the town of St. Clair, Michigan. There, the *Butler*'s owners went ashore, pleased with how well the new ship handled. For them, a safe train ride back home. For the *Butler*, a voyage toward an unexpected brush with history.

The next 24 hours were spent crossing vast Lake Huron, and the captain went below for some sleep. In the small hours of the 27th, he was called back to the bridge when the Detour Reef Light was picked up on the port bow. Flawlessly, the skipper navigated his great vessel up the St. Marys River, through the Soo Locks, and finally into grey Lake Superior. The barometer was still too high for the captain's liking.

The *Butler* was sailing smoothly, picking up speed as she passed the landmark Point aux Pins Lighthouse on the starboard bow, then the Point Iroquois Light on the port. Then, as the ship churned through Whitefish Bay, the barometer dropped like a lead weight. The breeze freshened and it began to snow. Captain Benham knew what those signs added up to. He told the lookout to keep a sharp eye for the Whitefish Point Light.

Ice pellets began to rattle on the windows of the pilothouse and the wind increased in strength. Just as the lookout picked up the Whitefish Point Light, a gust of snow obscured it from view. The men in the pilothouse could not see even as far as the ship's bow.

The *Butler* was pitching and rolling heavily. Her fog whistle blew constantly, warning any other vessels that might be nearby of her presence. The riveted steel plates of her new, untested hull groaned under the pressure of the pounding waves. There was no panic on board, but at the back of every mariner's mind on any given voyage is always the thought that this could be the last one.

Now the thermometer was dropping as fast as the barometer. Ice formed on the deck. Every pair of eyes in the pilothouse strained to peer through the darkness and the swirling snow, searching for a familiar light. Suddenly there was a series of flashes off to starboard. The captain counted the seconds between the blinks. It was the Caribou Island Light! That was all Captain Benham needed. He set a course for Keweenaw Point, which he

The Monkshaven, *one of 14 ships lost in a three-day gale on Superior in November 1905. Hunger and cold almost drove crewmembers mad before they were rescued from Angus Island.*

would know even in the hell of snow and wild water by the Gull Rock Light and the Manitou Island Light. At the same time he said a prayer of blessing for the lightkeeper on Caribou.

But the *Butler* was not out of danger yet. The ship was vibrating from the pummelling of the waves, and at times the propeller was out of the water, spinning dangerously in the open air. The steward called up to tell the captain that he had water pouring into the mess rooms. Benham acknowledged the report, but there was little he could do about it. He had to keep the ship moving forward, and out of the troughs created by mountainous waves.

By the morning of the 29th, no one had spotted the lights that were so vital to keeping a safe course. With no guiding beacon in sight and the storm still raging, Captain Benham did what any shrewd Great Lakes skipper would do. He turned for the wide open lake. Failing a safe harbour to run into, the *Butler*'s chances were better out there. Running close to shore would simply be inviting disaster on the jagged rocks. Captain Benham at this point had not slept for almost two days.

At last the storm seemed to be abating, though the lake was still extraordinarily rough. As another morning dawned, the captain caught the familiar flash of a distant beacon. "Outer Island Light!" he announced. A surge of relief swept through the ship. Now they could steer a straight course for Duluth.

As the *Butler* approached Duluth, an unusual sight greeted the crew. Huge bonfires had been lit along the waterfront to help guide storm-tossed ships into the safety of the harbour. Only when they were docked and able to go ashore did the crew of the *Butler* begin to comprehend the true severity of the storm they had just passed through, as they learned of ships missing or known to be lost. But the *Joseph G. Butler, Jr.* had made it, thanks in large part to those guiding lights on the shore.

LET THE LOWER LIGHTS BE BURNING

by Philip Paul Bliss

Brightly beams our Father's mercy
    from his lighthouse evermore,
But to us He gives the keeping
    of the lights along the shore.
Let the lower lights be burning!
    Send a gleam across the wave!
For to us He gives the keeping
    of the lights along the shore.

Dark the night of sin has settled,
    loud the angry billows roar;
Eager eyes are watching, longing,
    for the lights, along the shore.
Let the lower lights be burning!
    Send a gleam across the wave!
Eager eyes are watching, longing,
    for the lights, along the shore.

Trim your feeble lamp, my brother,
    some poor sailor tempest tossed,
Trying now to make the harbor,
    in the darkness may be lost.
Let the lower lights be burning!
    Send a gleam across the wave!
Trying now to make the harbor,
    some poor sailor may be lost.

This hymn was written in 1871, and has
become the sailors' anthem to lightkeepers.

BOOKS

Barrett, Harry B. *Lore and Legends of Long Point*. (Don Mills, ON: Burns & MacEachern) 1977.

Barry, James P. *Ships of the Great Lakes*. (Berkeley, CA: Howell-North Books) 1973.

Bowen, Dana Thomas. *Memories of the Lakes*. (Daytona Beach, FL: Dana Thomas Bowen pub.) 1946.

_____. *Shipwrecks of the Great Lakes*. (Cleveland: Freshwater Press) 1952.

Boyer, Dwight. *True Tales of the Great Lakes*. (New York: Dodd, Mead & Co.) 1971.

_____. *Strange Adventures of the Great Lakes*. (Cleveland: Freshwater Books) 1974.

Calvert, Rev. R. *The Story of Abigail Becker*. (Toronto: William Briggs Pub.) 1899.

Chisholm, Barbara & Gutsche, Andrea. *Superior: Under the Shadow of the Gods*. (Toronto: Lynx Images) 1998.

Clifford, J. Candace and Clifford, Mary Louise. *Nineteenth Century Lights*. (Alexandria, VA: Cypress Communications) 2000.

Donahue, James L. *Terrifying Steamboat Stories*. (Holt, MI: Thunder Bay Press) 1991.

Fischer, George, & Bouchard, Claude. *Sentinels in the Stream*. (Erin, ON: Boston Mills Press) 2001.

Floren, Russell & Gutsche, Andrea. *Ghosts of the Bay: A Guide to the History of Georgian Bay*. (Toronto: Lynx Images) 1998.

Fryer, Mary Beacock. *Battlefields of Canada*. (Toronto: Dundurn Press) 1986.

_____. *Volunteers and Redcoats/Raiders and Rebels*. (Toronto: Dundurn Press) 1987.

Gateman, Laura M. *Lighthouses Around Bruce County*. (Chesley, ON: Spinning Wheel Pub.) 1991.

Gibson, Sally. *More Than an Island*. (Toronto: Irwin Publishing) 1984.

Guillet, Edwin C. *Lives and Times of the Patriots*. (Toronto: University of Toronto Press) 1963.

Gutsche, Andrea; Chisholm, Barbara; Floren, Russell. *Alone In the Night: Lighthouses of Georgian Bay, Manitoulin Island and the North Channel*. (Toronto: Lynx Images) 1996.

Gutsche, Andrea & Bisaillon, Cindy. *Mysterious Islands: Forgotten Tales of the Great Lakes*. (Toronto: Lynx Images) 1999.

Hyde, Charles K. *The Northern Lights: Lighthouses of the Upper Great Lakes*. (Lansing, MI: The Peninsula Press) 1986.

Mansfield, John B. *History of the Great Lakes*. (Chicago: J.H. Beers & Co.) 1899.

Paterson, T.W. *Canadian Battles and Massacres*. (Langley, BC: Stagecoach Publishing) 1977.

Stone, Dave. *Long Point: The Last Port of Call*. (Erin, ON: Boston Mills Press) 1988.

Stonehouse, Frederick. *Haunted Lakes*. (Duluth: Lake Superior Port Cities Inc.) 1997.

_____. *Great Lakes Lighthouse Tales*. (Gwinn, MI: Avery Color Studios) 1998.

_____. *Haunted Lakes II*. (Duluth: Lake Superior Port Cities Inc.) 2000.

_____. *Women and the Lakes*. (Gwinn, MI: Avery Color Studios) 2001.

Wright, Larry & Patricia. *Bonfires & Beacons*. (Erin, ON: Boston Mills Press) 1996.

_____. *Bright Lights, Dark Nights*. (Toronto: Boston Mills Press) 1999.

NEWSPAPERS & PERIODICALS

The Dunnville Chronicle
The Fort William Daily Times–Journal
Kingston Whig Standard
The Manitoulin Expositor
The Mining Journal, Marquette, MI
Parry Sound North Star
The Toronto Globe
The Toronto Globe & Mail
The Toronto Star
Vogel, Mike. "Horseshoe Reef Lighthouse", *American Lighthouse*, Winter 1989.

INTERNET

Arenac County Historical Society, "Charity Island Lighthouse", Westwood, Brent. http://www.geocities.com/charityislandlight/articlebwestwood.html?200527

Buffalo Light: Guardian of the Harbor, Heverin, Aaron T., Oct. 1998. http://www-buffalofistoryworks.com/light

Great Lakes Shipwreck File: Official US Coast Guard Wreck Reports, Swayze, Dave, April 21/05 (update). http://greatlakeshistory.homestead.com/home.html

Great Lakes Shipwreck File 1679--1998, Swayze, Dave, 2001. http://www.boatnerd.com/swayze/shipwreck/w.htm

"History of Arenac County, Michigan", Ennes, Calvin, Arenac County MIGenWEB http://www.rootsweb.com/~miarenac/

Haunted Lighthouses, Wagner, Stephen. http://paranormal.about.com/library/weekly/aa032601b.htm

Inventory of Historic Light Stations, National Park Service, 2001. http://www.cr.nps.gov/maritime/1tsum.htm

Lighthouse Digest: "Our Women Lighthouse-Keepers", Gray, Mary Richards (Reprinted from Designer Magazine, 1904). http://www.lighthousedepot.com/Digest/StoryPage.cfm?StoryKey=657

Lighthouse Explorer Database, Lighthouse Depot Online. http://www.lighthousedepot.com/database/searchdatabase.cfm

Lynx Images: 50 Lighthouses, featured in book and video *Alone in the Night: Lighthouses of Georgian Bay, Manitoulin Island, and the North Channel.* http://www.lynximages.com/50lights.htm

Michigan History Magazine, "Mysterious Death at Sandpoint Lighthouse," Phillips, Kristin, Sept. 12, 2003. http://www.michigan.gov/hal/0,1607,7-160-18835_18896_20587-77124--,00.html

Seeing The Light, Terry Pepper. http://www.terrypepper.com/lights/index.htm

Sunken Treasures, The Wrecks of the 1000 Islands. http://www.1000islands.com/wrecks/wrecks.htm

Shipwreck Tours, Glass Bottom Boat Tour and Lake Superior Wreck Dives. http://www.shipwrecktours.com/

ACKNOWLEDGEMENTS

Brodie Resource Library, Thunder Bay, ON
Jere Brubaker, Old Fort Niagara, Youngstown, NY
Ron Dale, Fort George, Niagara-on-the-Lake, ON
Jack & Georgie Docker, Dunnville, ON
Jeff and Linda Gamble, Big Bay Lighthouse B&B, Big Bay, MI
Great Lakes Lighthouse Keepers Association
Guelph Public Library
Haldimand County Public Library, Dunnville, ON
Library of Michigan
Alexander McGillivray, Little Current, ON
Joseph Miller
Ontario Provincial Archives
Parry Sound Public Library
Terry Pepper
St. Lawrence County NY Historical Society
Tom Tag
United States Lighthouse Society
Larry Wakefield

PICTURE CREDITS

Apostle Islands National Lakeshore: 29 (tl,m,r)

Archives of Ontario: 65, 92

Arenac Historical Society: 146

Barrett, Harry and Barrett family: 117 (tm,i)

Beaver Island Historical Society: 188 (r,l)

Bowling Green State University: Historical Collections of the Great Lakes, 10 (t), 163 (t)

Bruce County Museum and Archives: 152 (l), 153, 154, 262

Canadian Coast Guard: 76 (r), 77, 112 (r), 138, 174, 175

Canadian Postal Archives: 24 (r)

Chantry Island Tours and Restoration Project (http://www.chantryisland.com/): 151

Chicago Historical Society: 16 (tr)

Coletti, Peter: 87

Collingwood Museum: 198

County of Grey-Owen Sound Museum: 29 (tl, tli)

Daily British Whig, Kingston, Ontario (November 26, 1920): 74

Docker, Jack and Georgie: 130

Eckert, Jack: 192

Forand, Michel: 64

Fort Malden National Historic Site: 120 (m)

Gora, Mike: 130 (b), 137

Great Lakes Historical Society: 112 (l)

Grimes, Marian: 258 (m)

Hamilton Public Library: 90 (t)

Hoyland, Dorothy: 239

Huronia Museum: 11, 27, 29 (b all), 166 (r), 168-170 (l,r), 171 (t), 253, 260 (all), 261 (all)

Isle Royale National Park: 28 (b,r,l), 225 (l), 229 (l), 241, 243

Johnston, Pat: 164, 245 (all), 246, 248, 251

Kennedy, Jack: 186

Knechtel, Art: 156

Lake Superior Maritime Archives, Lake Superior Maritime Coll. UW-Superior: 3, 10 (b)

Mansfield, J. B. ed., *History of the Great Lakes*: Vol II, Chicago: J.H. Beers & Co., 1899: 142

Leelanau Historical Museum: 193(b)

Lynx Images Inc.: 19 (i), 161, 162, 207 (b), 209, 232 (m), 240 (r), 256

Marine Museum of the Great Lakes at Kingston: 20 (b), 23 (t), 24 (l)

Marquette Marine Museum: 214, 215

McGreevy, Robert: 111(t)

McKenzie, Don: 28 (rt)

McMaster, Jamie: 26, 156 (l t,b)

Metropolitan Toronto Reference Library: 14 (t, m, b), 15 (t,b), 22 (t,i) 23 (i), 38, 40 (t,i), 44, 50, 54 (tm), 55. 57 (i), 58, 59 (i), 60, 61, 62, 66, 67, 68 (t, i), 70, 76 (l), 86, 89 (i), 90 (b), 91, 93, (t,b), 99, 100, 101, 103, 113, 117 (b), 120 (Ii, r), 121, 131, 132, 152 (r), 179, 201, 205, 212, 228 (r), 230, 240 (l), 242, 249

Michigan Travel Bureau (Judith A. Kubitz): 181

Michigan State Archives: 204

Milwaukee Public Library: 226

Mole, Erwin: 13, 72, 80 (r), 84, 110, 128, 140, 259

National Archives (US): 20 (t), 49, 51, 68, 104, 143, 228 (l), 252

National Archives of Canada: 16 (tl), 19 (m) 25 (l), 32, 34 (m,i), 36, 43, 45 (l), 54 (b), 57 (t), 89 (m), 119 (r), 120 (i,l), 156 (r), 159, 160, 171 (l), 173, 221 (all), 222 (r), 254

National Park Service: 182 (r)

New York Public Library: 98, 102

Norfolk Historical Society: 116

Oakville Historical Society: 86 (i)

Parry Sound Public Library: 163, 164 (t,b), 167 (all), 247, 248 (all)

Pelee Island Heritage Centre: 119 (l)

Port Colborne Historical Society: 141

Queen's University Archives: 31, 36, 39

Roscoe, Pearl: 135

Rico, Rudy and Alice (http://www.rudyalicelighthouse.net/): 45

Seawolf Communications, Cris Kohl: 263 (b)

State Archives of Michigan: 183

Stevens, Wanda: 155

Stonehouse, Frederick: 184 (l), 185(l,r)

Terry Pepper Great Lakes Collection: 189, 229

The Globe (& Mail): 53 (Dec. 7, 1926); 55 (Dec. 7, 1957), 63 (July 23, 1930), 80 (i)(August 8, 1955), 97 (Feb. 1, 1896); 124 (March 24, 1955); 145 (April 13, 1922), 166 (l) (Feb. 27, 1937), 177 (Dec. 7, 1926); 224 (May 29, 1933); 236 (Dec. 11, 1906); 255 (Nov. 17, 1920)

The Scanner, Monthly Bulletin of the Toronto Marine Historical Society, V. 6. No. 7, April 1974 (Bascome Collection): 202

Thunder Bay Historical Society: 231, 232 (t), 265

Toronto Daily Star: 79 (b), 126, 225

U.S. Coast Guard: 9, 16 (b), 25 (r), 134, 135(i), 180, 182 (l), 184 (r), 187, 191, 194, 197, 217, 223, 258 (b)

University of Detroit Marine Collection: 19

Unknown: 129, 131 (i), 129, 131, 199

US Army, Corps of Engineers: 136

Vermilye, Jon: 82

Washington Island Archives: 196 (m,i)

Western Manitoulin Historical Society Museum, Gore Bay: 6

Wilson, Tom: 48

Windsor Star: 139

Woodward Grant and Co.: 17

Key: r: right l: left m: middle B:bottom
t: top i: inset

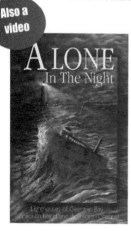

ALONE IN THE NIGHT:

Lighthouses of Georgian Bay, Manitoulin Island
and the North Channel

Alone in the Night peels back dusty layers of history, revealing the heroic and the scandalous, the gritty and routine aspects of this remarkable chapter of Canada's marine heritage. The book features over 50 lighthouses, and traces the fascinating evolution of lightkeeping. Stories, over 400 archival photographs, maps and relevant site information bring this era back to life.

ISBN 1-894073-14-2
292 pages, 9"x10"
CDN $39.95
ISBN 1-894073-15-0
video (70 mins)
CDN $29.95
ISBN 1-894073-16-9
video & book package
CDN $59.95

by Megan Long
ISBN 1-894073-31-2
176 pages, 6"x9"
CDN $24.95

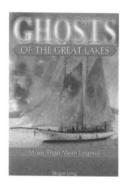

GHOSTS OF THE GREAT LAKES   More Than Mere Legend

Ghosts of the Great Lakes takes readers from the far western shores of Lake Superior to eastern Lake Ontario revealing haunting and strange tales. These whispers from the other side, however, are based in history and fact. Read these historical accounts of the Great Lakes' most fascinating ghost stories and judge for yourself—are they more than mere legend?

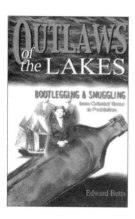

By Ed Butts
ISBN 1-894073-48-7
272 pages, 6"x9"
CDN $24.95

OUTLAWS OF THE LAKES

Bootlegging & Smuggling
From Colonial Times to the Present

A French bootlegger founded the city of Detroit in the eighteenth century. Two hundred years later, American and Canadian bootleggers supplied booze to the criminal empires of Al Capone, Dion O'Banion and the Purple Gang during the doomed experiment called Prohibition. Some became rich; others died with their boots on. Some were cut down by Coast Guard bullets; more were gunned down by rival bootleggers. All of them were brazen and ingenious (Rocco Perri had a front as a macaroni salesman) and they stopped at nothing. Whether they operated in defiance of unjust laws or out of pure greed, the smugglers and bootleggers of the Great Lakes and St. Lawrence River carved a legacy of violence and adventure, one that has had a profound impact upon the histories of Canada and the United States.

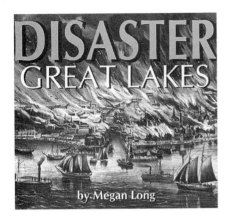

DISASTER GREAT LAKES

Violent, unpredictable weather has brought down ships from War of 1812 schooners to the legendary *Edmund Fitzgerald*. On shore, great fires have devastated the young cities of Chicago and Toronto, and cut huge swaths through the forests leaving thousands dead or homeless. Train wrecks, explosions and environmental disasters such as the Love Canal have become painful catalysts of change.

by Megan Long
ISBN 1-894073-26-6
148 pages, 8"x9"
CDN $24.95

The human core in all its complexity is revealed by the many compelling ways people respond in times of crisis. Richly told and illustrated, this book includes a concise list of the worst catastrophes in the history of the Great Lakes region, both American and Canadian.

MYSTERIOUS ISLANDS
Forgotten Tales of the Great Lakes

Mysterious Islands is an adventurous historical journey to islands found within the vast basin of the five Great Lakes. Standing removed and alone, islands have been central to some of the most important, outrageous and tragic events in Great Lakes history, from a decisive and bloody naval battle in the War of 1812, to Prohibition rumrunning, to harrowing tales of shipwreck and rescue. The waves of time have left many islands behind, but remnants of the past still mark their shores—burial grounds, grand hotels, abandoned quarries, lighthouses, strategic forts and even a castle.

ISBN 1-894073-11-8
294 pages, 6"x 9"
CDN $24.95
ISBN 1-894073-10-X
video (70 minutes)
CDN $29.95
ISBN 1-894073-12-6
video and book package
CDN $49.95

THE BOOK includes over 100 stories and over 500 rare photographs and helpful maps. **THE VIDEO** takes viewers to beautiful and intriguing places through remarkable cinematography and compelling archival footage and images.

Silver Screen Award,
U.S. International Film and Video Festival, 1999
Number 2 on the PBS Home Video Bestseller List

LYNX ⬯ TIME ...

LYNX ⬯ PLACE ...

LYNX ⬯ IMAGES ...

Lynx Images is a unique Canadian company that creates books and films filled with engaging stories and dramatic images from Canada's history.

Lynx projects are journeys of discovery, expeditions to sites where the past still resonates.

The company is comprised of a small, dedicated group of writers and film-makers who believe that history is something for all of us to explore.

CANADIAN AUTHORS   **CANADIAN STORIES**

EDWARD BUTTS

Ed Butts is author of *Outlaws of the Lakes: Bootlegging and Smuggling from Colonial Times to Prohibition*; co-author of *Pirates and Outlaws of Canada: 1610-1932*; and author of *Idioms for Aliens*, a humorous book on English grammar. He has also written a novel, *Buffalo: a Fable of the West*, and *She Dared*, a collection of true stories about remarkable women from Canadian history. His articles have appeared in numerous publications in Canada and the United States. For several years he taught at the Learning Center of Sosua, a school in the Dominican Republic, and wrote humorous articles for two multi-lingual Dominican magazines. He now lives in Guelph, Ontario.

JOIN THE ADVENTURE!

We are searching for powerful archival photographs, film footage, knowledgeable contacts, and stories from Canada's past for our future projects. We welcome your input and comments. Please mail, fax, or e-mail us at input@lynximages.com

---

COMMITTED TO A FUTURE
OF BRINGING YOU MORE OF THE PAST

Thank you for your support
—Russell Floren, Barbara Chisholm, Andrea Gutsche
WWW.LYNXIMAGES.COM